EUROPEAN POLITICAL THOUGHT 1600-1700

EUROPEAN POLITICAL THOUGHT 1600–1700

W. M. Spellman
Associate Professor of History
University of North Carolina
Asheville

St. Martin's Press
New York

St. Martin's Press, Scholarly and Reference Division, 175 Fifth Avenue, New York, N.Y. 10010

First published in the United States of America in 1998

This book is printed on paper suitable for recycling and made from fully managed and sustained forest sources.

Printed in Hong Kong

ISBN 0–312–21877–X clothbound
ISBN 0–312–21879–6 paperback

Library of Congress Cataloging-in-Publication Data
Spellman, W. M.
European political thought 1600–1700 / W. M. Spellman.
p.   cm.
Includes bibliographical references (p.   ) and index.
ISBN 0–312–21877–X (cloth). — ISBN 0–312–21879–6 (pbk.)
1. Political science—Europe—History—17th century.   I. Title.
JA84.E9S64   1998
320'.01'1—dc21   98–28242
                                                      CIP

In memory of my friend

William Joseph

CONTENTS

TIME-LINE
of key texts treated in this survey

Texts are arranged chronologically, followed by letters in parentheses indicating the paradigm into which the text best fits: (A) absolute monarchy, (CM) constitutional monarchy, (R) republicanism and (SC) secular contractualism.

1573   Francis Hotman, *Francogallia* (CM)
1574   Theodore Beza, *Right of Magistrates* (CM)
1576   Jean Bodin, *Six Books of the Republic* (A)
1579   George Buchanan, *The Right of the Kingdom in Scotland* (CM)
           (De jure regni apud Scotos)
1579   Philip du Plessis-Mornay, *A Defence of Liberty Against Tyrants* (CM)
           (Vindiciae contra tyrannos)
1593   Richard Hooker *Of the Laws of Ecclesiastical Polity* (CM)
1598   James VI of Scotland, *Trew Law of Free Monarchy* (A)
           Basilikon Doron (A)
1600   William Barclay, *The Kingdom and the Royal Power* (A)
1603   Johannes Althusius, *Politics Methodically Set Forth* (CM)
1612   Francisco Suarez, *A Treatise on the Laws and God the Lawgiver* (CM)
1625   Hugo Grotius, *Of the Law of War and Peace* (SC)
           (De jure belle ac pacis)
1644   John Milton, *Areopagitica* (R)
1648   Gerrard Winstanley, *The Saints Paradise* (R)
1649   Anthony Ascham, *Of the Confusions and Revolutions of Governments* (R)
1650   John Milton, *The Tenure of Kings and Magistrates* (R)
1650   Marchamont Nedham, *The Case of the Commonwealth of England Stated* (R)
1651   John Milton, *A Defense of the People of England* (R)
1651   Thomas Hobbes, *Leviathan* (SC)
1652   Gerrard Winstanley, *The Law of Freedom in a Platform* (R)

1656   James Harrington, *The Commonwealth of Oceana* (R)
1659   Richard Baxter, *A Holy Commonwealth* (CM)
1660   John Milton, *The Ready and Easy Way to Establish
              a Free Commonwealth* (R)
1660   George Lawson, *Politica Sacra et Civilis* (CM)
1660   Samuel Pufendorf, *Elements of Universal Jurisprudence* (SC)
1670   Baruch Spinoza, *A Treatise on Religion and Politics* (SC)
              (Tractatus theologico politicus)
1672   Samuel Pufendorf, *On the Law of Nature and Nations* (SC)
1673   Samuel Pufendorf, *On the Duty of Man and
              Citizen According to Natural Law* (SC)
1673   Baruch Spinoza, *Ethics* (SC)
1680   Robert Filmer, *Patriarcha* (A)
1680   Henry Neville, *Plato Redivivus* (R)
1689   John Locke (1632–1704) *Two Treatises of Government* (CM)
              A Letter Concerning Toleration (CM)
1696   Algernon Sydney, *Discourses Concerning Government* (R)
1702   Wilhelm Leibniz, 'Meditation on the Common Conception
              of Justice'
1704   Bishop Bossuet, *Politics Drawn from the Very Words of
              Holy Scripture* (A)
1714   Bernard de Mandeville, *The Fable of the Bees* (SC)

PREFACE

Humans have always struggled to respond to the conditions which nature has placed them in across the centuries. Be it the very basic search for nutritional sustenance, the attempt to shape explanations for the hard realities of illness, suffering and death, or the formulation of emotionally satisfying stories regarding one's place in the universe, each generation has sought to make sense of the immense variety of experience in this brief temporal setting. And a very important part of that larger undertaking has involved creating structures conducive to communal and collective social interaction. Indeed it might be said without too much distortion that the ability to live together in an orderly fashion is prerequisite to the successful utilization of nature for purposes of survival, just as it is preliminary to the development of refined ideas respecting the import of the human journey.

But living together successfully has constantly obliged humans to develop either formal or informal mechanisms by which to regulate individual conduct, to ensure that the behaviour of the one does not jeopardize the collective well-being of the many, the common good. This book, quite simply, is concerned with seventeenth-century explanations and analyses of the formal mechanisms, what we have come to term 'politics' from the Greek noun for the city state (polis). It surveys the efforts on the part of a wide range of European thinkers to discover the roots and the parameters of obligation in its broadest sense, the origin, appropriate structure, and limits of public authority, and the purposes or social ends to which that public authority should be directed.

The book is intended for the student and for the general reader who knows little about seventeenth-century European political ideas but who is interested in securing a broad overview of the subject. It is a very big topic, and in an effort to provide a useful survey I have doubtless oversimplified and compressed a number of complex issues in a manner that will appear wholly unsatisfactory to the many specialist scholars whose works I have shamelessly raided in assembling my own arguments.

Despite its intended audience, however, I have not written a textbook summary designed merely to recapitulate the current historiographical wisdom, or to provide yet another commentary on a series of canonical texts, as though an imaginary dialogue on perennial questions had been entered into by major thinkers across all chronological boundaries. Rather, by placing individual thinkers within a larger framework of broad ideologies or vocabularies, I hope to examine the interplay between divergent political ideas and the policies and resolutions pursued by princes, ministers, and administrators, by members of national assemblies and religious bodies, as well as the consequences of these ideas for members of all social groups. Four paradigms or modes of argument are presented: absolute monarchy, constitutional monarchy, republicanism, and what I have labelled secular contractualism. Each of these traditions of discourse will be treated within the larger setting of early modern state-building, territorial and religious aggrandizement, and interstate rivalry, processes over which the vast majority of the population of Western Europe had no influence, and for which they had no special enthusiasm.

Throughout the book, I have attempted to keep the discussion at an uncomplicated level while employing a style of exposition intended to bring out some of the dynamism of the period. I have, for example, avoided the now preferred use of non-sexist language specifically in order to remind the reader of the gender bias that was inherent in virtually all seventeenth-century discussion. The use of masculine nouns and pronouns is designed to highlight the exclusion of women from the arena of political discourse – and most importantly from political rights – in this period.[1] When the influential Cardinal Richelieu (1585–1642) intoned that women 'by nature indolent and unable to keep secrets, are little suited to government, particularly if one also considers that they are subject to their emotions and subsequently little susceptible to reason and justice', he was merely giving sardonic voice to a widespread male prejudice.[2] With this caveat in mind, we will look at political discourse at the level of formal, theoretical treatises, at new ideas appealing for the first time to a larger popular audience, and even at unoriginal ideas advanced by theorists who mirrored or elaborated other, better known thinkers. In addition to analysis, it is hoped that the book will provide historical sensitivity, placing ideologies in their appropriate social, religious, and cultural *milieux*.

There are of course plural contexts that one must consider when studying individual texts: family, religion, social class, economic interests, friendships, local allegiances. But following the advice of Brian Tierney, I believe that two frameworks are essential in the study of political theory: the intellectual inheritance of the author and the principal issues that the writer was trying to address or resolve. The former includes what Alfred North Whitehead once called the 'fundamental assumptions presupposed by all disputants', the unspoken picture of humankind's place in a divinely ordered creation, while the latter obliges us to know something of the immediate life issues confronting individual thinkers.[3] Treating these points in something approaching an equitable manner requires that we set aside as best we can our own sense of place and attempt to see the theories from the inside, to appreciate both the urgency of the moment in question and the legacy of ideas appropriate to each author. Chapter 1 seeks to provide this essential background, while the subsequent chapters pursue our four principal paradigms.

I would like to thank the Obert C. and Grace A. Tanner Humanities Centre at the University of Utah for electing me to a research fellowship during the 1995–96 academic year. This grant enabled me to begin the project in a congenial and supportive environment. Subsequent to that period, most of the work was carried out during the summer months at my home institution. I am indebted to the reference librarians at Ramsey Library, UNC-Asheville, for securing a number of hard-to-get texts via the interlibrary loan system, and for putting up with my unending queries and plaintive calls for help. As with earlier projects, N. E. Costello provided unselfish assistance and valued advice, especially at the editing stage. An essential starting point for anyone writing in this field is *The Cambridge History of Political Thought, 1450–1700* (Cambridge, 1991), edited by J. H. Burns with assistance from Mark Goldie, and containing articles from the leading scholars in their respective fields. My own heavy reliance upon this exceptional volume is evident throughout what follows. Finally, the ongoing student textbook series, *Cambridge Texts in the History of Political Thought*, under the general editorial direction of Raymond Geuss and Quentin Skinner, has proven to be an indispensable resource both in terms of primary sources and thanks to the critical introductions provided by the individual editors.

W. M. S.

INTRODUCTION

For most of us, it is difficult to think of political ideas as somehow separate from the events and processes of time and place, from the crises, problems, and larger trends confronting people at a particular juncture in the human experience. Changes in the political life of European society invariably inform political theory, as writers struggle first to understand the fundamental nature of these changes, and then work to defend, amend, or criticize what they take to be the long-term developments. And arguably the most significant development in European political life during the seventeenth century was the emergence of the sovereign state – at first confessional and then increasingly secular – as both impersonal object of allegiance and omnicompetent public authority within a clearly defined territory. The process had been inaugurated in the 1500s, but the full profile of the novel configuration only became apparent during the course of the seventeenth century. Whatever else characterizes life in the West three centuries after the period treated in this book, ours is without question a national state-dominated society where humans are divided into military-political-cultural units and where the sovereignty of the centralized political order over all other human associations is firmly established.[1] Moreover, the state has become self-justifying, wielding its authority without reference to any purported transhuman sanction. Beginning with the period treated in this book and continuing even today, political theory has concerned itself increasingly with the impact of this centralizing state both on society in general and upon the individual in particular.

Nineteenth-century scholarship often took for granted that medieval peoples organized themselves into sovereign territorial states much like moderns do, with every generation following the same eternal principles of centralized human association. This is perhaps one reason why imperial Europe found so little of lasting value in the stateless forms of human social organization 'discovered' in sub-Saharan Africa and parts of South Asia after 1800. This view has now been abandoned by researchers who are more apt to argue for the novelty of the 'state' in the Western experience, for its evolution as a powerful cultural concept over many centuries, more the product of human agency and device than of nature. Respecting the tremendously fluid term 'state' itself, the author of one recent survey suggests that 'it is difficult to see that it can be meaningfully employed to describe aspects of politically organized society in the medieval west before the twelfth century'.[2]

Medieval allegiances were, after all, mainly local; it was the exceptional medieval monarch who directly governed land and people in a conclusive and consistent manner. Personal alliances, personal power, the oath of the liege man: these predominant political behaviours guided the power elite across Western Europe. For the vast majority of medieval people, systems of authority were plural in nature and local in setting. Church, manor, monastery, guild, profession, village, town, kinship group: each claimed jurisdiction over its members in a complex and overlapping web of both informal and juridical relations. If a single central authority were conceded at all, that concession would go to the Roman Catholic Church, the sole organization whose universalist claims were felt across the Continent. But even here we must exercise caution, for whatever its wide-ranging pretensions in the spiritual arena, the church was incapable, practically speaking, of providing the type of material stability, security and order that was prerequisite to survival in an otherwise hostile environment.

Moreover, most reflections on political questions in the medieval period were to be found within works authored by theologians, philosophers and jurists seeking to address issues much more inclusive and less specialized than the sphere of the strictly political. Medieval writers, for example, included what we would today consider to be spiritual, ecclesiastical and theocentric matters in any discussion of earthly authority and jurisdiction. Authors spoke of 'rule' (*dominium*), the 'government' (*regimen*) of 'kingdoms' (*regia*), and control of 'land' (*terra, territorium*), but not of the state. True, students trained in the law at medieval universities learned the codification of Roman law known as the *Corpus Juris Civilis* or the Justinian Code. And this legal code did stress the importance of centralized administration and the superiority of the political order over all other formal associations. But its principles had little appreciable impact upon the custom and tradition of early medieval society prior to the thirteenth century.[3] Indeed before Niccolò Machiavelli (1469–1527) called for the ascendancy of the political and the secular over the religious and transcendent, the word 'state' was never used in context with the organization of political authority.[4]

This situation had changed dramatically by the opening of the seventeenth century, and the French lawyer and theorist Jean Bodin was one of the first to recognize the transformation. Thanks largely to the confessional civil wars launched in the wake of the Reformation, the process of state-building was now well underway, and political theory would increasingly respond to this unprecedented development of the institutional, the bureaucratic and the impersonal, with authors now focusing exclusively on these key aspects of government and society. Bodin himself, as a member of a politically active group of civil servants and writers known as 'Politiques', put to one side questions of theology and instead set himself to bolstering the claims of the monarch as a sovereign above all other – including religious – institutions of authority. It is, I believe, to this steady unfolding and then acceleration that we must turn our attention if we are to grasp the core concerns of seventeenth-century political thought. By the late sixteenth century, the Christian faith had lost its centuries-old claim to provide a unified centre, a common touchstone capable of coordinating the myriad intermediate authorities which had regulated the lives of Europeans since the early Middle Ages. A new model of authority was surfacing, and for good or ill it is with us even today, commanding an allegiance – and in some troubling mid-twentieth-century cases a fanaticism – unthinkable only 400 years ago.

Recent scholarly efforts to attach a general label or character to the seventeenth century have not been particularly fruitful – or for that matter very instructive. Compressed between the Renaissance and Reformation on one side of the chronological divide and the Enlightenment and American and French Revolutions on the other, historians over the years have utilized such eminently unsatisfactory terms as the 'age of scientific genius', the 'heroic age of rationalism', the 'century of revolution' and the 'age of religious wars' in order to package the century. More ambiguously, others have written of a continent-wide period of 'general crisis' or rather a set of crises, involving everything from a reorientation of intellectual pursuits to an economic upheaval preliminary to the birth of commercial and industrial capitalism, to fundamental demographic shifts and, most importantly, widespread political revolt brought about by the unprecedented changes in the relationship between state and society, between a decentralized feudal order and the growth of the first military-bureaucratic, and coercive state. In this last model, seventeenth-century political thought is most often associated with the secularization of public life and the gradual emergence of the individual out from under the twin shadows of orthodox spiritual authority and civil subordination.[5]

Missing from many of these discussions is an assessment and appreciation of major continuities, particularly religious ones. One of the features of our survey will be the argument that theological premises, despite the growth of the political state – and the state's dominance of now national Christian churches – remained close to the centre of most seventeenth-century theories concerning the organization of civil society. Chief amongst these premises were the twin beliefs that God's intentions were medial to the good government of peoples and that magistrates must, without exception, place divine purposes ahead of personal prerogative. As J. H. Burns has made clear in his introduction to the recent *Cambridge History of Political Thought, 1450–1700*, seventeenth-century states 'strove strenuously to be confessional states, in which membership of the political community was inseparable from membership of a coextensive ecclesial community'.[6]

Despite the cautions of Herbert Butterfield against progressive or 'Whig' views of the past, cautions first expressed almost 70 years ago, we are still too prone to embrace unilinear pictures of historical development where the outcome is foreordained, or at least where seventeenth-century theorists are seen as fighting bravely to bring about the modern democratic age.[7] Rejecting this temptation does not mean that our situation, 300 years removed from an earlier tradition of thought, prevents us from seeing connections that contemporaries were not aware of when they wrote. But it should serve to remind us that intellectual transitions, and in this case the transition from a religious to a predominantly secular model of political theory, were extended affairs, and that earlier patterns continued to inform discourse long after innovative theories had made their inaugural appearance in print. It is these earlier configurations, their principal defenders and the world which these persons inhabited, that we hope to explore in chapters 2 and 3. Only then will the gradual abandonment of these patterns under the strain of new circumstances, treated in chapters 4 and 5, make sense. How what was felt to be true for the bulk of the Christian centuries, how the direction of both the inner self and the external world by priests and natural, God-ordained superiors eventually gave way before a new model of civil society, one where the interests of the magistrate were no longer seen as opposed to the interests of the subject but instead reflected and legitimized those interests, is a story of continuing interest, not least at the close of a century where repeated assaults upon this latter set of political practices and institutions have been of profound consequence for the human prospect.

Two of the more engaging – indeed unprecedented – aspects of political thought during this century are that authors from a variety of backgrounds hoped to influence the immediate outcome of events with their arguments, while these same authors were hoping to politicize groups of people who had heretofore been excluded from any role in the concerns of rulers. Many of the writers to be treated here were working outside the traditional scholarly community and felt themselves to be immediately engaged in – or alienated from – the often tumultuous power state politics of the period. According to one social historian: 'There is much to be said for the view that between 1618 and 1648, more western Europeans were interested in politics than ever before. Affairs of state were impinging on people's lives and information about politics was circulating more widely then it had been.'[8] And the solutions being offered to long-standing political problems – in particular to the problem of authority and individual autonomy – were exceptionally diverse. French theorists such as Bodin and later Bishop Bossuet were addressing one particular audience in their respective works, while the English Levellers John Lilburne and Richard Overton reached out to quite another public, a following in large measure separate from the literate and privileged elite. We will examine these new voices in chapter 4 when we address republican theories and practices, paying particular attention to the manner in which republicanism reached back to a pre-Christian past in an effort to secure competent and accountable leadership.

These new republican voices, together with the naturalistic arguments put forward by Thomas Hobbes, Hugo Grotius, Samuel Pufendorf, and Bernard de Mandeville (discussed in chapter 5 and in the conclusion), represented largely secular, and in that respect distinctly modern, responses to the growth and consolidation of the territorial state. In basing their theories on the assumption that the main purpose of the centralized, political state is to protect the merely terrestrial interests – the physical security, the liberties, the rights – of a now equal citizenry, these writers confirmed the eclipse of a specifically Christian and otherworldly agenda which had failed to reconcile its own very diverse manifestations in post-Reformation Europe.

For these inventive theorists, natural law divorced from all theological preconceptions and based instead on the observable facts of human nature, provided the starting point for a rigorous new science of politics, a politics which was at once both anthropocentric and pragmatic. Its precision would match that of emerging natural philosophy, where the mysteries of the physical universe were being uncovered thanks in no small measure to the steady employment of an uncompromising empiricism. Hobbes, ignoring authority and precedent much as Descartes before him had done, would 'ground the civil right of Sovereigns, and both the duty and liberty of subjects, upon the known natural inclinations of mankind, and upon the articles of the law of nature'.[9] And the result would be a reaffirmation of centralized power, of the need for unimpeachable sovereignty rooted in the consent of equal citizens. No longer would birth, status and association dictate one's place in a hierarchical universe. Now citizens under the same impersonal law, now atomistic individuals without recourse to the protection and the privilege of medieval plural authorities – the church, the city, the guild, the university – stood before a sovereign state whose monopoly of coercive power and whose increasingly terrestrial and activist agenda conceded no opposition outside previously agreed constitutional means.

Typically this emergent state power came to be exercised largely through impersonal institutions: courts, legislatures, armies, bureaucracies. How this process unfolded, and how this unprecedented grant of power was permanently secured not by force, but through the agreement of free men who now determined the limits of legitimate state action, will be one of the key points of discussion in what follows. To the extent that 'man' was at the centre of this new constellation of ideas which elided Christian-Aristotelian fixed ends or purposes, we can say that political theory had arrived at the threshold of the modern age in the West. The *ancien régime* and the Christian anthropology which it embraced would, of course, continue to dominate the political landscape in Western Europe for almost another century after 1700, the point at which our survey must conclude. But while the power of precedent, corporatism, status hierarchy, and Christian absolutism would persist until the great ungluing of 1789, the intellectual underpinnings of this aged structure had been substantially debilitated by the close of the seventeenth century.

Religion – and the imposition of orthodoxy – still very much informed political praxis in 1700; the next world still counted for a great deal in the rhetoric of politics. Europe did not, to use Paul Hazard's famous compression of developments in France, one day think like Bossuet and the next day think like Voltaire.[10] But by any reasonable criterion it is difficult to deny that political thought by the close of the seventeenth century had become dislodged from its centuries-old intellectual moorings. Less than a century later, in 1776 and more dramatically in 1789, new theory would become new fact, altering basic assumptions about the origins and ends of public power in a manner that was both unprecedented and, thus far, irreversible.

1

CIVIL AUTHORITY IN AN UNFAMILIAR SETTING

Occupying a comparatively small geographical region at the far western extreme of the Eurasian land mass, Europeans had fashioned for themselves a remarkable patchwork of political forms across the centuries between the disintegration of Roman authority and the advent of an inchoate 'national' sense during the early modern period. More the product of reflexive contingency than the result of any thoughtful, planned construction, there was nothing to compare with the congeries of European governmental models in the Ottoman lands, in South Asia, or in the vast expanses of the East generally. By 1500 there were literally hundreds of more or less independent political units in Europe, each one headed by rulers who were more often than not first among equals, with sometimes hundreds of competing power holders within often shifting boundaries. This situation dictated that all prospective state-building programmes would involve a process of agglomeration and absorption, at the inevitable cost of affronting tradition and privilege, and prompting jurisdictional feuds, at almost every turn.[1] In an important respect political thought in the early modern period consists of 'a series of reactions to this political change', attempts both to justify and to oppose the expanding power of the state.[2]

At the start of our period the picture remained exceedingly varied. Hereditary monarchy dating back to the feudal centuries obtained in Spain, England and France, while some form of elective monarchy found favour in Poland, Hungary, and Bohemia. Strictly ecclesiastical states were instituted in parts of Germany and, most importantly, in central Italy, while working republics operated in the Swiss cantons, the United Provinces, and in some northern Italian cities. The Holy Roman Empire, stretching across some 300 bishoprics, free cities, and

8

principalities in Germany, combined the elective principle with respect to the imperial title, but also preserved the axiom of hereditary princely rule, and a large measure of autonomy, in the majority of the constituent provinces.[3] This political diversity was matched by linguistic distinctiveness, as national tongues superseded universal Latin just as territorial states had supplanted ubiquitous Rome.

Quentin Skinner has written that before the modern idea of the state could emerge and productive discussions about its nature, powers and relationships take place, certain essential preconditions had to be met.[4] In the first instance politics needed to be defined as a distinct branch of moral philosophy, a legitimate undertaking in its own right with important consequences for the well-being of the earthly community. The abundant concerns of the 'city of man', so much disparaged by those reared in an Augustinian tradition, only re-emerged as a worthwhile subject of study in Christian Europe with the thirteenth-century translation into Latin of Aristotle's *Politics*. By the sixteenth century, and especially after the dissolution of the Christian commonwealth brought about by the Reformation, the centrality of politics to the life of the body and spirit was put into sharp relief by writers who began to grapple with the implications of widespread religious division.

Also crucial to the idea of the state as the focus of political thought – and not unrelated to the Reformation crisis – was first the subordination and ultimately the elimination of all real and potential rivals to the autonomy and the social cohesiveness of the territorial kingdom. This included both external authorities, such as the Holy Roman Emperor in the German states and the international church centred in Rome, and domestic protestations against independent magistracy and centralized lawmaking as embodied in the feudal heritage. The external jurisdictional authority of the church was first undermined in the north German states during the Reformation, as the secular princes began to exercise their power over both public and private life.[5] But it was the domestic challenge which demanded the closest attention. The very idea of the state as a single unit where many contiguous regions were governed from the centre, and where the legitimate use of force was exercised under delegation from this centre, was innovative and considered to be dangerous by the plural 'estates' which formed the medieval constitutional norm.[6] Again this road to sovereign independence was already being travelled by many of Europe's temporal princes and magistrates well before the opening of the seventeenth century, but the process was greatly accelerated after 1600.

Preliminary Assumptions

Throughout much of the seventeenth century, and for that matter
for most of the medieval experience, political thought and political practice were not concerned with the individual's rights and his obligations
to the prince or magistrate who represented the power of the sovereign state. The focus on the individual and on individual freedoms
with respect to the state is in fact a very recent development in the Western tradition; in large part the quest for personal freedoms has been at
centre stage for no more than 250 years. Rather the bulk of political
thought during our period was concerned foremost with government
and its varied relationships with distinct orders, estates, corporate and
unequal interests. Whereas economic classes tend to constitute the common picture of modern stratified society, orders or estates based upon
status, honour and position formed the foundation of early modern social
gradations.

In this model social groups were identified not strictly by wealth, but
more importantly by the esteem and dignity attached to their public
function in society. Status was largely disassociated from wealth, while
non-economic criteria such as education, birth, titles, legal privileges and
office all provided the footings for power and prestige. Families whose
money was acquired through the production of goods, for example,
were ranked beneath poorer university graduates and magistrates.
The 'status' hierarchy, which also included a formal system of legal
inequalities and privileges, was viewed by its defenders as composing a
larger unity of interdependent groups, all of whom benefited from the
body politic.[7] A personal sovereign, not a bureaucratized and impersonal state, commanded different modes of allegiance from these separate
orders, thus there was no workable concept of a universal equality of
subordination to the magistrate. Writing in the late sixteenth century at
a moment when French sovereignty was in disarray as a result of pro-
tracted religious civil war, Jean Bodin affirmed that: 'There was never
commonwealth, were it true or but imaginary, or the most popular
that a man could think of; where the citizens were equal in all rights and
prerogatives; but that always some of them have had more or less than
others.'[8] It was a view clearly reflected in the words of the Cambridge-
shire gentleman and first governor of Massachusetts Bay Colony, John
Winthrop, who cautioned emigrants that 'in all times some must be
rich some poor, some high and eminent in power and dignity; others
mean and in subjection'.[9]

Even law codes stressed the fact that obedience entailed different sets of actions and proscriptions depending on one's place in the hierarchy of fixed social orders. Members of the clerical estate in France, for example, often enjoyed exemption from the civil judicial apparatus, while the second estate, composed of the nobility (totalling no more than 1 per cent of the overall population), monopolized not only all top positions in the church, the military, and the royal administration, but also controlled local administrative and judicial posts in the countryside. Together with this enormous political privilege, the nobility was entitled to exemption from the *taille*, the main direct tax of the old regime. René Descartes may have claimed the essential equality of human intellect in 1637 with his *Discourse on Method*, and Thomas Hobbes may have derided social hierarchy as an artificial construct in his *Leviathan* (1651), but neither pronouncement had much appreciable impact on the relationship between subject and sovereign before 1789. Here, perhaps more than anywhere else, distinctions between medieval and early modern civil society must be softened, while purported linkages between the seventeenth century and the modern West merit reappraisal.

The hierarchical paradigm which informed social relations was but one part of a much larger set of correspondences informing the whole of God's creation and into which the individual found his or her proper duty. Hierarchies in the celestial sphere, where angels took their place after God, were mirrored in the animal kingdom, where the lion was designed for pre-eminence, and in the human body, where the head commanded a hierarchy of lesser organs, and in the political arena, where the king presided over a series of descending magistrates. Dominance hierarchies, as Brian Tierney has pointed out, were not simply abstract theories, they were observable facts of nature.[10] Everyone was acutely aware that a rigidly stratified social structure, a world of rank where appearance, diet, housing and speech all told a story about one's place in the eternal order of creation, was both centuries-old and firmly endorsed by religious leaders across the Protestant–Catholic divide. The social structure, it was held, was simply another example of the natural gradations that God had elected to impose upon his handiwork for reasons not communicated to frail humankind. The twelfth-century English writer John of Salisbury had addressed these correspondences in his *Policraticus* (1159) when he compared the Catholic priesthood to the soul of the human body, soldiers and administrators to the hands, labourers on the land to the feet, with each part performing its assigned function in a set hierarchy.[11] And near the start of the century under consideration in this book, the Church of England divine Richard Hooker confirmed that: 'The whole world consisting of parts so many, so different, is by this only thing upheld; he which framed them hath set them in order.' God ensures that 'the lowest be knit to the highest by that which being interjacent may cause each to cleave unto other, and so all to continue one'.[12] During the course of the seventeenth century this Aristotelian conception of a Great Chain of Being would find itself under attack as a new, empirically based science replaced a 2000-year-old cosmology with one that removed humankind from centre stage, but it took time for the removal of hierarchy in the Galilean universe to recalibrate the centuries-old assumptions in more terrestrial compartments.

Something of this fundamental set of inequalities would be called into question in parts of Europe by the close of the century, but even in those places where legal equality and the primacy of the individual found tentative grounding by 1700, as in England, or where republics had been established, as in the Netherlands, the notion that society was layered into groups whose access to political power was largely set by their economic standing and, more particularly, by their ownership of landed property, remained a commonplace in thinking about what had always been a stratified and deferential culture. The republics of the seventeenth century were hardly creatures of the people or democracies as we understand the term today.[13] In 1689 John Locke would speak with confidence about the contractual nature of civil society and about government's responsibility to protect the individual freedoms agreed by all parties in the original contract, but at the same time he believed that the vast majority of the English male population, the landless labourers in town and country, must accept their group responsibility to cultivate the earth and provide rents for absentee landowners and gentlemen like himself, gentlemen who in cooperation with other members of the status elite, and with the monarch, defined the parameters of the public good. Educated men – that tiny minority of Europe's population – formed their deprecatory view of the common man on the basis of their reading in ancient authors, and these sources were unlikely to recommend themselves to anyone convinced of the essential sameness of human nature.[14] Inequality fixed by birth had been undermined by the time Locke published *Two Treatises of Government* in 1689, as his own brilliant career would illustrate, but this did not mean that practical inequalities in virtually every aspect of English life were not accepted practice.

Those fortunate few like the Oxford-educated Locke, who helped to define the nature of government's relationship with society, would not recognize the many assumptions about the functions of licit government that we take for granted today. No one in the seventeenth century expected that the dynastic state would use tax revenues to provide a range of social programmes for the infirm or the aged. Nor did the early modern state guarantee anyone rights to free expression, assembly, or movement. Individualism was neither defended nor valued. Magistrates were not obliged to provide their subjects with rights to representation, or to legal representation in criminal cases, or to the protection of a regular, impartial police force. Indeed presumption of guilt was normative in most judicial systems. The state was to be supported by taxation, but the use of these revenues had very little to do with the enhancement of the individual's place in what was thought to be a world of unchanging relationships and celestial correspondences.[15]

Monarchs

At the apex of most European political systems, systems which, as we have seen, contemporaries accepted as hierarchic and static in nature, and in which wealth and authority rested in the hands of a tiny minority, was the monarch. It is in this respect, as noted by a recent scholar, that: 'Political ideas in late-medieval and early-modern Europe were preponderantly, and inevitably, ideas about kings and kingship.'[16] However, princes during the seventeenth century were by no means rulers over tightly defined homogeneous states, despite the fact that the international frontiers of Europe before 1700 were quite close to their modern counterparts. Rather most rulers found themselves claiming increasing powers over a diverse, multilingual, and sometimes multinational collection of peoples and cultures, all eager to preserve their uniqueness and, if possible, their long-established autonomy. Marriage and inheritance often placed a ruler at the head of peoples who were expected to transfer their loyalty at the caprice of dynastic matchmaking and estate settlement. And no better illustration of the nature of the multinational dynastic state can be offered than that presented by the Habsburg possessions. The Spanish branch of the family, even as late as 1640, governed and misgoverned the Iberian peninsula, the southern Netherlands, Franche-Comté, Portugal, and New World dominions larger than Europe proper, while Naples, Sicily and Sardinia in Italy were also part of that unwieldy inheritance. To this mix must be added the separatist psychology of the landholding elites in Aragon, Valencia, and Catalonia, all deeply distrustful of creeping 'Castilianization' and keen to keep the crown out of their affairs.[17] By 1700 the Austrian Habsburgs, in addition to their significant German possessions and their elective title as Holy Roman Emperor, dominated Bohemia, Hungary, Transylvania and parts of modern Romania. The Russian empire, the 'Third Rome', simply dwarfed its Western European counterparts in terms of its hegemony over large and indefinable territories stretching eastward into Asia, while even in the more compact kingdoms of France and England, cultural and linguistic minorities remained very much a presence and a concern for government at the centre.[18]

Localist orientations aside, most subjects were at least aware of the ruling family which claimed their allegiance and whose coronation oath normally included elevated references to the general well-being of the population at large. And most accepted the propriety of the hereditary principle. In his well-known *Pensées*, Blaise Pascal (1623–62) asked whether anything 'could be less reasonable than choosing the first son of a king or queen to govern the state?' Presumably it would make more sense for all concerned if the ruler was both virtuous and skilful, but unfortunately every regal misanthrope pretended to these qualifications. However since 'civil war is the greatest of misfortunes', Pascal like so many others embraced hereditary monarchy as the best solution to the dilemma.[19] The principal objectives of most monarchs in the early seventeenth century – at least for those who were concerned about peace and economic development in their own states and about the pursuit of religious and dynastic interests in Europe – involved the formation of a loyal and efficient bureaucracy, the gradual abridgement of the multiple pockets of political and judicial power in the towns and in the countryside, the training and regular payment of a standing army sufficient to take the place of the old feudal levies (a monopoly over the physical means of coercion), and, more generally, the replacement of lineage and military skill with education and intellectual merit as prerequisites to service and counsel at Court.

This last ambition involved the interposition of Renaissance ideals of service to the state where previously the nobility had maintained its exclusive right to counsel the prince by virtue of its control over land, arms, and provincial affairs. Bellicose habits long associated with the aristocracy were increasingly placed at a discount by ambitious monarchs and in exchange a new civic-minded nobility was cultivated, one which associated all state interests solely with the person of the monarch.[20] It is important to acknowledge that no European head of state wished to level society by reducing noble wealth or influence at court; rather the entire royal programme was intended to undertake functional shifts in the political role of the king's fellow landowners, his natural allies, the customary leaders of society, in part to secure their social and economic hegemony in rapidly changing times. In return for giving up their private armies and *seigneural* jurisdictions, the crown promised continued tax exemption (England excepted), the opportunity to compete for a grab bag of lucrative appointive offices, and a more efficient exploitation of the governed in the interest and for the profit of the existing social structure.

Without exception, kings and their ministerial agents were the major advocates and practitioners of state-building throughout the period. Thus when seventeenth-century political theorists raised fundamental issues regarding the origins of civil society, why one ought to obey the prince, and the nature and extent of state power over its subjects, it is important to recall that the most dynamic monarchs of the seventeenth century were attempting to do something which was antipodal to established wisdom in political theory: very simply put, they were attempting to carry out change, to innovate, to adjust traditional political structures in a way that would make these structures more responsive to the expanding needs of the crown in an age of intense dynastic, commercial and religious conflict.

In particular, it was the dramatic augmentation of the military capacity of the seventeenth-century state which so unnerved the politically active elite outside the capital.[21] For these hereditary offspring of the decentralized feudal order, the central issue at the turn of the seventeenth century was the preservation of their local power – their much-cherished judicial and law-making authority – in the face of what many of them rightly viewed as a concerted attempt on the part of nascent government at the centre to abbreviate provincial patterns of leadership and autonomy. Indeed most of the serious revolts led by politically significant sections of the landed population during the course of the seventeenth century – in England, Catalonia, Portugal, Sicily and Naples, during the Fronde in France – were motivated largely by a fear that the monarch was attempting to alter the historic relationship between crown and locality, to jettison an ancient unwritten constitutional arrangement of power.[22]

The position of many provincial elites with respect to the crown was that the king should take responsibility for preserving the constitutive laws and traditions of the kingdom, however vaguely formulated these might be, and not with fashioning them anew. In France, for example, this meant the preservation and defence of some 360 customary laws in 1600, agglomerations of ancient liberties bound to frustrate any and all plans for integration and administrative efficiency, much less for a firm course of military modernization. The monarch, it was thought, should respect the diversity of the feudal past, including the existence of other loci of political and military power in the towns and in the countryside, and all attempts at altering the status quo in favour of distant government, standing armies, fortifications, and unfamiliar bureaucracies were interpreted as attacks upon aristocratic privilege and provincial integrity. The work of state-building in the seventeenth century was by no means applauded by a population which still associated all elements of change, in whatever department of human life, with decay and sinfulness.

Types of Counsellors

In most states assemblies representing three powerful interest groups: large landowners, municipal leaders, and the church, had historically enjoyed the right to consult with the king on matters of great importance, although the meeting of these assemblies was definitely on the decline throughout most of Europe between 1600 and 1700. The medieval tripartite division of European society into those members of Estates who fight, those who pray, and those who work, continued to inform the organizational breakdown of most of these legislative assemblies, both at the regional and at the national level. In England, hereditary lay peers and bishops of the Church of England sat separately from the gentry landowners, lawyers and other moneyed professionals who inhabited the lower House of Commons. In theory, at least, the latter group represented the interests of all non-nobles in the realm. Government ministers sat in both houses, normally setting the initiatives at the behest of the crown. In the Cortes of Aragon and Castile, in the Polish Diet, and in the Swedish Riksdag, lesser landowners dominated the proceedings in the lower chambers. The same was true in the provincial Estates in France, which continued functioning after the national Estates

General had atrophied. With the exception of the unique States General in the Netherlands, representative assemblies remained, by and large, creatures of the crown, occasional meetings summoned and dismissed by the monarch and charged solely with addressing issues introduced for their consideration by the prince. The social composition of those who sat in the non-noble chambers was changing as well. While enjoying neither the landed income nor the precedent status of the hereditary landed nobility, urban merchants, financiers and manufacturers whose personal wealth sometimes exceeded the income of certain members of the aristocracy were important, although by no means dominant, figures in the political life of the dynastic state. Urban society as a whole was becoming instrumental to the financial well-being of the major states of Western Europe. Many towns, ruled by narrow, self-perpetuating oligarchies, had acted as privileged corporations since the middle ages, enacting their own laws, monopoliz-ing access to political power, and regulating the social and economic lives of the labouring inhabitants. Central governments recognized the growing importance of commoners whose wealth was not derived from rents, however, and set in motion tariff and trade policies designed to foster and to protect commerce and native manufactures. Capital derived from the business activities of non-noble burghers or bourgeois subjects proved an important source of loans to the crown in all of the major states, thus the encouragement of new wealth-producing activities was seen to be in the larger interest of the nation. Wealthy common-ers, for their part, were permitted the opportunity to buy offices and titles in the new service-oriented state, thus solidifying their identifica-tion with the good fortunes of the crown. Affluence derived from com-merce and the law placed the many temptations of office, titles and the indolence associated with landownership within reach, a process which Fernand Braudel once described as 'the defection of the bourgeoisie'.[23]

When assessing the status of the aristocratic landed elite, the many dif-ferences in their respective conditions across Europe cannot be ignored, but some common features do stand out. From land management to seigneural justice, from the leadership of men in battle to the pleasures of the hunt, noble households and noble influence dominated the rhythm of life in the provinces from Muscovy to Madrid. Only the king could create new members of the titled aristocracy, and their numbers, in rela-tion to the overall population, remained quite small, with, for example, no more than 1 per cent of the population in France, between 5 and 10 per cent of the total in Spain, and between 8 and 15 per cent of the inhabitants of Poland numbered amongst the aristocratic ranks.[24] In England the early statistician Gregory King estimated that the combined peerage (titled aristocracy) and gentry (baronets, knights, esquires) constituted only about 3 per cent of those living in the Island Kingdom.[25] Exclusivity in numbers, however, was coupled with exceptional power, both military and political. Before the middle of the seventeenth century, the majority of fighting men in royal armies were members of feudal retinues raised on behalf of the crown by great territorial lords, men who in theory owed their highest allegiance to the king, but whose warlike culture and status pride posed a potential threat to the monarch. Only with Cromwell's New Model Army in the 1640s do we see the emergence of a disciplined national force in the pay of the centralized state.

Not enjoying anything approaching a monopoly of violence in their own kingdoms, monarchs needed to consolidate these disparate provincial forces if they were ever to put a stop both to noble violence in the countryside and repeated challenges to public order at the centre. The anarchic behaviour of portions of the French nobility during the era of religious civil wars was but one deadly illustration of the dangers of decentralized noble military might. Creating a national army did not mean the disarming of the nobility, however, since the aristocrats whose predecessors had led personal forces were now to become the exclusive officer class in the crown's armies, the ambassadors to neighbouring courts, and the diplomats in the emerging foreign service corps. Nobles were encouraged by the crown to settle whatever issues divided them by recourse to the expanding royal courts, and not to the field of battle. The medieval culture of violence, of personal impulsiveness and the public display of aggression, was antithetical to the job of state formation.[26] The idea of the monarch as the repositor of justice was no innovation of the seventeenth century, but by discouraging private violence while keeping opportunities open for aristocrats to lead fighting men, the monarch's position as lawgiver and judge was immeasurably enhanced.

The ranks of the nobility were changing during the seventeenth century as monarchs sought additional sources of income through the sale of titles while also recruiting a new, educated service elite. In England, the first two Stuarts increased the number of titled aristocracy from 81 to 126 and, citing only the most notorious example, a new title of baronet was put on the market in 1611 at the asking price of £1095.[27] The status of the service-oriented nobility was disputed by the older families whose

landed wealth and lineage was associated with warfare and not administration, but the unseemly commercial trend of granting peerages to
townsmen and professionals was not to be reversed.

This practice of selling titles and offices which conferred noble privileges, while it did not lead to fundamental shifts in the overall social
structure, did open up the ranks of the nobility to newcomers who felt
fewer inhibitions about engaging in a range of activities long thought
to be inappropriate for members of the titled aristocracy. Business,
finance, manufacture, trade and colonial development had normally
been associated with the money-grubbing existence of ambitious commoners, but increasingly activities divorced from the land and the collection of rents became more palatable to the noble station. Together
with court pensions, monopolies, tax farms and various annuities from
the crown, business investment ensured that noble families remained
solvent and in most cases prosperous. Despite much speculation by historians about 'the crisis of the aristocracy' and the rising economic fortunes of the gentry, by and large seventeenth-century society's natural
leaders maintained their tax-exempt and privileged position in the various dynastic states of Europe, while new members to the exclusive club
'established' suitable genealogies, immersed themselves in the culture of
the court, and began the difficult work of building a home in the capital
suitable to the requirements of fashion.

Access to high office remained open to those ancestral families who
exhibited loyalty to the crown and a willingness to exchange eminence
in warfare for distinction in the university lecture hall. And it appears
that many were prepared to do just that. On the continent over a dozen
new universities were established before 1600, while in England alone it
has been estimated that of those males who were literate in the population at large, one in fifteen undertook some university training, about
the same percentage as today. This newly educated aristocracy learned a
common language and absorbed a common Latin culture, all of which
made for a surprising degree of homogeneity amongst gentlemen aristocrats across Europe's many borders.[28] Taking up residence in the capital
or at Court for at least part of the year, office-holding aristocrats
spent less of their time on their ancestral estates, thereby decreasing
opportunities for provincial trouble-making and solidifying the identity
of interests between crown and nobility. Overall, then, magnates willing
to adapt to changing expectations retained their positions as royal
governors, generals, admirals, and most importantly, as counsellors to
the king. The governing class, as one scholar pointed out, 'changed far

less than seemed likely during the great conflicts of the century. Inherited wealth, family connection and patronage were still the essential means to success.'[29] During the last two decades of the seventeenth century in France, for example, the most important circle of ministers around Louis XIV 'consisted, with one exception, exclusively of members of the family clans of Colbert and LeTellier-Louvois'.[30]

The Ruled

Whereas the sixteenth century had witnessed an overall doubling of the population, the roughly 60–70 million inhabitants of Europe east of Muscovy in 1600 were not able to maintain this remarkable rate of expansion. At the close of the seventeenth century the aggregate population was in the neighbourhood of 85 to 100 million, with virtually all of the increase taking place in northwestern Europe – the Low Countries, southeastern England, and parts of northern France. Despite the inherent difficulty of estimating size where few quantifiable data are available, the population of central and eastern Europe appears to have remained flat over the course of the century, while places in Italy, Spain, and in some German states experienced actual declines. This slowdown in population growth was not unrelated to issues in political theory, for the cost of government was everywhere increasing dramatically during the century, and the proceeds from direct taxes on the peasant population at large constituted the bulk of revenues used by ever-expanding central governments.

The overwhelming majority of these 85–100 million souls played no direct role in the political life of the countries in which they lived and toiled, even though their unremitting labour constituted the backbone of the polity. Indeed the whole notion of the dynastic hereditary state was in some respects an irrelevancy for Europe's masses. In eastern Europe, serfdom was expanding on traditionally large estates during the seventeenth century, while west of the Elbe the decline of feudal bondage did little in practical terms to improve the economic position of the tenant farmer and landless labourer. And while conditions might differ enormously between, say, English yeoman farmers and Castilian agricultural labourers, peasant allegiances were in general fiercely local everywhere across Europe, and this was no more than the result of a pragmatic outlook on life. Loyalties to lord, priest, and community were, by and large, habits unreflectively adhered to, and were certainly much stronger than whatever feelings one might have toward the dynastic ruling family. Often the village community was synonymous with the manor or with the boundaries of the parish. Across the continent landowners and town councils dispensed local justice in their own courts over matters ranging from disputes between tenants to the transfer of property, while the church tribunals adjudicated a wide variety of activities deemed to be infractions of the moral order as defined by religious authorities. Rents (normally a proportion of the harvest) and fees for the use of stock, seed and mills were paid to the local landowning aristocrat, gentleman or *seigneur*, tithes were handed over to the local priest or minister, and taxes like the *taille* in France were appropriated by the representative of the ever-growing central state. This last deduction provoked the greatest resentment amongst the peasant population, perhaps because of its tendency to rise without apparent cause or benefit to the locals. Immediate self-sufficiency unencumbered by deputies of the crown was the great desideratum of village life, and it was this intrusion of the agents of the Court into the lives of the locale that provided one of the more significant trends in seventeenth-century state-building. Throughout Europe everyone was involved in an expanding relationship with the dynastic state and everyone supposedly received benefits from this set of institutions, security being paramount among them. But aristocratic landlords continued to monopolize political power and public functions in the countryside, while the peasantry, uneducated, largely illiterate, immobile, unskilled and without property of their own, provided a wide platform of service upon which the earthly order attempted to mirror the celestial one. The prerogatives of landownership were many for the few who successfully combined paternalism with economic exploitation.

What, then, do the concerns of the vast majority at the bottom of the social structure have to do with the political theories put forward by Europe's literate, comfortably housed, warmly clothed, reasonably (if not nutritiously) well fed, and sometimes bathed elite? At the very least men – and I must emphasize that I mean only men – who controlled land and enjoyed an even minimal access to political power, both at the local and at the wider state level, had a very immediate material stake in preventing disturbance from below. Habitual resistance to change was no monopoly of Europe's impoverished peasantry. The potential for social chaos resulting from extreme want was a serious and recurring worry for the aristocrat or gentleman whose lifestyle, in the words of

Richard Dunn, 'differed so radically from that of the lower orders that he seemed to represent a higher biological species'.[31] Throughout the seventeenth century the problem of poverty and underemployment had engaged the attention of increasing numbers of writers, as the poor migrated to population centres in search of opportunity. With rising numbers, the older view of God's poor as deserving of special charity was replaced by a greater focus on what amounted to alleged improvidence and lack of application on the part of those who had failed to provide for themselves and their families. Men who practised no useful calling found that their 'idleness' was increasingly linked not with economic deprivation but with the malfunctioning of one's own moral compass.

We can see some of this fear in the way in which seventeenth-century governments addressed the problem of increasing vagrancy, especially in the aftermath of a major crop failure when, exhausting the supply of bark, roots, straw and vermin in their locales, but wishing to avoid the cannibal option, ragged and angry refugees would flood into the towns and cities seeking relief from the pain in their stomachs and the chill in their extremities. One result was that charity was increasingly laicized by the start of the seventeenth century, taken out of the hands of clerical authorities and placed under the jurisdiction of tough-minded civil bodies, either municipal or centrally controlled. In England, where the issue came up in many sessions of parliament, responsibility for the poor was devolved onto local parishes. The workhouse provided the solution of choice for many in positions of local power, but this invariably led to additional taxes or 'poor rates' borne by gainfully employed residents. Therefore conditions in the workhouses were made harsh enough to 'encourage' the able-bodied to seek employment on their own.

In a society without policing, without institutional systems for controlling large masses of impoverished people, the time-tested ways of judicial violence had to suffice. Thus incorrigible vagrancy and petty crimes of property would be dealt with harshly: maiming, branding or the lash, while for serious criminals there was no room for correction or reform: their antisocial activities would keep the hangman at the level of full employment. There were 70 executions a year in London between 1607 and 1616, and while the punishment may not have been exacted, as called for in the law, for theft over two shillings, capital crimes were broadly defined and amply punished.[32] A public prosecutor in Paris, writing to Louis XIV's chief minister, Jean Baptiste Colbert, in September 1697 about a case in which a convicted counterfeiter was sentenced to the galleys for life instead of receiving the usual death sentence, regretted that such gratuitous leniency 'brings no credit to the court of which I am an officer'.[33]

Back in the rural setting, peasant unrest and even revolt, most often directed against tax collectors, undisciplined soldiers, and other unloved agents of the crown, had become annual, almost prosaic events by 1700, but to society's natural leaders they were by no means less disturbing for their regularity. And collective rural discontent, the results of which were always unpredictable, could easily exhibit itself at parish festivals, fairs, and religious processions. Popular revolt has been most extensively studied in France, where risings in the wake of crop failure, plague, lack of employment and the impact of war took place somewhere in the countryside every year during the first half of the century.[34] Provence, for example, an area with a total population of no more than 600 000 people, played host to 153 popular risings between 1635 and 1669.[35] Similarly in Aquitaine between 1596 and 1715 there were some 500 revolts, most minor, some not. The tax agents of Cardinal Richelieu were often the loathsome targets of rebellious French peasants when the hardship escalated after France's entry into the Thirty Years War, while poor harvests due to wet weather across Europe in 1646 and 1647 contributed to a number of popular risings against central government.

E. H. Kossmann's judgement that 'for the masses of the population in any period of history the form of government under which they live matters only in so far as they experience its material consequences' seems appropriate in this context.[36] In Spanish-controlled Palermo, Italy, for example, food shortages in 1647 led to an attack on the town hall and the destruction of tax records, while in Naples during the same year, resistance over the salt tax quickly spread to other parts of Southern Italy.[37] Religion also played a role in triggering peasant violence. In the north of Ireland, Catholics dispossessed of their land by state-sponsored Protestant settlers rose up in 1641 and, enlisting the support of the destitute peasantry, engaged in indiscriminate attacks upon the intruded newcomers, the extent of which were greatly exaggerated by the panicked authorities in London. Lutheran peasants in Austria took up arms in 1626 after Ferdinand II ordered conversion to Catholicism or emigration, but in this case the Bavarian army of occupation was able to overwhelm the ragged troublemakers.[38]

The fact that most rebels appealed over the heads of 'corrupt' officials to the goodness and justice of the king inspired little confidence in the fundamental loyalty of those wielding pikes, scythes and muskets. Even the local landed elite had much to fear, for as one author has observed, once the attack on outside authority had begun, 'the distinction between those who crushed the peasant with taxes and those who demanded rents, tithes, or labour dues could cease to matter'. The greatest concern for central government was the possibility that local revolt might become linked with larger issues of provincial autonomy, as was the case in Languedoc in 1632 when the provincial governor translated local discontent into a general attack against crown administration, or in Normandy in 1639, when the revolt of the *nu-pieds*, brought on by escalating war taxes and bad harvests, placed upwards of 20 000 peasants, townsmen, some nobles and clergy in arms against the agents of Louis XIII's government.[39] Looking to reclaim what had been lost to them by agents of outside change, peasant rebels sometimes posed a genuine threat to the existing social and political structure. Referring to the English situation, J. H. Plumb has written that by 1688 'conspiracy and rebellion, treason and plot, were a part of the history and experience of at least three generations of Englishmen. Indeed, for centuries the country had scarcely been free from turbulence for more than a decade at a time.'[40] In such an unsettled environment, political theory would be obliged to revisit timeless questions respecting the nature of legitimate authority, deference and obedience in a period of recurring want and, more immediately, in an age of intense religious conflict. Maintaining order in the face of desperate disturbance from below was one of the paramount concerns of writers from across the ideological spectrum in the seventeenth century.

Principal Objectives

The three chief functions of the Christian state, at least since the start of the Reformation in the early sixteenth century and continuing through to the end of our period, were thought to be the maintenance of internal order through the administration of justice, the protection of all subjects from foreign aggressors, and, perhaps most importantly, the enforcement of religious orthodoxy – control over individual conscience – in the name of saving wayward souls from eternal damnation. This final charge, involving as it did 'the interpenetration of spiritual and temporal realms', had developed out of an early Christian perspective which had emphasized the prince's role as minister to the true church.[41] Throughout the middle ages princes had seen themselves as front line defenders of the faith, and this duty was raised to new heights in the wake of the Protestant reform movement.

The accepted view of the nature and purpose of the state at the start of the seventeenth century, then, was quite remote from modern liberal and permissive conceptions. This outlook, centuries in the making and accepted by most in an unreflective fashion, was articulated forcefully at the middle of our period by the English Puritan minister and, after 1660, prominent nonconformist Richard Baxter. In *A Holy Commonwealth* (1659), Baxter made it clear that the fundamental purpose of all temporal government is to advance the eternal welfare of souls and to glorify God. 'In a Divine-Common-wealth, the Honour and Pleasing of God, and the salvation of the people are the Principal ends, and their corporal welfare but subordinate to these.' The everyday temporal concerns of magistery are important only in so far as they forward a subject's prospects for the afterlife, and the authoritarianism that was characteristic of most governments constituted the basic ethos of society at every rank and station.

There was to be no salvation outside the true church, however, and Baxter remained a firm advocate of an established, obligatory national communion. For Baxter, for his medieval predecessors, and for the majority of his contemporaries, church and state were two interrelated aspects of the same incorporated community; the political and the ecclesial were one. It was the duty of the state to support the church in its work of glorifying God and in its care of souls. 'The Happiest Commonwealth is that which most attaineth the Ends of Government and Society', he wrote, 'which are the public good, especially in matters of everlasting concernment, and the pleasing of God the Absolute Lord and King of all...'[42] It cannot be emphasized enough how the religious (ingenuous or otherwise) and dynastic preoccupations of Europe's political elite affected the great mass of the population in profound ways, especially when it came to the use of state-sponsored organized violence against one's neighbours. In the words of one recent scholar: 'War and Diplomacy were conducted by the few in the interests of the many, whose mute consent was all that was required of them.'[43]

It is perhaps understandable that in a century when science and philosophy took unprecedented and unfriendly aim at the purposeful, teleological, and providential world of the scholastic mind, the image of developments in political thought offered by scholars should stress the emergence of subjective natural rights over conventional duties, contract over divine ordinance, individual autonomy over corporate responsibility, the secular over the sacred. The view of the state and the church as something other than two organizations existing alongside many others in a complex social structure would come under increased scrutiny during the course of the seventeenth century, and gradually a new understanding of the role of the state as an institution limited by law, unconcerned with the parameters of individual conscience, and protective of certain personal rights – a picture more familiar to our own liberal assumptions – would emerge in the writings of a number of theorists by 1700. It will be one of our tasks to trace the contours of this fundamental shift through the turbulence of Europe's internal and international conflicts. But the significance of the change can only be fully appreciated by reminding ourselves of the potency of the earlier paradigm, the resilience and, for many, the attractiveness of a view of civil society where the state was divinely commissioned to forward the ends of an even greater kingdom at a cost in human lives and human decency that we, while not unfamiliar with many other forms of systematic, state-sponsored cruelty, can nevertheless only blench at.

Perhaps most important, especially for those who believed that they had discovered the eternal truths contained in Scripture and had succeeded in building a confessional church around them, was the issue of determining the obligation of the faithful towards those in error, those countrymen and foreigners alike who, either out of ignorance or malice, gainsaid the dominant, state-supported definitions. The numerical significance of these dissenters was undeniable. At the start of the century the Holy Roman Emperor claimed the allegiance of a large number of Lutherans, the king of France was the leader of a sizeable Huguenot community, the Catholic king of Spain wielded authority over a growing Calvinist population in the Netherlands, and in England a Catholic minority had as their temporal head a Protestant queen. The answer to this problem, at least since the time of the first Christian Roman Emperor Constantine I, had been to employ righteous force in the higher work of saving souls. The record since that time had not been an especially ennobling one, at least in terms of its overall alliance with the ancient Gospel message. Persecution and forced conversion may have enabled the Roman church to maintain its militant ascendancy throughout the long course of the middle ages, but the Reformation crisis seriously complicated matters by opposing the patrons of emphatic certitude against the exponents of dogmatic assurance. Calvin, for example, had argued that all political authority would expire at the day of judgement, but before that final great assize its role was 'to foster and maintain the external worship of God, to defend sound doctrine and the condition of the church, to adapt our conduct to human society, to form our manners to civil justice, to reconcile us to one another, to cherish peace and common tranquility'.[44] Few seventeenth-century writers were apt to disagree with this formulation.

Throughout most of Europe at the turn of the seventeenth century, the principle established by a war-weary Holy Roman Emperor Charles V and his Lutheran princely opponents at Augsburg in 1555, whereby the convictions of the temporal ruler determined the faith of the people, was adopted as the only plausible, if theologically suspect, solution to internecine and stalemated civil conflict. It was the rare author who, like John Bergius, spiritual adviser to the Calvinist Electors of Brandenburg from 1624 to 1658, counselled tolerance toward Lutherans and the use of persuasion over force and violence.[45] It was accepted everywhere that religious minorities, in addition to forfeiting any chance for personal salvation, represented a fundamental threat to the integrity, to the very survival of the state, and in the interest of the greater good these spiritual malefactors had to be rooted out.[46]

Examples of the vital work abounded. In England and in Protestant Ireland, anxiety over Catholic subversion filled the century, from the Gunpowder Plot of 1605, to the rebellion triggered in Ulster in 1641, to the Exclusion Controversy of 1679–81, and concluding with the ouster of the Catholic James II in the revolution of 1688.[47] Indeed it can be said that no episode in English political life during the century was without its nefarious Roman dimension. In France under Louis XIV (1643–1715) the toleration which had been accorded the Huguenot minority under Henry IV back in 1598 was gradually eroded, and loyalty to the state was once again equated with conformity to the confession of the prince. Louis XIV's support for the banished James II after 1688 placed his regime at the centre of English anti-Catholic animus, a position that had previously been occupied by the now lamentable Spanish kingdom. In the German Empire of the Habsburgs, the efforts on the part of Bohemian nobles to create a Protestant majority in the college of imperial electors by offering the Bohemian crown to a non-Catholic in 1618 precipitated three decades of bloody international conflict, leaving the scarred survivors to erect permanent camps – and resonant hatreds – across a fundamental religious divide. Nowhere in Europe, with the possible exception of the United Provinces, was pluralist tolerance an accepted standard by which Christian political action was to be guided. Religious war, be it internal or external, was all too often viewed as an unfortunate but necessary preliminary to the good life.

Indeed many pious Christians, following accepted patterns of providential thought, believed that the ordeal of war was itself a divine punishment for sin, for the routine violation of God's mandate for humankind.[48] Given that there were only four complete calendar years when peace obtained throughout the continent, the theory would seem to suggest that seventeenth-century Europeans were very deeply immersed in the worst sort of Augustinian depravity. In estimating the human consequences of Catholic rebellion in Ireland and Cromwell's subsequent pacification, for instance, William Petty arrived at the figure of half a million dead between 1641 and 1652, out of a total population of no more than 2 million.[49] At the very least such shocking numbers made God's providential purposes very puzzling indeed – making exception of course for supremely confident Calvinists like Cromwell who knew just what the divine Father was about in permitting such lopsided victories.

The truly exceptional year in the seventeenth century, then, was the year without the lawless brutality euphemistically advertised as Christian warfare. Mostly dynastic in character but more often than not with a common religious denominator, wars which destroyed the lives of those who had neither stake nor interest in the ostensible occasion for the quarrel were very much the norm in seventeenth-century Europe. The near constant state of conflict, both civil and international, between the middle of the sixteenth century and the end of the seventeenth placed enormous financial strain on all of the major powers, and in particular upon those in society least able to shoulder the financial burden, the impoverished peasantry. In France the per capita tax burden on the Third Estate sextupled between 1620 and 1640, years when the country, thanks to the geopolitical vision of Richelieu, was engaged in the Thirty Years War.[50] During this century roughly one half of the income collected by the respective early modern states was spent on war, preparation for war, or in servicing debts contracted while prosecuting a war.

Given these activities, it should not surprise us to learn that between the 1590s and 1700 increases in military manpower across Europe were enormous. The little Dutch Republic, for example, increased the number of men under arms from 20 000 to 100 000, while the French army grew from 30 000 to almost 400 000 under the direction of Louis XIV. Similarly in Russia, a 35 000-man force in the 1630s became a behemoth of 170 000 by 1700, while in England where Queen Elizabeth had only managed to assemble a 30 000-man complement during the height of war with Spain in the 1580s, William III could place almost 90 000 in the field and on the seas in the aftermath of the Glorious Revolution.[51] In 1700, at the height of the struggle against Louis XIV, some 5 or 6 per cent of the entire English population were engaged in the armed forces of the Island Kingdom. Increased taxes on a peasant population whose numerical expansion had slowed considerably over the course of the century created additional hardship and resentment within the ranks of Europe's poor. But from the rulers' perspective, the build-up in military power enabled states to preserve and even to extend the faith, to control their frontiers, to repel aggressors and, not insignificantly, to maintain their own hegemony within defined borders. New domestic taxes may have bred simmering discontent, but they also furnished the armies which could control events when that discontent transformed itself into open rebellion.

Shared Perspectives

Despite the tripartite division of leadership in most European states, all segments of the ruling elite in seventeenth-century European society – monarchs, landowning aristocrats (including clerical interests) and prosperous burghers – agreed that some model of organized community was imperative if even the most elemental temporal objectives – the preservation of person and protection from hostile outsiders – were to be maintained. Very few accepted the Florentine Machiavelli's notion (now current for over a century) that politics was an autonomous end in itself, separate from all larger aspirations. Jean Bodin, writing at the end of the sixteenth century, spoke for the vast majority of writers in our period when he asserted that the prince's laws must be 'framed unto the model of the law of God'.[52] This God was both a divine father and king whose office and power were, not surprisingly, reflected in the daily operations of the best earthly governments.

And the form which the law of God took had been articulated for centuries. Although it may be uninventive and tiresome, we must constantly remind ourselves that 400 years ago people thought differently about most things, including the source of political obligation. Throughout the course of the seventeenth century, the overwhelming majority of

Europeans acquired their political views from the pulpit, where the explanations in Scripture put forward on Sunday mornings were carefully glossed by the ministry. And the essential message taught in those countless pulpits involved a number of constants which cut across the otherwise mortal Protestant–Catholic divide. Husbands and wives, sons and daughters, servants and apprentices, all learned that the origin of government lay in God's unalterable fiat, promulgated after the Fall of our first parents when Adam and Eve, repeating the contumacy of Satan, rebelled against their Maker and thus forfeited the felicity and perfection originally granted to them in Paradise. Had there been no Fall then, there would be no sickness now, no poverty, no inequality, no death, only men and women in a state of continuing bliss. In other words had obedience, that cardinal virtue, been maintained in Paradise, had due subjection and conformity to an easy rule been observed, then the myriad hardships in the post-exilic state and the sting of death at its close would have been avoided. But in the words of one English homily, 'neither heaven nor paradise could suffer any rebellion in them, neither be places for any rebels to remain in'.[53]

Thus it was that Adam's descendants were subject to death and damnation for the fault of their first parents, and the execution of the sentence would have been carried out were it not for the undeserved and loving sacrifice of God's only child. Under the new dispensation God ordered a revised model of subjection: that children obey their parents, that wives obey their husbands, and that everyone obey the temporal governor and his subordinate magistrates. All persons were naturally under the authority of a God-ordained superior; there was nothing artificial, nothing fashioned by man in legitimate temporal authority. There was no thought given to mediating the power of the magistrate with the autonomy of the individual.

Early Christian writers had largely agreed in viewing the origins of the state, although mandated by God, as essentially the product of human sinfulness.[54] Perhaps the most powerful root of this common sentiment was the Christian Augustinian picture of human corruption and incapacity for justice first articulated by the great bishop of Hippo late in the fourth century, a position much ameliorated by Thomas Aquinas in the thirteenth century but nonetheless still current in theological circles and given repeated empirical confirmation by the behaviour of men whenever structures of authority were placed under strain. Both Luther and Zwingli insisted that God had ordained the secular authority of princes and magistrates, and sanctioned their employment of physical coercion, because of the inherent sinfulness of humankind. God's rule over a fallen and disobedient world necessitated the instrument of state power; absent the declension of our first parents, there would be no need for the sword or the magistrate. According to the Elizabethan churchman Richard Hooker, human corruption since the Fall was so great that 'to take away all kind of public government in the world, were apparently to overturn the whole world'.[55] Government was thus one of the principal repercussions of Adam's contumacy; from the pulpit it was announced regularly that the state was an unfortunate but necessary organization which performs no positive functions but simply restrains human corruption.[56]

It is worth recalling in this context that political thought before 1700, although slowly emerging as the sort of autonomous intellectual inquiry advocated by the innovative and infamous Machiavelli, remained largely attached to influential and enduring theological concerns. Ideas about the state, its origins, functions, and claims to our obedience, retained their centuries-old affinity with the spiritual and the eternal. There was no room in this other-worldly political theory for the concepts of personal liberty or individual rights which have become so embedded in Western culture since the Enlightenment. The subordination of the merely terrestrial well-being of individuals to the unyielding mandate of heaven was the essential measure of the good state, and mention of 'quality of living' always referred to comportment with divine purposes rather than material comfort or happiness.

Interestingly, the individualism which was lacking in contemporary political discourse found a welcome home in the Christian doctrine of final things, where individual consciousness and universal dignity awaited the chosen in the heavenly estate. In the still-influential scholastic hypothesis, humankind's nature or form was to seek that which was proper to its design: beatitude or personal communion with the Creator. Seventeenth-century politics remained a 'God-conscious' and instrumental enterprise where natural superiors were charged with maintaining an order and balance in the social arena comparable to the harmonies in the heavens. The particular and contingent actions of the state would afford the conditions under which subjects might enjoy the sort of security needed for the contemplation of the absolute and the eternal. Again Richard Hooker had this convention in mind when he stated that it is a 'gross error . . . to think that regal power ought to serve for the good of the body, and not of the soul, for men's temporal peace and not their eternal safety. Government had a higher charge than 'only to fat up men like hogs and to see that they have their mash'.[57] Indeed mash might have its place in a century where want and warfare were the constant companions of most Europeans, but it was not the business of those in power to assure the subject population a full stomach at the expense of forfeiting the intemporal soul.

The Best Form

In the early medieval period, two antithetical conceptions of the law and licit authority within the state had emerged, one a descending theory which located power in the ruler who is beholden to no other human agent or judge, and the other an ascending theory where power was believed to derive from the people who delegate it upwards to a mutually agreed superior on condition that the ruler respect the ancient laws and traditions of the people.[58] The problems which engaged political thinkers on both sides of this divide during the seventeenth century had been set by developments whose origins can be traced to the first decades of the Protestant Reformation, but the broader medieval inheritance also played its part in the solutions which were offered.

The variegated political map of Europe suggested that the most effective means to the agreed end of godly government, or for that matter the precise duties of rulers and ruled, were by no means subjects of broad consensus in the decades after 1600, and we shall examine a very wide spectrum of thought in the following chapters. When studied within the context of the severe dislocations experienced across the Continent during the seventeenth century, dislocations brought about by war, religious friction, dynastic antagonisms and global imperial ambitions, the question of what form of polity, and what set of obligations, anchored one's commitment to a particular authority, presented political theorists and political actors alike with difficult choices, choices more often than not conditioned by time and place.

In the seventeenth century most writers believed that political legitimacy rested on precedent, on the patterns already established, on history when viewed as a broad canvas of examples. The conclusions of one's predecessors were largely felt to be prescriptive, the wisdom of an earlier age setting the unalterable standards for current deliberations and problem-solving. This is why so many revolutionaries claimed that their actions were nothing more than a defence of traditional practice against the innovations of ambitious monarchs and their agents. The word 'revolution' itself was a metaphor borrowed from astronomy in order to describe either a turn in the political wheel of fortune or the restoration of an earlier condition, not a fundamental shift of power away from a privileged elite to a long-suffering majority. Seventeenth-century revolutionaries, be they Catalan peasants or English gentry, were normally fighting to restore what they took to be ancient constitutional arrangements, their elemental habits of the ages.[59]

Whatever form of political order was embraced by seventeenth-century writers, whatever view of human nature in the pre-political state was offered, whatever understanding of the historic constitution and God's will was promoted, all writers predicated their models on the assumption that civil society informed by a higher law – God's law – was a requirement for orderly living in the present, and for any hope of securing everlasting life in the future. Throughout most of the century the second objective clearly took pride of place in the language of serious political discourse. The ideal of a church-state where religious uniformity was enforced in the belief that its absence was a recipe for discord, such an ideal continued to animate political thought long after the worst horrors of the Thirty Years War had been concluded. The indispensable source for anyone wishing to express views on the civil order remained the Bible, its specific directives increasingly open to the subterranean ways of individual conscience. Some of the more important results of this personal exegesis – and the subsequent inauguration of a process whereby the text was finally set aside in favour of a more pedestrian and all too human standard – are outlined in the chapters which follow. That the overwhelming majority of seventeenth-century writers continued to ask the question 'how is a Christian society to be ordered?' betokens the strong continuities with the confessional centuries. That the enforcement of religious orthodoxy could begin to be replaced with the protection of property as perhaps the pre-eminent responsibility of the state signals the enormity of the challenge presented to the confessional agenda during the same 100 years.

2

CONTOURS OF ABSOLUTE MONARCHY

While writers in *ancien régime* France did not use the word *absolutisme* to describe their government, apologists for the great revolution during the decade of the 1790s found this neologism to be an accurate assessment of the monarchical political order that was overthrown by a newly liberated and enlightened people.[1] Indeed French absolutism was in some respects 'defined to fit the case of Louis XIV', making the word synonymous with the alleged innovations and policies of one man, instead of regarding it as 'a broad historic phenomenon'.[2] The word first made its appearance in England even later, in the radical literature of the 1830s.[3] But in seventeenth-century England, doctrines of absolute sovereignty were very often associated by its critics with the narrow power-seeking interests of the Stuart monarchy and the privileged clergy in the state-supported Church of England. In either case monarchical absolutism was pejoratively linked with unlimited power, tyranny, despotism, fanaticism, the rule of one against the interests of the many. Until recently some historians have been willing to accept the harsh judgement registered by the French revolutionaries and English radicals against the first promoters of the idea of absolutism, while accepting the notion that absolutist forms of government enjoyed their definitive flowering in the seventeenth century.

It is perhaps to be expected that a more democratic age would look back and describe seventeenth-century apologists for royal absolutism as retrograde and unenlightened, the self-interested defenders of *ancien régime* privilege and spectacular inequality. The historian Perry Anderson, for example, interpreted the emergence of absolutism as nothing less than the result of a deliberate compact between the landed aristocracy and the prince, a compact whose purpose was to stymie the expansion of capitalism. In the east, especially in Prussia and Russia, this agreement purportedly involved noble support for the crown and service in the bureaucracy in return for extended rights over the peasantry in the form of the institutionalization of serfdom. In the West, where a free peasantry and an urban bourgeoisie were already in place by the start of the seventeenth century, the aristocracy adapted itself to state service while the prince promised to use the coercive power at his disposal to pre-empt popular unrest and to preserve noble status and landed wealth.[4] Such analyses offer a powerful indictment of a system thought by some to be at the foundation of later forms of arbitrary rule. But we must be cautious to avoid ascribing too much to what was a varied set of phenomena, the sum total of which sought to address pressing needs and popular sympathies. It may be that such a critical position, especially in light of political circumstances at the time, takes insufficient account of a unique range of problems facing all European governments after 1600.

Why Absolutism?

Before turning to the work of some seventeenth-century exponents of absolutist theory, it may be useful to touch upon some underlying assumptions and developments. In the first place, we must recall that the security of the prince had been seriously compromised by the intensity of contemporary ideological and religious conflict. In the closing decades of the sixteenth century, resistance theorists on both sides of the religious divide provided scriptural grounding for acts of regicide when conditions warranted, and works like the *Vindiciae contra tyrannos*, and George Buchanan's *De jure regni apud Scotos*, both published in 1579, enjoyed a not inconsiderable readership. There had been more than twenty attempts on the life of Henry IV before the French king was finally assassinated by a Catholic fanatic in 1610. In England, every Tudor monarch faced at least one major rebellion, while the first Stuart king, along with the members of the House of Lords, narrowly escaped death when the Gunpowder Plot of 1605 was thwarted. The second in the Stuart line, Charles I, was less fortunate. An extra-legal show trial condemned the king to death as an enemy of the people after Charles failed to prevail against parliament's forces in the Civil Wars of the 1640s.

Another significant inducement to move in the direction of absolutism at the start of the seventeenth century concerned the enormous costs associated with the 'military revolution' of the period, when the training and mobilization of larger armies was seen to be imperative to the very survival of the state. In this respect one could argue that centralization was driven by external aims and ambitions and not, primarily, by internal pressures created by competing social groups in late feudal society.[5] Monarchs needed to increase regular revenue from domestic sources, to override the ingrained parochialism of regional assemblies and the taxpayers who were represented by these assemblies, for the good of the state lest hostile powers, motivated by religion or by simple ambition for additional real estate, destroy the persons and property which the monarch was sworn to defend in his coronation oath. If, as Thomas Hobbes had averred, heads of state were constantly 'in continual jealousies, and in the state and position of gladiators; having their weapons pointing, and their eyes fixed on one another', then the escalating cost of military preparedness was simply a burden that had to be accepted, even at the distress of an unprecedented and unsettling centralizing programme.[6]

Finally, in the face of an obvious breakdown of government in France during the third quarter of the sixteenth century, chronic aristocratic factionalism in Spain, Sweden, Poland and, to a lesser extent, in England, and the anarchic horrors of the Thirty Years War in the German states, it was thought that absolute rulers, if afforded the opportunity, could most effectively place the corporate interests of the nation ahead of the myriad oppressions of overmighty subjects, the selfish demands of specific landed interest groups and parvenu urban money-bags. Only such a fount of justice and military power could transcend the different customs and prejudices of the provinces and shape a larger, more coherent unity. Across a Europe unique for its multiplicity of political forms, there were unmistakable signals that a new sense of urgency respecting the need for undivided sovereignty was directing the thought and action of writers and political actors alike.

Working from Jean Bodin's definition of sovereignty as 'the most high, absolute, and perpetual power over the citizens and subjects in a Commonweal', the heads of dynastic states increasingly came to believe that they could no longer afford to share command with other powerful interest groups if the duties of ensuring domestic tranquillity, international respectability, and religious orthodoxy were to be met.[7] No one, for example, wished to slip into the localist bedlam of the seventeenth-century Polish state, where an elective kingship an∢ fractious aristocracy guaranteed the triumph of provincial misrule dangerous and ideologically charged times, a fundamental redefin⟩ of sovereign power, one where no institution, no noble privilege or ical corporation or representative assembly would be allowed to challenge the chief magistrate, seemed obligatory. Only under such an arrangement of power, where legislation, taxation, judicial power, and the means to make war were controlled by an undivided authority, could the material and spiritual welfare of subjects be assured.

Heralded by its supporters as progressive and community-oriented, absolutism stood for efficiency in government, for the promotion of trade and industry, for sound administration and for the security of vulnerable frontiers in a Europe of atavistic and competing powers. In absolutist thought the state was not simply one organization among others, but was constitutive of the whole social order, and the will and power of the king was the glue which held society together.[8] To make the ruler dependent upon the cooperation of his most powerful subjects, especially those who clung to feudal precedent and localism, was counterproductive to the swift and equitable resolution of pressing domestic and international problems, and to the oversight of what all observers acknowledged was an increase in the workaday administrative, financial, judicial, and international functions associated with the central state. Colbert needed more and better reports from his *intendants* in the provinces, not dissonant and distracting voices in a legislative assembly; Louis XIV, when the public good required it, must have the right to raise taxes without wider consent and not be obliged to dispute the merits of the call with members of the three Estates who were competent only to estimate their own particular needs.

Only in this manner could the civil and religious disorder that had been part of the French experience from 1560 to 1660 be reversed. Troubles and disorders similar to the French case might be identified in every European state during the course of the seventeenth century. The birth of the military-bureaucratic state with the absolutist prince at its apex appeared to many theorists to be the best solution to the fact of a divided and competitive Christian Europe, a Europe where, according to absolutist writers, no single state could afford to maintain an earlier tradition of decentralization and medieval constitutionalism. Qualities associated with the Sermon on the Mount were all very well for individual sinners; applied to the crystallizing nation-state these same principles invited certain disaster. A godly absolutism was, for its defenders in print, the only means to the type of collective security prerequisite to the redirection of human interests heavenward.

Appearance and Reality

On the surface, the evidence of a pointed shift towards absolutism after 1600 seems not insignificant. Representative institutions consisting of the three great orders of clergy, nobility and affluent townsmen appeared to be falling into desuetude in a number of countries. The Englishman James Harrington, looking back at mid-century, lamented: 'Where are the estates, the power of the people in France? Blown up. Where is that of the people in Aragon, and the rest of the Spanish kingdoms? Blown up.'[9] In France the historic Estates General was not called into session by the monarch between 1484 and 1560, and after the 1614 meeting it did not convene again until the great Revolution of 1789. Indeed it was during the last meeting of 1614 that the Third Estate requested the king to proclaim: 'That, as he is acknowledged Sovereign in his state, holding his crown only from God, there is no power on earth, of whatever kind, spiritual or temporal, that has any right over his kingdom, to deprive it of the sacred persons of our kings, or to dispense or absolve their subjects of the fealty and obedience that they owe them, for any cause or pretext whatsoever.'[10]

The king's ability to impose the *taille* on his own will, together with the royal preference for meeting separately with the provincial estates when in need of a general subsidy, ended any argument in favour of the idea that a larger community of the realm had a voice in matters of taxation, a right which even Bodin had affirmed. Crown introduction of the *intendants* into provincial administration during the 1630s countered local intransigence respecting the need for efficiency in government and accountability to the king, while doing not a little to curb the traditional fleecing of the peasantry by local *seigneurs*. Cardinals Richelieu and Mazarin, although challenged at every opportunity by local landed elites, worked tirelessly to make the Bourbon dynasty master in its own house.[11] That work reached its consummation long after the deaths of these dedicated royal servants, for when the *parlement* of Paris lost its right to remonstrate before registering royal edicts in 1673, and when the Catholic clergy affirmed the independence of the crown from papal oversight in 1682, Louis XIV appeared to have achieved the elusive goal of governance unhindered and unchallenged by his quarrelsome subjects. Cardinal de Retz, who had on more than one occasion sided with rebels against the crown, observed laconically that 'France has had kings for more than twelve hundred years, but these kings never had the absolute power they enjoy nowadays'.[12] During the final three decades of the king's reign, there were no major revolts against the growing burden of taxation, and religious dissidents (namely Jansenists and Huguenots) had been silenced or driven out of the country.[13] The ceremony, pageantry and spectacle associated with court life at Versailles, not to mention the overall architectural impress of the baroque pile itself, were designed to remind everyone of the qualitative distinction between monarchy and mere aristocracy, to reaffirm the mystical rightness of the subordination owed by the liegeman.

Across the Channel the Stuarts found little joy working with an always loquacious parliament and avoided meeting that body whenever alternative sources of income permitted. Between 1629 and 1640 Charles I attempted to rule without convening the Lords and Commons, and when not in session there were no standing committees or regular officers to give voice to opinion outside the Court. The crown enjoyed significant prerogative rights, including the power to suspend parliamentary statutes when in the king's estimation the safety of the kingdom was at stake. As head of state the king called and dismissed parliament at his own discretion, controlled foreign affairs (including issues of war and peace) and coinage, appointed common law and prerogative court judges, designated members of his privy council, selected bishops and presided as head of the national church, and regulated industry in the interest of the national defence. Charges that Charles I and his sons, Charles II and James II, were very much enamoured of absolutism were commonplace during the tenure of each man upon the throne. For later Whig historians, the execution of the first Charles in 1649 and (the Stuarts being slow learners) the deposition of James in 1689 saved the day for all doughty champions of consultative government.

In the same year that monarchy was restored in England after the failure of Cromwell's republican experiment (1660), the Danish Estates ceased operation. Twenty-three years later, a new Danish law code announced that the king alone enjoys 'supreme authority to draw up laws and ordinances according to his will and pleasure, and to elaborate, change, extend, delimit and even entirely annul laws previously promulgated by himself or his ancestors'.[14] At about the same time (1680), the three non-noble Estates in the Swedish Riksdag, furious over the land-engrossing penchants of the nobility, sided with King Charles XI in his successful efforts to 'resume' previously alienated royal lands. In that year some two-thirds of the peasants were tenants of the nobility, while twenty years subsequent only one-third remained in that status. The Diet of 1693 declared, with widespread popular backing, that 'by God, Nature and his high hereditary right' the king and his heirs 'have been set to rule over us as absolute sovereign kings, whose will is binding on us all and who were responsible for their actions to no man on earth, but have power and authority to govern and rule their realm, as Christian kings, at their own pleasure'.[15]

To the south, Frederick William of Brandenburg-Prussia, levying taxes by personal decree in Cleves, Mark, Brandenburg, and, after 1673, in Prussia, inaugurated the process whereby the civil and military affairs of later Prussian governments would be guided by the crown and its advisers alone. In the Iberian peninsula, the kings of Castile remained masters of a global empire unhindered by any constitutional requirement to consult with representative institutions, and after 1667 his 'most Catholic majesty' made the talkmasters in the Cortes of Castile permanently redundant. Not to be outdone by these precedents, Tsar Alexis (ruled 1645–76) undertook to shape a justificatory ideology of absolutism which drew increasingly from the Byzantine model. With the patriarchs of Moscow confirming that the Holy Ghost was actually in their emperor in order that he might better govern men, the Romanov tsars aggressively pursued an autocratic programme. A thorough codification of the laws began in 1649, serfdom was imposed on the peasantry, the old system of according court and military offices on the basis of precedent was abandoned, and the composition of the tsar's council shifted to include a majority of members from a service gentry background, leaving the aristocracy with a diminished voice in politics. The reign of Alexis' youngest son, Peter (ruled 1700–25), witnessed a dramatic acceleration of these and other consolidating trends.[16]

At a preliminary level, then, these tendencies across Europe were both portentous and alarming for those who cherished the feudal and medieval notion of consultation and advice. But the underlying problem with using the word 'absolutism' in order to describe these and other seventeenth-century developments is that in practice there were no monarchs who actually enjoyed complete freedom of action without the advice and consent (tacit or active) of local elites. No prince could act in an arbitrary fashion outside the law and not expect serious opposition from very powerful members of the noble, burgher and clerical estates, the very segments of the population whom monarchs were keen to ally themselves with in the programme of centralization and bureaucratization.[17]

Taking only the best known example, during the second half of the century in France Louis XIV was always careful to cultivate the allegiance of the nobility, for he realized that the power to enforce law and collect taxes in the countryside was more often than not held by local bodies headed by the baronage. The coronation oath, where the monarch pledged to protect the liberties of the church and the Estates, together with an undertaking to dispense justice to all subjects, distanced the monarch from arbitrary power. The king was a source of enormous patronage for the aristocracy, and noble cooperation with crown interests in the countryside ultimately forwarded the social and economic preoccupations of both parties.[18] Key to that patronage system was the sale of offices, a sort of royal privatization scheme which expanded enormously during the seventeenth century. The number of offices in France stood at about 4000 in 1515, ballooning to 46 000 by 1665 as the rage for appointment – and exemption from taxation – reached its apogee.[19] And while this system of venality was of some short-term advantage to the crown in terms of producing a ready infusion of much-needed revenues, over the long term these holders of office, who in essence had purchased a portion of royal authority, could also frustrate the king's will on a wide range of issues.

Throughout the long reign of the 'Sun King' (1643–1713) a clearly delineated hierarchy of power remained in place throughout France, and if the king could issue edicts without consulting his subjects, the enforcement of those commands remained in the hands of sometimes uncooperative local magnates and judicial bodies. As one scholar has observed: 'Even at the height of Louis XIV's ascendancy, in the 1670s, pockets of privilege, custom, and exclusion flourished in France.'[20] The judicial functions associated with the provincial *parlements* were never upset or redefined during this period, seigniorial jurisdiction over one's tenants was never abridged, while the preference of the *noblesse d'épée* to settle disputes by extra-legal recourse to duelling, while repeatedly condemned by the crown and the law courts, continued with relative impunity. Bishop Bossuet, tutor to the Dauphin and author of *Politics Drawn from the Very Words of Holy Scripture* (1704), might employ divine-right formulations of absolutism in order to anathematize notions of resistance, but with a total bureaucracy amounting to only 1000 overworked individuals, there remained plenty of room for the type of give and take between the provinces and Versailles to sharply qualify the transfer of absolutist theory into practice before 1700.

In England the crown was too impoverished to pay for a system of regular salaried officials whose exclusive allegiance was to the monarch and whose tenure in office depended upon performance. James I received around £400 000 in income at the start of his reign in 1603, a figure which eventually was increased to some £900 000 thanks to the extra-parliamentary machinations of his son Charles I in the 1630s. But in real terms (adjusting for inflation) the regular income secured by Charles was equivalent to that garnered by that notorious spendthrift Henry VIII in 1510, this despite the fact that the population of the Island Kingdom had doubled in the interim. Unpaid amateur officials, most of whom were the same people who sat in the House of Commons when that body was called into session, served the crown as Justices of the Peace in the countryside. There was no national army to coerce these unsalaried bureaucrats, only various militia raised locally. Under these conditions the effective power of the monarch depended very much upon the collaboration of his property-owning subjects.[21]

When we turn to the case of Spain, the problem is shown in even sharper relief. The sixteenth century is often portrayed as Spain's 'golden age' of empire, economic prosperity, and crusading military might, while the succeeding 100 years is described as a period of decay or irreversible decline. At one level the picture is indeed compelling. Compared to a French state racked by religious civil wars, a feeble monarchy, and financial disarray, Spain at the time of the death of Philip II in 1598 was master of an overseas empire larger than Europe itself and stretching from America to possessions in Africa and the Far East, and the new king, Philip III, commanded what was still the most impressive military force in Europe. The kingdom of Portugal had been annexed in 1580, for the first time bringing the entire Iberian peninsula under Habsburg control. In addition, the Spanish nobility had remained, comparatively speaking, united behind the crown throughout the sixteenth century, and whatever small pockets of religious dissent may have gathered clandestinely, a climate of submissiveness was moulded by the 'familiars' of the Inquisition so that religious issues never posed a serious threat to the stability of the state.[22]

The image of Spain as the irredentist Catholic ogre of Europe, ruled by fanatical absolutists in the persons of Philip II and his successors, and home to Jesuit political theorists who peddled shop-worn papal supremacy while simultaneously condoning regicide if the prince should deviate from the true path, certainly resonated with early seventeenth-century English writers on politics. Spain's wealth and military resources, it was held, were at the beck and call of the Counter-Reformation madmen in Rome, and its bigoted and mystery-mongering monarchs provided the model for the type of leadership destined to obtain throughout Europe should the Protestant states fail in the great struggle against the Catholic nemesis. Yet despite the fears – and the hyperbole – of those who recalled the Elizabethan era of heroic struggle against Philip II, there were a number of facts about the Spanish monarchy which did not comport with the model of tyrannical rule outlined by its opponents, and political theory originating in Spain reflected these realities.

First and foremost, the Habsburg rulers of Spain exercised their extensive powers solely in their home kingdom of Castile, the largest, most populous and traditionally the most productive of the Iberian dominions. When one adds Aragon and Portugal to the mix, languages, currencies, and representative institutions multiplied and royal authority diminished.[23] During the 1620s, Philip IV's dedicated chief minister, the Count of Oliveres, attempted to consolidate government functions by opening more high offices to non-Castilians, encouraging intermarriage, restricting the autonomy of regional viceroys and, most importantly, establishing a reserve army staffed by recruits from all of the king's dominions, but the effort was successfully resisted by the outlying provinces.[24]

Of greatest importance, perhaps, is the fact that the king did not enjoy the right of collecting extraordinary taxation outside of Castile. Of the 16 million Europeans under the Spanish crown, only one-third of these, mostly living in Castile, bore the costs of global imperial administration. Respecting the traditions of the peripheral kingdoms was a very costly gesture indeed, for Philip III, who reigned from 1598 to 1621, received no subsidies from the assemblies of Estates (Cortes) in Aragon, Valencia, Portugal, or the Basque provinces.[25] And despite the great wealth extracted from mines in the New World, only one-quarter of total crown revenues were covered by American bullion. During the seventeenth century, shipments of bullion from the American empire fell dramatically, while in the colonies themselves the Amerindian population continued its unprecedented decline, mercantilist restrictions against Dutch, English and French traders were ignored by venal customs officials and their hangers-on, and American agriculture receded to subsistence levels. If one of the defining criteria of the absolutist state involves bureaucratic centralism and territorial consolidation with the intention of introducing uniform legal and administrative procedures, then seventeenth-century Spain, with its Iberian pluralism and imperial diversity, clearly does not qualify.[26]

General Assumptions and Specific Impediments

Not surprisingly, the most vocal – and influential – supporters of the king's absolute power in each of the dynastic states were the clergy of the predominant churches. Where for centuries the Catholic Church had been the most important rival to the emerging states, with the Reformation the Protestant churches lost their right to exist autonomously, while the Roman Catholic communion found itself allied firmly with the Catholic princes. The age of nationalist churches had begun. In France and in Austria, the Catholic hierarchy consistently defended the growth of royal power as a check to religious dissidence. Further East, the Russian Orthodox Church became the principal bulwark of the tsarist state, while in England the bishops, whose preferment rested with the monarch, naturally looked to the supreme head of the church to sustain their claim to divine authority in the spiritual realm.

These same English Church leaders relied upon royal backing in their ongoing struggle with Calvinist reformers who wished to abolish the remaining Catholic traditions and practices within the national communion. Calls for the continued reform of the church had been issued in parliament throughout the reign of Elizabeth, and it was only expedient for the clergy to magnify the prerogative of the crown when many members of the Commons appeared eager to dictate ecclesiological and ceremonial 'purity' for the church on their own terms. Institutional, professional, and spiritual self-interest all pointed clergymen clearly in the direction of absolutist theory. The doctrine of non-resistance was a staple of the Anglican pulpit both before the Civil War, and even more emphatically, after the return of Charles II in 1660. Rebellion, in the words of one of Charles I's chaplains, 'causeth all sin in general, and is as great as the foulest sins in particular, even as witchcraft and idolatry'.[27] Submission to natural superiors, on the other hand, was in the words of another preacher 'proper to man, not instituted by man; for it hath its beginning from God'.[28]

It was on this point of natural superiors that writers focused a great deal of their attention. For theorists of absolutism, elevating the power of the seventeenth-century prince comported perfectly with the predominant popular picture of an ordered universe created by God where all things held their appropriate place in an unalterable hierarchy of correspondences. Contained within the larger macrocosm of the physical universe were subordinate bodies or microcosms whose arrangement mirrored the larger structure. In the heavens, in the church, and in the social order, all was conceived by an omnipotent God who had set the proper place for created things. One of these hierarchical microcosms was the political order, whose structure 'was held to reflect the gradational form characteristic of the universal scale of creation: society was a hierarchy of social degrees and ranks'.[29] To challenge the natural hierarchy, at whose apex stood the monarch, was to engage in sin of a very serious nature, for the monarch's position in the microcosm was akin to God's position in the macrocosm, and to upset that paradigm was to invite ill fate.[30] The Englishman Thomas Wentworth, loyal servant of Charles I and chief bogeyman of the parliamentary opposition, expressed this view succinctly when he announced that: 'The authority of the King is the keystone which closeth up the arch of order and government, which contains each part in due relation to the whole, and which once shaken, infirm'd, all the frame falls together in a confused heap of foundation and battlement, of strength and beauty.'[31] That a benevolent and providential God had ordained princely government for humankind was foundational to a larger constellation of assumptions which served to situate man in a world of purpose and striving. 'Take away Kings, Princes, Rulers, Magistrates, Judges, and such states of God's order, no man shall ride or go by the high way unrobbed, ... and there must needs follow all mischief and utter destruction, both of souls, bodies, goods, and commonwealths.' Such was the resolution of the Church of England's 1547 *Book of Homilies*, and the appeal was repeated across Europe for the next 150 years.

In addition to the 'correspondence' factor, for most Europeans a strong monarchy was 'felt' to be the true form of executive leadership because it reflected, albeit imperfectly, the wisdom of God's paternal oversight and the remedy for humankind's sinfulness in the wake of the Fall. Broader theological and anthropological assumptions thus helped to sustain absolutist theorizing. In particular, an Augustinian estimate of corrupt human nature, where cooperation and kindness to one's neighbours were the exceptions to normative conduct, suggested the need to concentrate power in one person or one body. Indeed a key feature in the medieval lineage of the absolutist idea can be traced back to the thought of St Augustine, the fourth-century bishop of Hippo, who made it quite clear that classical conceptions of political society as a community of men seeking a rational ordering of their collective temporal affairs were, from the Christian standpoint, unattainable.

In a world of iniquitous and destructive individuals, coercive political structures were essential bulwarks against chaos and insecurity. St Paul had indicated as much in Romans 13:1,4 where the minister ordained of God was 'a revenger to execute wrath upon him that doeth evil'. Political order, as we have seen, was the consequence of the Fall, thus political authority had to be placed well beyond the reach of common men lest their anarchic and sinful dispositions plunge God's special creation into the abyss of mutual destruction. The ruler, and even the tyrant, was appointed by God to curb the worst behaviours of subjects whose proclivity for evil was not to be remedied in this life.[32] Whatever sufferings and injustices might be inflicted by the evil ruler were to be endured in silence, for the earthly tenure was of little significance in comparison to the heavenly home. Addressing King James I of England in 1624, the clergyman John White affirmed that the king 'is more than an ordinary man: God hath set his own image, as it were upon his gold, in an eminent manner upon you, which he hath not done upon other men: your cause is God's cause, your zeal and constancy is for Gods truth'.[33]

Absolutists believed that only the undivided sovereign could hope to apply the principles of natural law which were implicit in the definition of the human soul but which, in the wake of the Fall, had little appreciable impact on the behaviour of most men and women. Anarchy and disarray were now the natural penchants of the descendants of sinful Adam and Eve, and mixed governments where sovereignty was compromised only fuelled the destructive and rebellious tendencies of creatures who knew the law but whose base appetites led them to defy its directives. Augustinianism provided strong Christian credentials to a theory of politics which denied subjects a capacity for personal disinterest requisite to the job of guaranteeing the good of the entire population. The unchallenged authority of the prince was a part of the scholastic 'science of Being' because it satisfied a deeply felt need for personal security in a community of inveterate sinners.

Before absolutism could become a viable political model in Western Europe, the centuries-old pretensions of the Roman pontiff to definitive rule in both the spiritual and temporal arenas needed to be addressed.

Originating with the cult of St Peter, the popes of the early middle ages struggled vigorously against the claims of Byzantine imperial authority by alleging that the 'keys to the kingdom of heaven' (Matthew 16:18–19) first entrusted to Peter, could be transmitted to his heirs at Rome. In the landmark bull *Unam Sanctam* in 1302, Boniface VIII elaborated on the theory of papal supremacy by stating that while temporal authority had been delegated to princes by the successors to St Peter, each ruler remained ultimately responsible for his actions to the Roman Curia. Under this theory 'universal sovereignty was claimed for the pope and his court; the medieval theorists of papal monarchy leaned heavily on the terminology and ideology of Roman imperial law and precedent'.[34]

Oversight and the right of deposition, including the power to release subjects from their allegiance to the erring prince, were the exclusive perquisites of the spiritual head of the Christian community. Commissioned as God's anointed during the act of consecration, kings could lose their sacral character by disobeying God's law as interpreted by the Church. Kingship was not a God-descended right, but an office legitimated by the Roman Catholic Church. This concept was given renewed affirmation by a number of Spanish Jesuits in the late sixteenth century. In particular, the writings of the theologian Francisco Suarez (1548–1627) defined the contours of much Catholic thinking on politics throughout the entire course of the seventeenth century. Spiritual authority was superior to its secular counterpart, according to this leading figure in Counter-Reformation thought, because matters spiritual had the Creator for their end, and the Holy See was charged with ensuring that princes ruled in accordance with the spiritual well-being of their subjects. The temporal felicity and security afforded by the well-ordered state was a worthwhile end, but it must always be subordinated to the definitive end of humankind. According to Suarez,

> both the corrective and punitive functions are proper to the office of a pastor; and it frequently happens that censures alone do not suffice for these purposes, an inadequacy sufficiently brought out by daily experience; therefore, one must conclude that Christ did bestow the power in question upon His Vicar, since he made that Vicar pastor over Christian princes no less than over the rest of Christendom.[35]

The state was a part of the divine order set by God, and the successor to St Peter must guarantee that the lesser realm is not misdirected by ambitious princes.

Attempts to give this theory practical application after 1600 included an episode in 1606 when Pope Paul V forbade English Catholics to take an oath to James I in the aftermath of the failed Gunpowder Plot. James, like his Protestant Tudor predecessors, rejected the papal power to depose, claiming instead that his kingly authority proceeded directly from God, and demanding the oath as a test of his subjects' allegiance. Subjects were required to 'swear that I do from my heart abhor, detest and abjure as impious and Heretical, this damnable doctrine and position: That Princes which be excommunicated or deprived by the Pope, may be deposed or murdered by their Subjects or any other whatsoever'.[36] In fact James's position was little more than a restatement of Luther's assertion that ecclesiastical authorities had no jurisdiction in temporal matters, and that subjects, while not obliged to obey a heretical prince, had no right to resist him and must endure tyranny in silence. Writing his *History of Passive Obedience* at the conclusion of the seventeenth century, Abednego Seller identified the origins of absolutism with 'the infancy of the happy Reformation' when 'the most eminent of the reformed divines' took a stand against both the pretensions of Rome and the radical ambitions of the peasantry.[37] Recently Quentin Skinner has concluded that 'there is no doubt that the main influence of Lutheran political theory in early modern Europe lay in the direction of encouraging and legitimating the emergence of unified and absolutist monarchies'.[38]

Ironically, Protestant princes were not the only ones balking at Rome's extended claims. As early as the fourteenth century, at a time when pope Boniface VIII was affirming the legitimacy of the hierocratic principle, the Chancellor of the University of Paris, Jean Gerson (1363–1429) and the English Franciscan William of Ockham (c.1280–1349) were insisting that secular government must be distinguished and separate from ecclesiastical control. In the early sixteenth century the Sorbonne scholar John Mair argued that the spiritual and secular jurisdictions must be separate and that 'kings are in no way subject to the Roman pontiff in temporal affairs'.[39] The Council of Trent had asserted the church's right in France to fiscal immunity and to jurisdiction in cases involving attacks against the faith, but Henry IV's Parlement of Paris refused to accept this decree.[40] Many Catholic apologists for absolutism insisted that the clerical estate had no brief to interfere with the decisions of princes on temporal affairs, that indeed the prince, in cases where public necessity demanded it, was permitted indirect control over the church in his kingdom.

Everybody – even the vast majority who were excluded from a role in Europe's many and disparate governments – acknowledged that the fundamental human duty was obedience to God. This office of submission to our principal superior, always a medial theme in pastoral teaching, overrode all forms of obedience to man. At one level this elemental duty might appear to diminish the prerogative powers of one's social superiors, at least in terms of regulating conduct, but in practice the centuries-old claims of the Roman Catholic Church to final jurisdiction over the actions of men, by virtue of its apostolic mandate to oversee the cure of souls, had under Protestant auspices devolved into a situation whereby individual territorial princes inherited the mantle of supervising both church and state affairs. Indeed the divine element of the princely office had always been an accepted part of Christian political theory, illustrated by the fact of clerical participation in the ceremony of royal consecration.[41] The various Germanic princes who had fought their way into positions of power after the collapse of Roman imperial authority, and who had accepted Christianity, for example, held the temporal sword under the jurisdiction of the Holy See.

Anointed with holy oils at his coronation, widely acknowledged to possess special healing powers by virtue of his sacred appointment, the prince was charged with maintaining – even extending – the one true faith across his domain.[42] In its monarchical form absolutism built upon the already strong medieval tradition of according the chief feudal lord of the kingdom a special relationship with God. Members of the parliamentary opposition to Stuart royal prerogative in England shared a deeply held conviction with their royalist opponents that the king was commissioned by divine ordinance to lead the nation. Even the lawyer Sir Edward Coke, no complacent yes-man for the monarchy, conceded that the king 'is over us the Lords anointed, and in these his Realms and Dominions, in all Causes, and over all Persons, as well Ecclesiastical as Civile, next under Christ Jesus our supreme Governor'.[43] Before the actual outbreak of civil war in 1642, parliamentary opponents of the king joined with Anglican clergy and crown allies in affirming the divine origin of Charles I's power and the superiority of monarchy over every alternative form of government.

Absolutist theory in its English context affirmed the already considerable powers enjoyed by the monarch and acknowledged as legitimate by the vast majority of the political nation. Parliament was seen by absolutist authors as the king's extended council which, when called into session, granted special taxes and passed laws which the monarch requested.[44] Writers in this tradition agreed that an absolute prince was not responsible to his subjects for actions taken in an executive capacity, but only to God and only then at the moment of judgement after death. In the words of an anonymous pamphlet published during the Fronde in France, the king 'is obliged, and promises at his Consecration, to render Justice, and to govern his Kingdom according to right and reason; when he does not keep his promise God, who is sole Judge of his actions, will not leave his injustice unpunished, but it does not belong to subjects to take cognizance of them.'[45] The prince was God's anointed, His temporal vicar whose duty was to administer divine justice, and in the tradition of St Augustine no amount of tyranny could justify sedition or rebellion.

Duty, Moderation, Natural Law

It is important for us to recognize that proponents of absolute rule, and there were many during the course of the century, did not equate absolutism with arbitrary or tyrannical government, with the expropriation of property and the collapse of legal precedent. Opposition nobles accused the Polish King Sigismund III of seeking absolute dominion when, at a meeting of the Diet in 1606, the monarch called for the establishment of a permanent tax and a standing army. But the charge in this case was misplaced, reflecting the nobles' primary interest in maintaining their own individual sovereignty, a sovereignty best illustrated by the establishment of the Liberum Veto in the sixteenth century, whereby a single noble could dissolve an entire assembly.[46] In England this erroneous conflation was made most forcefully in 1689 by John Locke, who in the opening of his rebuttal to Sir Robert Filmer's *Patriarcha* connected absolute rule with 'the utmost Misery of Tyranny and Oppression' and the reduction of the population to 'slavery'.[47]

Contrary to Locke's misleading allegation, writers who supported absolutism agreed that the supreme giver of life, whose every direction for his special creation was bound up with the promise of eternity, placed enormous responsibility on the ruler (and in most instances this meant the monarch) to govern in accordance with the postulates of divine and natural law, to adhere to standards of justice and conduct appropriate to a larger sacred mandate. Martin Bucer had articulated this position clearly from the city of Strasbourg as early as the 1530s.

During the early centuries of the church, Bucer claimed, when temporal rulers were non-Christians, God had relied on the power of the Holy Spirit to strengthen the church. Since the conversion of secular authorities, however, 'he wished them truly to serve him with their office and power, which derives from him, and is committed to them only for the good of Christ's flock'.[48]

It was this same concern with the common good which animated the thought of Jean Bodin at a key moment of crisis in late sixteenth-century France, when religious differences threatened to plunge society into an unending cycle of violence. And one century later, in more propitious circumstances, Bishop Bossuet was still at work reaffirming the sober message. Although the king's power comes from on high, he wrote to the Dauphin, 'they must not believe that they are the owners of it, to use it as they please; rather they must use it with fear and restraint, as something which comes to them from God, and for which God will ask an accounting of them'.[49] As one of Christ's deputies on earth, then, the prince more than any of his subjects was obliged to illustrate the qualities associated with the King of kings. St Paul had affirmed the gravity of the princely charge when he announced that: 'Every soul must be submissive to its lawful superiors; authority comes from God only, and all authorities that hold sway are of his ordinance.'[50] But in order to merit the unflinching obedience of one's subjects, princes under Christ were bound by a universal and knowable law, the law of nature or natural law, and their favourable reception at the day of final judgement was contingent upon their scrupulous adherence to this inflexible standard.

Natural law doctrine had long preceded the arrival of Christianity. Greek philosophers, speculating on the regularity which they had observed in the forces operating in the natural world, together with the rules and customs which appeared to be common amongst all peoples, concluded that there must be an intelligent organizing principle guiding both nature and humankind. But the vocabulary of medieval Catholic, later Protestant and even secularized natural law theory was set in pre-Christian Roman culture and society. In *De legibus* (On the Laws), Cicero described nature as the source of primordial eternal principles whose purpose was to guide human conduct, a source accessible to everyone through the exercise of natural reason, and originating in the being of an abstract God who was separate from the deities of the ancient pagan world.[51] For Cicero 'law is the highest reason, implanted in nature, which commands what ought to be done and forbids the opposite. This reason, when firmly fixed and fully developed in the human mind, is Law.'[52] Human ordinances merely make manifest a law which is already in place, and those statutes which defy the higher natural law represent base injustice, 'the most foolish notion of all' being the conviction 'that everything is just which is found in the customs and laws of nations'.[53] Origen (c.185–c.254) called the law of nature the law of God written in every human heart, and insisted that the positive laws of the state were invalid if not in conformity to these higher principles.[54]

In the thirteenth century, the Dominican Thomas Aquinas associated natural law with that small part of God's eternal law which humans, through the exercise of reason, are able to perceive irrespective of material circumstances, and in the sixteenth century Jesuit theorists like Suarez affirmed the Thomist perspective in their struggle against Lutheran deprecations of natural reason.[55] Human law and natural law were different in degrees, not in kind, and all law had as its end the advancement of divine justice.[56] It was widely accepted by seventeenth-century theorists that God had instilled basic precepts of the natural law, particular moral absolutes, into each rational being, and correct political truths were to be deduced from these absolutes.[57]

By placing universal reason anterior to all man made law, the absolute ruler could secure for his subjects, who like himself were but pilgrims on this earth, the conditions of peace and security, of law and order, of strong and unified government requisite to the more important work of pursuing the great gift of residence in the City of God. When the speaker of the English Parliament declared in 1604 that the commands issued by the king must be just, 'for he sits in the Judgment Seat of the absolute King of Justice', he was reminding his audience of the king's obligation to ensure that human law reflected the unchanging principles of the natural law.[58] According to Sir William Fleetwood, 'to make a law contrary to that [natural law] is to make a void thing'.[59] And when Francis Bacon urged that 'all national laws whatsoever are to be taken strictly and hardly in any point wherein they abridge and derogate from the law of nature', he was defining the limits of political obligation using the same universally accepted standard, a benchmark which, if adhered to, guaranteed that humans would maintain their proper relationship to God.[60] Even in Castile, a kingdom which Englishmen of Bacon's generation instinctively associated with the worst form of absolutism and Catholic irredentism, and where the input of the representative body, the Cortes, was not constitutionally required in the making of laws, the monarch was viewed first as a minister of the people bound by reason and natural law, all exercised in the name of the common good. Luis de

Molina's conclusion that the state is not made for the king, 'but the king for his country – to defend, administer and direct, not for his own whims, vanities and convenience, but for the common good' was embraced by absolutist writers throughout the seventeenth century across all territorial borders.[61]

Jean Bodin and James VI and I

We can profitably illustrate some of these restraints on absolute power in the political theories of two key figures of the late sixteenth and early seventeenth centuries. As we have already noted, Jean Bodin clearly had the problems and the needs of his own country in mind when he composed his greatest work, *Six Books of the Republic*. But it was much more than a work of mere political convenience, or a propagandistic statement suitable to a single time and place. Published in 1576, while he was serving as a deputy of the Third Estate to the Estates General, ten French editions of the book, together with three Latin ones, would appear in print before the author's death in 1596.[62] In 1606 Richard Knolles translated the text into English, and from that point forward to the outbreak of civil war in 1642 Bodin was cited by English writers of all political outlooks.[63] The *Republic* was written in response to the new forms of constitutional theory emerging in the immediate aftermath of the 1572 St Bartholomew's Day Massacre and in the shadow of four separate outbreaks of civil strife over the religious issue in France during the previous 10 years.

The Huguenot Calvinist minority had been winning dedicated adherents from across the social spectrum, including members of the aristocracy, since the middle of the sixteenth century. Their desire to maintain a toleration was supported by elements of the Catholic majority eager to avoid civil turmoil, but by the late 1560s the Huguenot preference for passive resistance had become impractical in the face of a growing threat from a militant Catholic interest at Court led by the House of Guise. In the absence of strong royal leadership after the death of Henry II in 1559, the crown, under the ineffective regency of Catherine de Medici, was unable to contain the more belligerent voices on both sides of the Catholic–Protestant religious partition. Ultimately convinced that the Huguenots were subverting the dynasty, the government decided to eliminate the leadership of the Calvinists in one brutal sweep. In the

weeks following the massacre in Paris, attacks on Huguenots throughout the country resulted in the deaths of an estimated 10 000 people.[64]

It is no surprise that the groups most likely to stress the contractual
nature of government were those suffering from the capricious actions
of the state. Most often the claim to resist was based upon a desire for the
right to practise one's faith without molestation rather than with specific
charges of misgovernment on the part of the magistrate. Huguenot
resistance theorists (to be treated in the next chapter) built upon notions
latent in the Calvinist tradition. While not condoning individual resistance to the ungodly prince, the early followers of Luther and Calvin had
not precluded other magistrates having the right to take action and use
the sword in defence of God's higher laws.

Although officially a Roman Catholic, and while never publicly calling
for religious freedom as a right owned by all Frenchmen, Bodin nonetheless agreed with the Huguenots that religious persecution was both
ineffectual and divisive. In Bodin's view religion was a personal affair
over which the state could contribute nothing, thus forms of religious
worship were best handled in the interests of expediency and social harmony.[65] In the opening pages of the *Republic* he lamented the triumph
of those Machiavellian ministers who 'instruct princes in the rules of
injustice to ensure their strength by tyranny' for these counsels always
led to the ultimate breakdown of political order. Despite this concession,
however, he was unwilling to affirm that resistance was legitimate under
any circumstances, for taking action against one despot simply results in
the elevation of multiple tyrants. 'Many, indeed, would be the tyrants if
it were allowable to kill them' leading to 'licentious anarchy, which is
worse than the severest tyranny that ever was'.[66]

The *Six Books of the Republic* popularized the word 'sovereignty' for the
seventeenth century, linking it with an indivisible power in the state
which could not be challenged by any other temporal or spiritual
authority. In a definitive and unprecedented fashion, Bodin's work
spoke to the process of consolidation which was taking place across
Western Europe at this time, setting aside the tangle of plural allegiances represented by the medieval world of feudal personal and property
relationships. According to Bodin (and according to most modern
notions), the indivisible, untrammelled, absolute, and perpetual sovereign, be it an assembly, a small group or (Bodin's preference) an individual monarch, makes all law for the well-being of the entire community,
appoints all inferior officials and magistrates, declares and concludes
war, and serves as a court of final appeal for every person regardless of

rank. Law is simply the 'command of the sovereign touching all his subjects generally on general matters', with the important provision that these commands always conform to natural and divine mandates. In the medieval frame of reference, the very notion of the ruler as lawmaker was insignificant in comparison to his judicial and administrative functions. But in a rapidly changing social, military and economic environment, the legislative functions of the sovereign, the power to create new law in response to new conditions, became paramount. Active resistance to this sovereign lawmaking authority was not permitted under any circumstances, for to allow the possibility of defiance implied that there was a power in society higher than and independent of the sovereign, and this was a recipe for chaos. Bodin did make allowance for passive disobedience since it did not claim a power of correction, but defiance of the sovereign always carried penalties which were at the discretion of the magistrate. In an important respect Bodin stripped allegiance of any practical ethical dimension, since the tyrant does not forfeit his sovereignty in light of his evil actions. He will of course face divine retribution for his misdeeds, but so long as he holds his absolute sovereignty, the allegiance of all subjects was obligatory.[67] The *Six Books of the Republic* inaugurated the modern supremacy of the political nation over all other competing loci of power, and in the process made equal subjection to a single temporal sovereign the main attribute which all citizens shared in common.

We should emphasize, however, that Bodin was not an advocate on behalf of despotism; he believed that a wise king must respect divine law, customary law and property rights, and that such a prince would regularly seek the advice and consent of the representative estates of the realm, especially when the issue of taxation was involved. In this respect he would have agreed with the Englishman Richard Baxter's later caution regarding princes whose power was unlimited: 'Greatness will have great temptations; And when there is no restraint, this will make the Greatest to be the worst.'[68] Sovereign prerogative power, however, was in Bodin's view an absolutely inalienable property; it might be delegated to inferiors for the sake of greater efficiency, but this entrusted authority is always exercised on the sovereign's behalf and is never inherent in the lesser magistrate. Both spiritual and temporal lords may exercise certain seigniorial jurisdictions and hold offices as a grant, a revocable trust from the crown, but Bodin wished to make clear to elites upon whose support and cooperation the crown depended, that jurisdictions and offices were not rights of personal property.

The author of the *Six Books of the Republic* insisted that a legitimate sovereign power could not tax without the consent of the estates or take a subject's property at will, that in fact 'there is not a prince in all the world who has it in his power to levy taxes on subjects at his pleasure, any more than he has the power to take another's property'.[69] But at the root of what appears at one level to be a significant fiscal limitation on the prince, Bodin – like many of his contemporaries – was convinced that the sovereign could and should live on the income from his own royal domain. Outside those rare cases when the security of the state was threatened and when the prince 'should not wait for the Estates to assemble, or for the consent of the people' before raising taxes, the normal rental income from the royal patrimony (if it were rented at market value) should provide more than enough income for salaries and regular government functions.[70]

The depletion of the treasury occasioned by crown expenditure on generous pensions for favourites and tolerance of corrupt officials had been a common complaint as early as the meeting of the Estates General of 1560 and 1561.[71] Permitting the Estates the right to consent in matters of extraordinary taxation was not intended to alter the formal relationship between the crown and the subject. Full sovereignty remained undivided as long as financial solvency was possible without new and exceptional taxation. In the end legitimacy was not based upon respect for individual rights, economic or otherwise; rather it was established solely by how well government maintained public order and provided for the good of the community.

King James I of England (James VI of Scotland) was the author of a number of important works in political theory, and his writings perhaps more than any other represent the theory of moderate or practical absolutism that we have been discussing here. The fact that Thomas Hobbes, Sir Robert Filmer and even Bishop Bossuet praised this first Stuart king may not surprise us, but that John Locke could also speak approvingly of James, 'that Learned King who well understood the Notions of things' in *Two Treatises of Government*, is strong testimony indeed to James's moderation.[72] Coming to the throne as a child-king in the wake of his mother's deposition in 1568, James's early thinking was shaped by Scottish Presbyterianism and its claim to set limits over royal authority. The young king's close relatives in France, members of the Guise family, were principals in the religious civil wars which afflicted that country, and James was not unfamiliar with Huguenot and Catholic League resistance theories which endorsed armed action against heretical

rulers. Nor was he ignorant of papal claims to exercise spiritual authority, including the power to depose heretical rulers, should the prince act
in a manner contrary to Catholic teaching.[73]
In the 1590s, the future king of England authored two books whose
controlling objective was to rebut the contractualist arguments of Scottish Calvinists, French Huguenots and Catholics throughout Europe.
After his accession to the English throne in 1603, James was keen to
demonstrate that the 'ancient liberties' of Englishmen were to be traced
to the free grant of kings, and not, as the common lawyers and anti-
quaries held, to a sacred inheritance from their collective ancestors,
later codified in documents such as Magna Carta.[74] James's Scottish
tutor George Buchanan had written in defence of the proposition that
the prince was akin to an administrator chosen and evaluated by the
people, while the Jesuit Robert Parsons insisted in *A Conference about the
Next Succession to the Crown of England* (1594) that James, as a heretic,
had no legitimate claim to succeed Elizabeth, that indeed the crown by
right must pass to the Spanish infanta. Elizabeth I had earlier (1570)
been excommunicated by the pope, an action which led some Catholics
to view the queen as a usurper who should be assassinated. The danger
was a very real one, for in France King Henry III was killed by a
Catholic fanatic in 1599, and his successor Henry IV would suffer
the same fate in 1610. Thus James was concerned to address the dangerous implications of all resistance theories when he first appeared in
print.
In *The Trew Law of Free Monarchies* (1598) and *Basilikon Doron* (1598),
James set himself the task of vindicating the divine right, absolutist
claims of hereditary princes independent of papal suzerainty. The king
was convinced that only a strong executive could prevent the type of
religion-inspired civil conflict which racked late sixteenth-century
France. The latter work was actually a best-selling advice book written
for the king's elder son and heir Henry. It was quickly translated into
Latin, French, Dutch, German and Swedish, and it was often quoted
approvingly by contemporary theorists. *The Trew Law of Free Monarchies*
was published anonymously and it has subsequently been viewed as
the most absolutist of the king's efforts. It was certainly the more theoretical of the two books, utilizing illustrations from Scripture, history
and reason to advance the case for royal power subject to no human
restraint.[75]
According to James, because they 'sit upon God his throne in the
earth, and have the count of their administration to give unto him',

kings are not made by subjects, nor do the laws constrain the prerogative
of the ruler whose first concern must be the overall good of the
commonwealth.[76] The sovereign must be obeyed in all things, 'except
directly against God' for royal commands are the commands of God's
minister, and the king 'having the power to judge them, but to be
judged only by God, whom to only he must give count of his judgement'.[77] For the Gunpowder plotters of 1605, as for the Catholic zealot
who assassinated Henry IV of France in 1610, James's claims of kingly
accountability to God alone shattered the pope's charge to protect the
souls and direct the actions of the faithful in the face of heresy. The wise
king will in fact shape his actions in correspondence to the law, 'yet is he
not bound thereto but of his good will, and for example-giving to his
subjects'.[78] These ideas were very familiar to the political elite in England by the time that James assumed the throne in 1603, and the print-
ers were kept busy producing copies of these two works as the old queen
entered her final year.[79]

Despite this initial stridency, however, James was careful to stress in
both of these works the ruler's duty to govern according to established
law and in the best interests of his subjects. 'Think not therefore', he
advised his son, 'that the highness of your dignity, diminisheth your
faults (much less give you a license to sin) but by the contrary your fault
shall be aggravated, according to the height of your dignity.' The glory
of kings has been established for a purpose by God, 'that their persons as
bright lamps of godliness and virtue, may, going in and out before their
people, give light to all their steps'.[80] James distinguished between the
true Christian monarch, who 'acknowledgeth himself ordained for his
people, having received from God a burthen of government, whereof he
must be countable', and the tyrant who is prey to his own passions and
appetites, and who believes that the people are ordained for his pleasure
alone.[81] The great contentment of the Christian king lay in the well-
being and prosperity of his people, while the evil tyrant builds his
personal happiness at the cost of his people's misery. In a speech before
Parliament in 1610, James distinguished between the state of kings
in primitive societies, where unlimited power was necessary due to the
lack of agreed laws, and the state of 'settled Kings and Monarchs'
where the ruler binds himself 'to the observation of the fundamental
Laws of his kingdom'. He assured MPs that while it was sedition for
subjects 'to dispute what a King may do in the height of his power',
Christian kings like himself would always rule their actions according to
the law.[82]

James combined his Bodinian emphasis on the responsibility of kings to uphold the established law with an unqualified opposition to the opinion that subjects possess a right of resistance to their monarch, even if the ruler were to act in a tyrannical manner and command things which overturned divine law. *The Trew Law of Free Monarchies* begins with the assertion that, next to their knowledge of God, 'the right knowledge of their allegiance, according to the form of government established among them' is essential if men are to live in a peaceful condition.[83] Addressing Star Chamber in 1616, the king compared the atheism and blasphemy of those who would dispute with God to the presumption and contempt in a subject who disputes a king's prerogative.[84] Although monarchy 'approcheth nearest to perfection', James allowed that one could disobey a tyrant. But those who engage in this passive resistance must always suffer in silence whatever penalties the king imposes on them for disobedience to his will.[85]

Bossuet, Filmer and Scripture

James's views were widely shared throughout Europe in the new century, and the king extended his support to a number of continental scholars who similarly affirmed that monarchs were not to be made accountable to any earthly restraints. Still, we should be careful to recognize that absolutist writers did not adhere to a single explanation of either the occasion for the transfer of undivided authority or the precise nature of its civil embodiment. While most often arguing that the sovereign's office was a direct commission from God (the divine right of kings), some thought that the position was an irrevocable grant from the community. Under the latter reading, it was even held that kings might be elected by the people, but royal authority, once an individual had been selected, always sprang directly from God. Sir Robert Filmer acknowledged the prestigious lineage of this theory when, at the outset of *Patriarcha* (1680), he observed that: 'Since the time that school divinity began to flourish, there hath been a common opinion maintained as well by divines as by divers other learned men which affirms: "Mankind is naturally endowed and born with freedom from all subjection, and at liberty to choose what form of government it please, and that the power which any one man hath over others was at the first by human right bestowed according to the discretion of the multitude".'[86]

The archetype of this elective principle or 'designation theory' was the papacy, where the occupant of the chair of St Peter was initially selected by his peers, but ruled only under the headship of Christ himself. The same basic formula was thought to apply to those kings who had secured their office by conquest; William of Normandy's successful invasion of England in 1066 may have demonstrated that hereditary right was not indefeasible, but even foreign usurpers owed their power to a single heavenly Master. 'By me kings reign, and princes decree justice' was the familiar message repeated from Proverbs 8:15, and designation merely identified the particular holder of the divine trust. Some writers thought that the powers of the absolutist prince were most effectively utilized when in the hands of one man, while others preferred to situate the locus of sovereign authority in an aristocratic or legislative body. The English Parliament during the Interregnum (1649–60), for example, exercised absolute sovereignty in the sense that no human law was superior to its decisions.

The varieties of absolutist theory were considerable indeed, but contained in each of them was the clear acknowledgement that sovereignty was indivisible and that government was a divinely appointed instrument for the realization of that good order essential to a redirection of human interests toward heaven. Writing against late sixteenth-century resistance theorists, Catholic and Protestant alike, William Barclay insisted that kings enjoyed 'this prerogative of authority, which is superior to all power of the people'. Barclay's *The Kingdom and the Royal Power* (1600) acknowledged that sovereign authority may come by way of divine appointment or by popular commission, but once in place it was unimpeachable.[87] Subjects must obey the commands of the prince as long as these directives comported with the law of nature and positive revealed law, while active resistance to a ruler, even an unjust one, was never to be condoned since it was thought to be the first stage toward mobocracy. Under no conditions could the absolute prince be removed from power, either by the subject population however represented, or by the leadership of the church, even one that claimed, as the Roman Catholic Church did, the right to dispense divine, life-saving grace. Once commissioned to make law and to adjudicate disputes for the good of the state community as a whole, the prince became the permanent custodian of the nation's temporal well-being. Undivided and indefeasible sovereignty was for the theorists of absolutism the surest, indeed the only, guarantee of order and stability in a otherwise violent world.

Without overlooking the importance of 'designation theory', then, we can turn our attention to the supporters of patriarchalism, those theorists who employed Scripture in an effort to ally princely power with paternal authority over the family. Like political theorists of almost every persuasion after 1600, patriarchalists wished to demonstrate how their position not only corresponded with supernatural design, but how it also reinforced existing social theory. The family had always been regarded as the source of larger social groupings, and as historians have made clear in recent years, fathers and husbands possessed enormous authority over women, children, servants and apprentices during the seventeenth century. Before a man became the head of his own household, he was an inferior to his father, his master, his teacher, his employer, and his minister.

Subordination and resignation to structures of authority growing out of the family unit were a normal part of the maturation process, and insubordination to one's natural superiors, as exemplified in Shakespeare's *King Lear*, led inevitably to social chaos.[88] It was not a difficult step, then, for writers to extend conventional social practice into the political sphere, to argue that the state had evolved naturally from the primary familial association. Just as the child was enjoined by the Fifth Commandment to honour and obey his parents, so the subject's solemn obligation to the head of the state was analogous to the personal bond within the household, a bond which was clearly the will of God. If one accepted this parallel between private and public where the state was viewed as an extended family – and the argument was being made for the first time in the seventeenth century – then all contractual theories, including the alternative absolutist notion that the office of the sovereign was originally a grant from the people, were invalidated.[89]

Bishop Bossuet's *Politics Drawn from the Very Words of Holy Scripture* remains, in the estimation of its most recent editor, 'the most extraordinary defence of divine-right absolute monarchy in the whole of French political thought'.[90] It was a defence built upon very familiar foundations, however. In 1625, for example, the bishop of Chartres had proclaimed in the name of the Assembly of the Clergy of France that: 'besides the universal agreement of peoples and nations, the Prophets announce, the Apostles confirm, and the Martyrs testify that kings are ordained of God, and not only that, but they are themselves gods...No one may deny this without blasphemy or doubt it without sacrilege.'[91] Bossuet completed the first six books of the work in 1679, near the close of a ten-year service as tutor to the Dauphin. He then set the entire project aside for 22 years, before completing the final four books in 1704, the year of his death. The finished work, half of whose 500 pages are taken up with verbatim extracts from Scripture, was first published in 1709.[92] For this intolerant defender of the Catholic Church, the *Politics* takes as its starting point not the traditional Thomist acceptance of both scriptural and pagan sources on an equal basis, but rather the Lutheran assumption that the Bible alone provides fallen humanity with all essential political principles.[93]

Bossuet was convinced of the insufficiency of reason to the task of understanding the true origin and nature of licit political authority. Fortunately the Bible, and in particular the Old Testament, provided adequate direction, historical and divine, in the field of civil life, and that direction pointed unmistakably to the propriety of absolute monarchy ordained by an interventionist and providential God, one far removed from the disinterested prime mover of the mechanical Cartesian universe. Bossuet equated rationalist notions of a general order in creation with the height of human arrogance, treating God as if he had 'only general and confused views, and as if the sovereign intelligence could not include in his plans particular things, which alone truly exist'.[94]

Of course, as Christopher Hill has pointed out recently, the Bible, although central to all seventeenth-century intellectual activity and the source of divine wisdom on all subjects, could mean different things to different people: 'It was a huge bran-tub from which anything might be drawn.' Even the notorious Thomas Hobbes, whose *Leviathan* had assayed to derive the principles of politics from the book of nature alone, could include citations from more than 657 biblical texts in his chief work, while over 1300 biblical quotations are to be found in his six major political works.[95] Citing scriptural warrant for one's political ideas constituted perhaps the most persuasive marshalling of evidence available to any author. And access to the Bible was expanding dramatically beyond the ranks of the literate and well-to-do. As early as 1546 Henry VIII was complaining that the Bible was 'disputed, rhymed, sung and jangled in every alehouse and tavern'.[96] Direct access to God's Word proved to be an irresistible draught with several unforeseen consequences.

Bossuet was thus not unique in exercising his considerable ingenuity in fitting the life-saving text to his particular political position. For example the *Politics* contains 73 references to the book of Judges, but chapter 21, where 'in those days there was no king in Israel: but every one did that which seemed right to himself' is passed over in silence.[97]

The bishop did not deny that several places in Scripture locate authority in the community, or that 'in the beginning the Israelites lived in a kind of republic', but he does insist that they later voluntarily reduced themselves to monarchy. Similarly he found evidence in 'profane histories' to support the thesis that ancient Greece, ancient Rome, and all current republics were at first governed by kings. 'Men are all born subjects: and the paternal empire, which accustoms them to obey, accustoms them at the same time to have only one leader.'[98]

After describing an anarchic state of nature in the first book of the *Politics*, the search for unity led men to civil society under a single ruler, and hereditary monarchy descended from David and Solomon proved the most durable. Perfection is not to be achieved in this world, but while there is no human institution without flaws, 'whoever undertakes to overthrow them is not only a public enemy, but also the enemy of God'.[99] Placing the state in peril by threatening the public peace cannot be permitted, but the prince must listen to his people when they submit respectful remonstrances. The quality in Christ that Bossuet stressed most emphatically was his passive acceptance of constituted authority, especially his recognition of Pilate's power over him. The same submissiveness and passive obedience was highlighted in Julian 'the Apostate', and conforms to the warnings in St Paul (Romans 13) to obey the powers that be.

The arguments advanced in what is perhaps the best known of the texts in this genre, Sir Robert Filmer's unimaginatively titled *Patriarcha* (1680), were actually current in England during the first part of the century, in particular the refutation of the idea of man's original freedom in a state antecedent to the formation of civil society. In 1593 the clergyman Hadrian Saravia published his *De Imperandi Authoritate*, a work dedicated to the Bodinian precept that divided sovereignty was a contradiction in terms, and one which drew upon Scripture to account for the origins and nature of government. The author denied the resistance theorists' contention that men were created in a state of natural freedom from which they subsequently removed themselves by voluntarily transferring authority to a king.

The liberty associated with a state of freedom was for Saravia 'the cause of the fall of Adam'.[100] Rather everyone was born into a family, and from these families early political institutions emerged guided by the principle of primogeniture so that 'men did not elect but received princes'.[101] It was not necessary for contemporary monarchs to trace their direct descent from Adam, for God always reserved the right to transfer power to a new ruling family, or indeed to forego monarchy and replace it with an aristocracy or even a democracy. Whatever the specific workings of divine providence, paternal power always remained with the ruling authorities. In Filmer's estimation: 'There is, and always shall be continued to the end of the world, a natural right of a supreme father over every multitude, although, by the secret will of God, many at first do most unjustly obtain the exercise of it.'[102]

In England, patriarchal theory was inculcated most forcefully at the popular level by the Church of England, although dissenting ministers promoted the idea as well. In canons adopted in 1606 by representatives of the entire clergy in Church Convocation, Adam and his successors were held to have been granted both fatherly and royal power.[103] And the catechism employed in the instruction of children expanded the umbrella of the Fifth Commandment to include all superiors; obedience to masters, teachers, ministers and lesser magistrates was just as crucial to one's fulfilment of God's law as conformity to the will of parents and princes.[104]

It was in the course of attending to their religious obligations that largely illiterate subjects learned about political authority as a natural state whose origins can be traced back to the creation, not a contractual or voluntary one built upon the shifting sands of mere convention. Indeed one of the attractions of patriarchalism was that it provided a compelling and familiar historical account of the origins of political society, from the power of the first father Adam over his immediate off-spring to the acceptance of wider responsibilities as society expanded and disputes arose. Adam's title to political authority was grounded in the divine will at the moment of creation; the purportedly 'historical' state of nature advanced by consent theorists, where freedom and consent preceded the formation of civil society, was simple myth.

In *Patriarcha*, Filmer deliberately eschewed the Church Fathers and later scholastic commentators on the Bible and focused instead on the text itself, especially the Old Testament. He opened his discussion with a rebuke of 'school divinity' for having 'hatched' the dangerous idea that mankind is free from all subjection and permitted the right to choose his government. For Filmer, Genesis was of central relevance to political truth, and Adam's possession of the earth as a divine charge, detailed in the story of creation, left no room for government by consent of free and equal individuals. The desire for liberty which he found so widespread amongst his contemporaries was itself the cause of Adam's fall.

In place of this alarming liberty Filmer offered a theory of natural subjection, the belief that all political power rested with a monarch to whom all lesser bodies and individuals were subject. Political power is identical with the arbitrary and absolute power that fathers enjoy over their offspring, their wives, their servants, and their apprentices. Filmer, who had composed *Patriarcha* during the tumultuous 1640s, believed that the invariable result of consent theories was civil unrest and popular sedition. Doubtless taking the Civil War period of the 1640s as a touchstone, he concluded that there could be no end to rebellion and religious upheaval without the firm inculcation and acceptance of the doctrine of natural subjection.

Celestial Mandates

There were, of course, other important writers who embraced absolutism as the most appropriate form of political organization in this century of emerging, and highly competitive, nation-states. I have omitted them from our treatment here because these individuals raised fundamental objections to the model of a God-ordained civil society accepted by the overwhelming majority of the population of seventeenth-century Europe. The apologists for absolute command treated in this chapter all reflexively assumed that how men organized themselves here on earth – and before God – was not a matter of volition, of choice based upon mere human convenience or utility. Instead it was believed that the roots of obligation to one's temporal superior, and the form which that superior order assumed, were intimately allied to a more comprehensive and significant allegiance.

God's purpose in investing absolute rulers was to secure a harmonious political order.[105] Simply put, absolutism was the product of divine ordinance, a mandate informed by the troublesome fact of human sinfulness, of primal disobedience in a paradisiacal state where instruments of coercion were absent. Now those instruments were compulsory, solemn reminders of human depravity and spiritual declension. Our moral duty to obey the state, and our responsibility to acquiesce in the guardianship of those who hold their power from God, testified to the resilience of a Christian anthropology that is no longer extant in the modern West.

This model of absolutist thought, steeped in centuries-old assumptions about the precarious place of humans in a purposeful and value-laden universe, shared little common ground with men who embraced the model of rulership while simultaneously rejecting its theological underpinnings. We shall turn to the exponents of this secular alternative in chapter 5, after considering some anticipations of this man made politics in the voluntarism of constitutionalist and republican writers. But we should be reminded that while challenges to divine right absolutism were mounted after mid century, the attraction of a theory of earthly rule which seemed to mirror the common understanding of the nature of God's rule in the transcendent sphere remained both compelling and comforting. As long as the interests of this world remained less meaningful than those of the next, as long as this journey was simply preliminary to a greater destination, then government of and by the people was an impertinence.

3

CONSTITUTIONS AND CONSENT

In his end-of-the-century plea for Protestant legislative autonomy in England's most proximate – and most problematic – colonial possession, the Irishman William Molyneux cautioned that the rights of parliaments should be nurtured at all costs in every country. 'This kind of government, once so universal all over Europe, is now almost vanished from amongst the nations thereof. Our king's dominions are the only supporters of this noble Gothick constitution, save only what little remains may be found thereof in Poland.'[1] For Molyneux, and for not a few like him who surveyed the political landscape of Europe at the close of the century, the ideal of the 'Gothick' constitution was being rapidly and insidiously eroded by the exaggerated claims of overly ambitious princes. The future of Europe seemed destined to follow the path of augmenting monarchical prerogative at the expense of broader consultation and consent, and inattention to this dangerous trend could only result in the eradication of all institutional and legal bulwarks against tyranny.

But whatever the more extreme ambitions of absolutist monarchs might have been, and whatever the fears of observers like Molyneux, the simple reality throughout Europe during the seventeenth century was that princes, as we have seen, needed the good will and cooperation of the hereditary nobility and the landed gentry if they were to rule effectively. This had always been the case. 'There has rarely if ever been a government absolute in practice' is the judgement of one recent scholar of the medieval period. 'A ruler or ruling group has always to consider the interests and actions of the ruled, if only to repress them, and generally it must limit its own desires in order to survive for long.'[2] It was therefore unrealistic for writers to moot the advantages of princely decision-making unhindered by the regional prejudices of landed interests if for no other reason than the fact that orderly governance in the countryside hinged upon the concurrence of men whose social standing in their respective locales was unimpeachable.[3]

Both the king and his most powerful subjects recognized that if their hegemony over the labouring population was to remain secure, then mutual dependence upon each other's good offices was imperative. Deliberative assemblies, at the village, town, provincial and state levels, had been an important part of the fabric of European political life throughout the medieval period and while, as noted earlier, none of these institutions represented individuals in the democratic sense of the last two centuries, the men who sat in these bodies worked unfailingly to protect the liberties and privileges enjoyed by powerful landed groups and urban oligarchs. To many writers, mixed sovereignty, 'bounded government', offered the best hope for maintaining the stability of the state and good order in society by assimilating the concerns of distinct interests into an agreed set of wider policies and objectives. This idea of constitutional restraints on executive power – both legal and institutional – is one of the exceptional features of European development, and arguably 'can be seen to lie at the very heart of Western cultural singularity...'[4]

To speak of constitutions in the seventeenth century is a bit like discussing normative principles of morality in the Western world at the close of the twentieth; each discussion must proceed without a documentary touchstone, a written set of universally agreed conventions and rules around which one might negotiate and reference. Before the revolutions of the late eighteenth century, European constitutions were, by and large, composite entities, made up of historic and customary patterns of securing community goals, together with a host of written laws handed down from across the centuries and interpreted in keeping with current needs. Sweden was perhaps unique in possessing a rather sketchy fourteenth-century 'Land Law' which defined kingship as limited and contractual, but even this text was much amended during the seventeenth century in favour of allowing the monarch greater discretionary power.[5] Not even the two largest governments wrestling with chronic disorder during the medieval age, the Holy Roman Empire and the Roman Catholic Church, based their considerable temporal authority on a formally structured and readily accessible code.

In feudal society it was impossible to identify a central power capable of focusing the individual wills of subjects, especially when powerful vassals possessed extensive lawmaking and judicial competence over their usufruct lands. There was certainly little clarity respecting the precise locale and scope of sovereign power in later 'constitutions', beyond the more obvious convention that power ought to remain within certain historically conditioned limits. Nor did monarchs put much effort into formulating systematic statements on the matter, preferring instead to forward their claims within the context of particular situations as the need arose.[6]

The main task of seventeenth-century consent writers was to show that sovereign political power, while derived from God, was mediated at first to the community – and not to a privileged individual or group – and that under certain adverse conditions this power, after it had been transferred to an agreed individual or group, might revert again to its communal roots. As we have seen in our discussion of absolutism, many proponents of the unlimited power of the prince (Filmer being the most prominent exception) had allowed that an initial transfer of rights from the people lay at the foundation of legitimate rule, implying that originally men and women were without a political master. It was thus plausible for opponents of absolutism to argue that the intention of this original transfer of power had been to secure effective government, and that no one had intended to yield himself up entirely to the dictate or caprice of the ruler, to forego the liberties associated with his station or the property which afforded him maintenance and freedom from servitude.

At the heart of the consent position, then, was the highly controversial notion that all social relations beyond the family, including all political forms, were non-natural and voluntary arrangements, deliberate conventions, designed and adopted by men for their mutual advantage and convenience. Most importantly, consent signified that the monarch was not beyond the reach of human control, that the office was, in the end, a man made institution, not a divinely designated and thus unalterable one. Disturbingly implicit in this family of ideas was the prospect that kings, under particular circumstances, could be resisted by their subjects. In particular, proponents of the idea of original contract held that when the king violated natural law, he could be actively opposed, coerced, by the subject population, or by the duly appointed representatives of the subject population. Those who justified such resistance were labelled 'monarchomachs' by their critics, a charged term which literally meant 'king-killer'. And while many constitutionalists were ready to acknowledge with their absolutist opponents that political authority was the result of man's sinfulness brought on by the Fall, still they insisted that the community was antecedent to the erection of the kingly office, and that subjects had a legitimate – indeed pivotal – role to play in the initial appointment.

Appeals to Tradition

What precedents, what established body of thought could seventeenth-century advocates of limited government point to in their encounter with emergent absolutism? Direct innovation was of course impermissible, the manifest sign of one's refusal to work within time-tested and God-ordained parameters of intellectual discourse. Seventeenth-century people were accustomed to being bound by precedent, whether this involved the transfer of land, the inheritance of goods, or the framework of civil order.[7] As Brian Tierney has cautioned in a recent work, the constitutional ideas of our period 'did not pre-exist eternally as Platonic abstractions; they were not engendered suddenly out of nowhere in the crises of the seventeenth century; they have a history'.[8] That history ranged widely and eclectically, absorbing and refining ideas from the ancient world of Greece and Rome, from the feudal heritage, from medieval Catholic debate over papal power, and from sixteenth-century resistance theories put forward by Catholics and Protestants alike. Each of these strands helped to shape a perspective on politics where the various estates or orders of society could claim rights of representation in formal assemblies, where an ascending model of government embracing a community's consent stood against the descending model of all-powerful princes.

(a)   Aristotelian anthropology

Anti-absolutist thought in the early seventeenth century owed not a little to the fact that most educated gentlemen, regardless of their country of origin, were familiar with ancient Greek and Roman authors who had extolled the virtue and sense of fulfilment associated with active participation in the life of the city-state or republic. While outright republicanism was not popular with the educated elite after 1600, the idea of non-military service to the prince enjoyed a growing constituency. Classical learning, especially as represented in the works of Cicero, Tacitus and Plutarch, disposed one to defend the importance of consultation in political life, while a strong civic humanist tradition kept alive the ideals of ancient participatory governance.[9] Perhaps most importantly, the thirteenth-century revival of the works of Aristotle served to counter an earlier Augustinian penchant for freeing rulers from the control of subjects. St Augustine's picture of the origins of political authority, we recall, dominated thinking throughout the early middle ages. Slavery and political authority were the products of sinful human nature. God permitted the rise of men who imposed their wills on the weak for two related reasons: subjection is a just punishment for sin, and the discipline accompanying subjection was useful in restraining sinful beings from their evil proclivities.[10]

Beginning in the thirteenth century a radically different picture was presented. The translations into Latin of Aristotle's *Ethics*, *Rhetoric*, and most importantly the *Politics*, 'introduced the ideas of the mixed constitution, of the citizen, and of participation in government...into the medieval world'.[11] Aristotelian studies affirmed the ability of rational and naturally social individuals to conform themselves to the precepts of natural law and therefore to realize their full potential in civil society.[12] The state reappeared as a natural product and man was described as achieving his highest human potential only as part of political society.

For Aristotle, civic association was an organic, normal development, something designed to forward the good life, what constituted the purpose and perfection of humankind in the bodily state. Humans have an instinct to combine into families, village units, and finally into city-states, the latter aiming 'at the most authoritative good of all. This is what is called the city or the political partnership'.[13] What distinguishes this human community from its animal counterpart is that man alone 'has a perception of good and bad and just and unjust and other things [of this sort], and partnership in these things is what makes a household and a city'.[14] Thus for Aristotle men did not associate out of fear of one another in a natural condition without a common superior and judge, but rather in order to advance their own perfection as rational beings. The formal state existed solely to promote the public good, and for Aristotle the key question was what form of constitution best served that end over the long term.

The reintroduction of Aristotelian political ideas at this time also encouraged the notion that formal political authority need not be seen solely as a remedy for human sinfulness and depravity, but might instead be employed in the pursuit of universal moral imperatives, and

even a modicum of earthly happiness, as defined by natural law. But un-
doubtedly the most significant result of the return of Aristotelian ideas
during the High Middle Ages was to encourage the exploration of alternatives and adjuncts to monarchical rule. Aristotle's acknowledgement
that 'The many, of whom none is individually an excellent man, nevertheless can when joined together be better – not as individuals but all together – than those [who are best]', allowed for the possibility that the
collective reason of community might be superior to the unfettered discretion of one man in forwarding the public good.[15] In Book 3 of the
Politics there are three forms of lawful political rule outlined. Pure forms
of monarchy, aristocracy, and polity can degenerate into tyranny, oligarchy, and democracy, but humans have the capacity to avoid these
outcomes. Writing at the end of the thirteenth century, Thomas Aquinas
affirmed that monarchy, while the best form of government, was apt to
degenerate into tyranny, and suggested that a constitution combining
Aristotle's three forms, with monarchical, aristocratic and popular input
shaping the law, was the best means of avoiding injustice and instability.[16] The general trend of Aristotelian political discourse, then, placed a
special emphasis on the unity and well-being of the community through
the employment of collective reason, communal involvement, and monarchy limited in accordance with law.

(b)   Medieval constitutionalism and conciliarism

Three important social factors contributed to the development of constitutional political ideas in the High Middle Ages. Of primary significance
was the fact that medieval Europe, unlike the other major world civiliza-
tions – China, Mughal India, the Islamic kingdoms – never witnessed
the formation and consolidation of a monolithic theocracy where all
temporal and spiritual power was concentrated in one person or in a single
institutional structure. Beginning with the Investiture Controversy
at the close of the eleventh century, a dual pattern of authority emerged
in the northwestern peninsula of the Eurasian land mass, one where
royal power contested the broad temporal claims of the papacy and
where the church worked to desacralize kingship by diminishing the
divine right pretensions of imperial leadership. When the eleventh-
century monk Manegold of Lautenbach, speaking on behalf of his superior Pope Gregory VII against the insouciant Emperor Henry IV,

maintained that 'the people is justly and reasonably released from its obligation to obey' whenever the emperor begins to act the tyrant as defined by the church, the enormous implications of the church–state rivalry for the question of determining the source of conclusive political power under God became apparent across Western Europe.

Related to this larger framework of competing claims to authority, chronic internal tensions within each respective camp hampered the efforts of religious and secular princes to construct loyal and disciplined regimes. Feudal barons and feudal-minded bishops resisted the consolidating penchants of their respective overlords, preferring instead the immediate perquisites of localism, petty jurisdictions and personal rule. Indeed the image of the king who must cooperate with his leading subjects had clearly informed most medieval coronation oaths, where kings promised to do justice to all social orders and to rule in conformity with established law. The feudal heritage, and the reciprocal pledges at the heart of that multilayered system, had emphasized the need for consultation and for mutual support in the interest of the common good. The same can be said for the earlier Germanic tradition of judgement by peers and elective kingship. Bilateral obligations based upon sworn oaths, protection in return for allegiance, the imperative nature of a common defence; these things allowed the notion of consent to remain part of the vocabulary of government throughout the medieval centuries.

By the thirteenth century, Europe's nascent kingdoms, duchies and bishoprics featured a wide array of representative assemblies which made government by consent a reality. Issues of war and peace, taxation, the rule of law, were each settled with increasing frequency by king, nobles and burghers meeting together. By the early fourteenth century these assemblies had secured a measure of coherence and protocol, and while it would be difficult to assign institutional status to such meetings, these bodies did manage to survive changes in leadership while forming accepted patterns for resolving issues of common concern.[17] Thus when Marsilius of Padua took up the argument for consent as the basis for legitimate political rule in his famous *Defender of Peace* (1324), for example, insisting that 'the elected kind of government is superior to the non-elected', he was voicing a perspective which found practical expression throughout Europe and which could trace its roots to earlier feudal practice.[18]

Finally, within the larger hierarchical structures of church and state, there emerged new groups whose equal members found themselves bound together by common interests and agendas. These corporate groups or collegial associations included cathedral chapters, confraternities, monasteries, universities, guilds and lay charitable associations, and the membership of each group shaped their own constitutional structures, deliberated over and controlled their own affairs, and delegated specific powers to their chosen leaders. The collegial relationships within these organizations were not without their influence in the secular political arena, as corporative structures proved their effectiveness in managing the affairs of large associations within society. Indeed collegial relationships and consensual practices were part of the very fabric of medieval life, from the ceremony of the feudal oath, to the workaday management of towns and cities, to the more solemn task of electing popes and emperors. Virtually all members of Europe's politically active minority were members of one corporate group or another, and their experiences in these self-governing societies profoundly influenced thinking about all forms of government.[19]

All three of these social factors were at work in the conciliarist movement born of the late fourteenth-century crisis within the Roman Catholic Church, a crisis known to us as the Great Schism (1378–1415). As early as the twelfth century church lawyers or 'canonists' were discussing models of authority within the church where the pope exercised his greatest power in concert with a general council of the clergy. Some of these early canonists went so far as to conclude that an erring pope could be held accountable for his notorious sin or heresy before a meeting of cardinals and bishops 'because in matters which pertain to the faith he is less than the college of cardinals or a general council of bishops'.[20] These ideas found immediate application when, after 1378, two and eventually three rival claimants to the chair of St Peter threatened the Universal Church with permanent division. The split was only settled in 1414 by a general council of the entire church meeting in the Italian city of Constance (1414–18).

Jean Gerson (1362–1428?), chancellor of the University of Paris, provided the conciliarists with their strongest argument at this critical juncture, although he was by no means the only voice pursuing the twin themes of corporate rule and mixed constitution. Gerson borrowed extensively from the ideas of his predecessors, and his works were widely read by constitutional theorists in succeeding centuries.[21] He turned to Aristotle at the close of his treatise *On Ecclesiastical Power* (presented to the Council in 1414) in order to represent the whole church as a form of mixed monarchy. The pope, Gerson argued, stood for the monarchical element, the cardinals the aristocratic, and the council the democratic, with the entire council forming the ideal mixture of power.[22] The author maintained that the highest lawmaking and governing authority in the universal Catholic community rested with the General Council, while the pope, who was a trustee for the Christian commonwealth, exercised his powers as a matter of administrative convenience to the whole church.[23]

For Gerson a parallel model of governance existed in the secular sphere. Here ultimate power rested with the body of the community as a whole, and rulers acted as ministers or trustees, bounded by the laws and governing for the good of the whole in all circumstances. Those who willingly established a monarchical system could only transfer those powers that they possessed as individuals. The king, who was seen as an administrator for the community, promoted unity and concord while operating under legal restraint. Nicholas of Cusa (1401–64), writing his *De concordantia catholica* (On Catholic Concordance) at the Council of Basel in 1433, confirmed Gerson's position when he announced that all legitimate authority 'is judged divine when it arises from a common concord of the subjects'.[24]

The conciliar movement did not long outlast the early fifteenth-century crisis in church governance, however, and it was almost completely silenced during the Reformation when Catholic apologists for unity turned once again to doctrines of absolute papal monarchy.[25] But as J. N. Figgis pointed out almost 100 years ago, the conciliar idea in the ecclesiological domain took root in secular constitutional theory, in particular offering persecuted religious minorities a useful argument in their struggle for survival in an environment of persecution.[26] Indeed during the sixteenth century the most influential works of political theory were constitutionalist in character, and the most radical of these grew out of the late medieval conciliarist tradition.[27]

In the early decades of that century, for example, Jacques Almain and John Mair both asserted that kings were instituted for the good of the commonwealth, and that subjects could never alienate their original sovereign power to preserve themselves against aggression, a position that would be forcefully reiterated by John Locke at the end of the seventeenth century. Almain and Mair even claimed that a tyrannical ruler might be deposed by the members of a representative assembly of the three Estates.[28] Thus when writers such as the Roman jurist Mario Salamonio stated in 1511 that princes did not always exist, that they were in fact instituted by equal partners in a pre-civil community, they were building upon an already important legacy. It was a legacy not lost on the seventeenth century, and certainly not lost upon the English parliamentarian William Prynne, who one year after the start of the Civil War (1643) wrote that 'King, Lords, and Commons by the Common Law make but one entire Corporation'. The king may be superior to individuals, but he was less than the two Houses, just as 'a General Council is above the Pope, the Chapter above the Bishop, the University above the Chancellor'.[29]

The German jurist and Calvinist Johannes Althusius, who for 34 years (1604–38) was syndic (legal secretary) of the imperial city of Emden in East Friesland, near the frontier of the Dutch Republic, brought medieval conciliarist ideas of federalism and constitutionalism together in his *Politics Methodically Set Forth, Illustrated with Sacred and Profane Examples* (1603). It was 27 years after Bodin completed his call for the monopoly of sovereign authority in the institution of monarchy when Althusius published his remarkable defence of political pluralism, corporate authority and popular sovereignty. The enlarged second edition of the work was dedicated to one of the Dutch Republic's constituent members, the States of Friesland. The author had only recently settled in East Friesland, a territory still officially within the empire, but long a haven for Calvinists suffering under Spanish persecution in the Low Countries. The Dutch rebellion against Spain, now some 30 years from its inception, had been predicated on the notion of contractual rule, where corporate bodies controlled the towns and elected members to the States General, and Althusius clearly sympathized with the rebels.[30]

Critical of Bodin's attribution of sovereign power to the magistracy, Althusius saw political society not as a sum of atomistic individuals, an all-encompassing and monistic institution, but rather as a series of ascending communities, each with a vital role to play in the larger life of the citizenry. The character of the ideal polity was decentralized in nature, based in the end on the integrity of these formal but local associations. In this key respect Althusius continued to advance two of the core assumptions of the medieval polity: the value of plural communities and diverse networks of power interests in arresting the aggrandizing tendencies of the central state, and the hierarchical structure of these communities, a sort of great chain of being in the ascent from private to public. Embracing Aristotelian naturalism, Althusius argued that despite mankind's natural sociability and interdependence, a voluntary act was required before any human association, including civil associations and formal government, could be established.

Sovereignty, wrote Althusius, inheres in the people, and while they might temporarily delegate specific powers to kings and other leaders, they can never voluntarily alienate their sovereignty to the head of the state on a permanent basis. Consent among equals was always 'the efficient cause of political association' and 'God assigned to the political community' the right of selecting their leaders. For Althusius, this popular sovereignty did not reside with the autonomous individual, but instead with people as members of a series of organized collectives – the family, the guild, the church, the village, and on to the city, the province and the realm. The strain of medieval pluralism or federalism can be found in his insistence that society consists of these indispensable corporate groups, organized into symbiotic communities, soldalities, collegia. According to Althusius: 'The public association exists when many private associations are linked together for the purpose of establishing an inclusive political order. It can be called a community, an associated body, or the pre-eminent political association' whose existence is not altered by the change of individual members but 'perpetuated by the substitution of others'.[31]

Local units of governance, beginning with the family and later including guilds and other voluntary associations, agreed to form a city-state, the first truly public association where so much of medieval self-government had evolved. At the next stage is the provincial association, including groups of villages, towns and cities, where problems of common concern are once again addressed by rulers who shape their decisions on the basis of input from the assembly which represents the larger membership. Finally there is the commonwealth or empire, the most inclusive of the public associations. However, its powers extend only to those matters which cannot be effectively treated at one of the lower levels. At every tier government decisions were reached in a collegial fashion, with assemblies and councils consulted by the supreme magistrate. Most importantly, a permanent council of state representing the entire sovereign population was responsible for preventing tyranny, and as a corporate group it might declare a king in violation of the law of the realm and remove him from his public duties.[32] Since sovereignty for Althusius was always located in the people, the power wielded by this highest association could be withdrawn whenever the rulers exceeded their charge. The check would be applied by the people as they are organized into the lower levels of the federative system. These groups predate the commonwealth, and in the end can exist without the guiding influence of the highest association. Althusius insisted that sovereignty or 'a supreme right of jurisdiction' always inhered in the whole people as a corporate association, while rulers and all subordinate officials were ministers of the community. The people were always antecedent and 'superior to its governors' and all were subject to the same rule of law.[33]

Government at every level represented and was in the end responsible to such groups, thereby creating a federal arrangement where political power was dispersed out from the centre. Althusius took as his model that which was most familiar to him: the decentralized structure of medieval society in general and the Holy Roman Empire and the Dutch Republic in particular. Rather than reject the principles of medieval political organization as Bodin had done in the face of religious civil war, Althusius defended what he took to be its many salutary features. He envisioned a German Empire where cities and provinces continued to enjoy significant autonomy, and where the emperor ruled within clear constitutional guidelines. Inspired by the progress of the Dutch rebellion against Spain, Althusius believed that 'the spirit of liberty is retained through [the] right of holding assemblies' similar to the Dutch States General, and he held that one of the principal tasks of the German electors was to hold the emperor accountable for his actions.[34]

(c)   Reformation debate

Initially, neither Luther nor Calvin had allowed for any form of active resistance to established magistrates. Citing St Paul's admonition that 'the powers that be are ordained of God'(Romans 13.1) both men believed that the magistrate was God's representative in the secular sphere, and that the primary purpose of government was to uphold the laws of God in the true faith.[35] In Luther's view even tyrants might be ordained of God in order to punish the wickedness of the people. But almost as soon as the former monk's reforms won acceptance in the northern states of the Holy Roman Empire, it was necessary for proponents of the new faith to defend the right of individual princes to preserve their churches. In 1530, in the aftermath of the failure of the imperial diet in Augsburg to settle the religious split between Catholics and Lutherans, the Emperor Charles V decided to make holy war against the Protestants. In response, lawyers for the Schmalkaldic League, the alliance of Lutheran principalities committed to defending the member states against imperial aggression, argued that as an elected official of the member states, the emperor's power was both partial and conditional. In particular, it was maintained that individual princes reserved the right to regulate religious affairs in their respective jurisdictions. Imperial interference in this area, it was claimed, was illegal and the offender forfeited his overall agreed authority.

Luther came to accept this reasoning by 1530, confident that by restricting the right to resist to inferior princes and magistrates there would be no repeat of the serious peasant uprisings of the mid 1520s. When the first Schmalkaldic War erupted in 1546 (the year of Luther's death), the imperial forces secured a swift and decisive victory which suggested the possibility of stamping out the Lutheran menace. But dogged resistance continued, led especially by the elected officials of the city of Magdeburg, who in 1550 issued a *Confession* which stated that when a magistrate (in this case the emperor) 'begins to be a terror to good works and to honour the bad' he can no longer be assumed to enjoy God's favour and ceases to be a legitimate ruler.[36] In 1555 the emperor conceded the principle of individual princely discretion. The Religious Peace of Augsburg allowed solitary princes, or in cities the working council, to select either Catholicism or Lutheranism for their respective populations. The treaty ended the need for future Lutheran resistance, and the more familiar modern association of Lutheranism with political passivity, so central to Luther's original thinking, began its long and troublesome career.[37]

In Strasbourg and in Geneva, Protestant exiles from Mary Tudor's grudgingly penitent England struggled to find a message that would strengthen the resolve of the godly who suffered under a papist queen. These Marian exiles were joined by Scottish refugees who had fled the Francophile rule of Mary of Guise. Both groups offered drastic solutions to the problem of Catholic rule, and both came under the influence of Calvinist theology during their years abroad. John Ponet, bishop of Winchester under Edward VI, was one of those who fled to Frankfurt after Mary's accession. In *A Short Treatise of Politic Power* (1556), Ponet maintained that a ruler who violated his or her trust should be treated like an ordinary criminal, a perspective unlikely to find much endorsement in the new Court.[38] Obedience was important, but only in moderation, 'for too much maketh the governors to forget their vocation and to usurp upon their subjects'.[39]

From Geneva the Englishman Christopher Goodman and the Scottish theologian John Knox fired off broadsides calling for individuals of any rank to follow the text of Acts 5.29, obey God rather than men, and

commit themselves to tyrannicide. Divine vengeance awaits the community loath to erase the 'Monstrous Regiment of Women', to use the
title from Knox's violent polemic against Mary Tudor, later to be
applied against Mary of Guise and Mary Stuart. Knox was declared a
heretic and ordered to be executed by the Catholic Church of Scotland
in 1556, but it was not enough to obstruct his return to his homeland in
1559 or to prevent him from playing a role in the organization of a
Reformed Church dedicated to the overthrow of the government of
Mary of Guise. In the long term, however, the embarrassment caused by
the misogynist elements in Goodman's and Knox's work (the Protestant
Elizabeth I of England obviously found nothing redeemable in either
man) minimized the impact of the call for popular action in subsequent
Calvinist offerings.

Returning to the more restrained notion of resistance at the magis-
terial level, the successors to Calvin structured their political thought in a
manner consistent with the hierarchical norms of contemporary society.
When Mary Stuart, who had returned to Scotland in 1561 to assume her
royal inheritance, was expelled in a rebellion by Scottish nobles under
the leadership of her brother the earl of Moray, George Buchanan came
to the defence of the rebels. Obedience, Buchanan insisted, can only be
commanded by kings who rule by the law as made by the estates of the
realm, the natural advisers to all princes. Buchanan's *De jure regni apud
Scotus* was only published in 1579, but it had circulated in manuscript
shortly after the deposition of the queen in 1567.[40] The king must rule
'like a guardian of the public accounts' on behalf of the people who had
designated him their ruler, and that 'whatever privilege the people hath
given to any, the same may require again very justly'.[41]

The start of the French wars of religion in 1562 signalled yet another
departure in Calvinist political thought. During the first decade of the
conflict the minority Huguenots professed steady allegiance to the monarchy, urging the Court to rid itself of its malevolent and usurping Catholic advisers, in particular members of the Guise family. But the murder
of an estimated 10 000 Huguenots in French cities, begun in Paris on
St Bartholomew's Day 1572 and continuing for a number of weeks, put
to an end all hopes that the Protestant minority in Calvin's homeland
might continue to win the acceptance and perhaps even the further conversion of the majority Catholic population. It was apparent that the dis-
solute young king, Charles IX, had ordered the attacks, and Catholic
mobs had eagerly joined in to complete the work of religious cleansing.
These crisis conditions, where the very survival of French Protestantism

lay in the balance, occasioned some of the most powerful and, in the long term, influential theories of resistance which were put to use repeatedly in the following century.

Along with a number of merely polemical pamphlets and anti-Court diatribes, Francis Hotman's *Francogallia* (1573) appeared soon after the infamous pogrom, and it has remained one of the more considered responses to the violently changed circumstances in late sixteenth-century France.[42] In what was really a work of historical jurisprudence dedicated to describing the constitution of ancient Gaul prior to the Roman conquest, Hotman stated that kings 'were not hereditary but were conferred by the people on those who were reputed just'. These appointed rulers 'did not have boundless, absolute and unchecked power but were bound by settled law, so that they were no less under the people's power and authority than the people were under theirs'. These kingships, indeed, seemed to be 'nothing but magistracies for life'.[43]

Hotman provided abundant historical evidence to make his case that, from the very beginning of the recorded past, Frankish kings were the creatures and agents of their subjects. Even more central to his overall argument was the assertion that a public meeting of the realm had been in place since the earliest days of the kingdom, an 'annual public council of the nation, which was later called the Assembly of the Three Estates'.[44] The Estates originally had the power to create and depose kings and to engage in activities normally reserved as part of the royal prerogative: declaring war and peace, regulating religion, conferring honours, appointing governors, regents and all other court officials. The very prerogative powers that Bodin would associate with the essence of sovereignty four years later in *Six Books of the Republic*, Hotman firmly vested in the historic public council whose powers had been undermined by the rising power of the Catholic establishment and new courts like the parlements. The author made no overt call for resistance in his scholarly work, but the implications of his reading of French history were obvious to his contemporaries, especially those noblemen and city leaders in the south and west of France who organized their own institutional assemblies, called *assemblées politiques*, which in turn mobilized armies to fight against the crown. At one of these *assemblées*, copies of Hotman's inflammatory work were distributed to the participants.[45]

Huguenots could not but take heart with the restorative antiquarian researches contained in *Francogallia*. Theodore Beza, successor to Calvin in Geneva upon the latter's death in 1564, consulted with Hotman in the spring of 1573 while he was composing his own work on the nature of legitimate resistance, the *De droit des magistrats* (Right of Magistrates), but like so many Calvinist writers who were sensitive to their minority status in Germany and France, Beza did not wish to inflame the suspicion amongst Catholics that Protestant religious beliefs were politically subversive.[46] He refused to acknowledge any right on the part of private individuals to resist a legitimate sovereign who had become a tyrant, possibly recalling the peasant jacqueries during the civil wars and the fear of social upheaval which accompanied them. The oppressed individual 'must either go into exile or bear the yoke with trust in God'.[47] On the other hand, lesser magistrates 'who have public or state responsibilities either in the administration of justice or in war' may resist any 'flagrant oppression of the realm' by virtue of their sworn duty to preserve the law and in light of the higher allegiance that all persons owe to God.[48] This call to arms for magistrates appeared in 10 French editions between its initial publication in 1574 and 1581, and before the mid point of the next century, 17 Latin translations had appeared in print.[49] Beza's 'office theory of kingship' directly challenged all proprietary notions of the dynastic state and helped set the stage for the expansion of the right of resistance to a wider circle of Christians.[50]

Beza's arguments were extended, and the call to rebellion made more direct, by Philippe du Plessis-Mornay, the probable author of the 1579 *Vindiciae contra tyrannos* (Defence of Liberty Against Tyrants). Significantly, the *Vindiciae*, which was often published together with *Du droit des magistrats*, is less reticent about highlighting the religious dimensions of the struggle against tyranny.[51] First translated into French in 1581, the *Vindiciae* appeared in English in 1648, one year before the execution of King Charles I. 'Kings and magistrates', its author claimed, 'who have received the sword from the people as a whole, should make sure that the general body of the Church is rightly governed; private individuals, that they are members of the Church.'[52] And while the author agreed that inferior magistrates were the ones with the duty to resist should the executive threaten tyranny, in an important departure it was conceded that on occasion select individuals, free from all ambition and filled with 'genuine and earnest zeal, conscientiousness, and finally, learning', might be called by God to lead a resistance in the name of the true faith. 'I do not say that the same God who has sent us Pharaohs and Ahabs in this age may not inspire liberators also, in some extraordinary way.'[53] The primary obligation of the king was to be 'guardian, minister, and protector' of laws which have been received from the people, not to lord over what he mistakenly takes to be his own private property. Subjects should not expect their prince 'to be a god and to demand divinity from merely human and unsteady nature'.[54] Injustices will always be allowed, but patterns of wilful disregard for the people must be rejected. All should recognize that of the two essential contracts around which our lives are regulated, one between God and the people, and a second between temporal ruler and ruled, it was the first which took precedence, and the king who freely and consistently violated his charge forfeited any claim to his subjects' obedience.

After the Protestant Henry of Navarre became the heir presumptive to the French throne in 1584, members of the Catholic League recycled the resistance theories of the Huguenot minority and made explicit the radical intimation in the *Vindiciae* that individual action in the face of heretical rule was permissible. These ideas were quickly embraced by English Catholics, many of whom had trained in the seminary at Douai. The League had been first formed in 1576, and was motivated largely by the conviction that the 'true' faith was being endangered as a result of concessions extended to the Huguenots. For this reason, and in light of Henry's hereditary claim after 1584, the League was opposed to any notion that the king, and especially one who compromised with heresy, wielded unchecked supreme power.[55]

In 1588, at a meeting of the Estates General, the leader of the League, Henri de Guise, together with his brother the Cardinal de Guise, were murdered. Henry of Navarre's efforts to establish his title after 1589 (he had been excommunicated by the pope in 1585) meant war with the League and with its papal and Spanish backers, and in an effort to nullify the king's hereditary claim, pamphlets issued by supporters of the League described the French crown as an elective office, the appropriate electorate being the members of the Three Estates. In addition, it was proposed that the estates should nominate members of the royal council, oversee all taxation and official appointments, and enjoy the right to meet without the king, who would be denied a veto power.[56] Religious uniformity was for the League the only sound basis for political stability, and despite Henry's 'conversion' to Roman Catholicism in 1593, League supporters, backed by a decision of the Sorbonne, questioned the sincerity of the monarch's new-found faith. They insisted that God would not have true Catholics submit to a heretic king unless the Divine Father had willed the damnation of men.[57] Papal deposition and the propriety of tyrannicide thus became staples of League opinion during the 1590s. In England the publication of two works in 1584 by leading Catholic exiles, Robert Person's *Leicester's Commonwealth*, and William Allen's *A true*, *sincere, and modest defense*, signalled the shift from passive resistance to public opposition to the heretic Queen Elizabeth I, a shift clearly influenced by similar developments in France.[58]

The Jesuits were also forceful voices in the Catholic school of resistance theory at this time, and some later scholars have even credited the society with first formulating the notion of the social contract. The leading Jesuit theorists of this period – Robert Bellarmine, Francisco Suarez, Juan de Molina – each confirmed the right of the community to challenge the prince when a clear pattern of tyrannical conduct was evident. According to one of their number, the Spanish Jesuit Juan de Mariana, tyrannicide could be justly undertaken 'by any private person whatsoever who may wish to come to the aid of the commonwealth'.[59] Especially disturbing to Jesuit theorists was the Lutheran claim that men were so deeply impaired by the stain of original sin that they could no longer apprehend the will of God and shape their temporal order in harmony with it. Suarez condemned 'the blasphemous suggestion of Luther' that men could not conduct their personal and collective lives in conformity with God's eternal law, that the law of nature could not be taken as an appropriate starting point for the formation of political life.[60]

According to these Jesuit neo-Thomists, God had implanted the natural law in men in order that they might better understand His designs and shape their political order accordingly. In restoring the place of natural law, the Jesuits rebutted the Lutheran claim that all political power was by direct ordination. Secular commonwealths could once again be viewed as conveniences organized by equal citizens living in a pre-political state of nature in order to better provide for earthly needs. Like John Locke at the end of our period, the Jesuits concluded that fallen man, although provided with the dictates of the law of nature, would never follow these commands in all instances. Therefore peace and justice would best be served in a state of civil society.[61] Through the process of voluntary consent, all men agreed to limit their natural liberties in return for the protection of the state. According to Suarez, 'the power of political dominion or rule over men has not been granted, directly by God, to any particular human individual'. Instead 'the power in question resides, by the sole force of natural law, in the whole body of mankind'. And while monarchy was the best form of government in Aristotle's well-known triad, 'other forms of government are not [necessarily] evil, but may, on the contrary, be good and useful...this determination [as to the seat of the power] must of necessity be made by human choice'.[62] While it would be too strong a claim to associate the Jesuits with the start of modern democratic and liberal constitutionalist theory (they were, after all, keen to retain for the pope the right to depose heretical monarchs), their discussion of the relationship between free contract and political obligation 'came to exercise its decisive influence in the course of the following century'.[63]

This rich output of late sixteenth-century resistance theory was concluded rather abruptly in France after the accession and subsequent reconversion to Catholicism of Henry IV in the 1590s. The Catholic League had never enjoyed widespread popular support in France, and its perceived links with Spanish imperial policy further diminished its appeal amongst the Catholic political elite. For their part the Huguenots were content with the generous policy of toleration put forward by the new king with the Edict of Nantes in 1598, accepting Henry's reconversion as a necessary expedient in light of majority sensibilities. Half a century later, and despite the attacks of Cardinal Richelieu against their political freedoms, the Huguenots continued to support the personal monarchy of the Bourbon kings. They played no role in the mid-century Fronde, and an appreciative Louis XIV reaffirmed the Edict of Nantes in May 1652.

The Civil War in England may have suggested to some that Calvinists were monarchomachs at heart irrespective of borders, but French Huguenots supported royal absolutism throughout the period of the English Republic. It was only during the 1660s that the king began his long series of encroachments against Protestant dissent, culminating in 1685 with the fateful revocation of the Edict of Nantes, an act which Paul Hazard once referred to as 'the high-water mark of the counter-reformation'.[64] In the wake of that decision and the persecution which followed, late sixteenth-century Huguenot resistance theory was revived, led by the exile pastor of the Walloon Church in Rotterdam, Pierre Jurieu. For Jurieu and the thousands of émigrés who had been deprived of their liberties and forced from their homeland, the king had declared himself an outlaw by using force against his subjects' conscience. They hoped to see the success of the Glorious Revolution in England spread to French soil.[65]

In England, on the other hand, the Catholic resistance theories which had provided justification for the plots against Elizabeth I in the late sixteenth century continued to inform action during the early tenure of her Stuart successor. The failed Gunpowder Plot of 1605 fuelled much anti-Catholic hysteria in England, leading directly to the requirement that all subjects take a new oath of allegiance to their Protestant monarch. And when Henry IV of France was assassinated by the Catholic fanatic François Ravaillac in 1610, the deepest reservations about Jesuit resistance writers seemed to be given sober confirmation. This act of regicide, following five years after the abortive Gunpowder conspiracy, locked English popular opinion into a virulently anti-Catholic posture for the duration of the century.

Ancient Constitutions

Another approach to the problem of sovereignty taken by moderate royalists or constitutionalists, especially by English writers trained in the law, was to insist that the monarch was bound not only by God's laws but by the fundamental positive laws, the established ordinances of the land observed by earlier kings and founded upon an ancient and unwritten common law. Hotman in France, Buchanan in Scotland, Grotius in Holland – all appealed to notions of the ancient constitution in order to criticize current regimes. Indeed outside England ancient constitutionalism became the key ideology of opposition groups, although it was by no means their monopoly. In 1590, one year after assuming the French throne, Henry IV accused his detractors of resisting 'reason, natural duty, and the ancient laws and constitutions' in questioning the legitimacy of his title.[66] And five years after Louis XIV revoked the Edict of Nantes, the anonymous author of *Soupirs de la France esclave, qui aspire après le liberté* (1690), revived the theory of the ancient constitution in claiming that the monarchy was originally elective, and that 'nothing of any importance was done in the kingdom without the advice and consent of the Estates'.[67]

In England the same ideology played mainly a preservative role.[68] The English legal profession represented a significant barrier to the absolutist notion that law was the exclusive product of the royal will. Lawyers were well represented in parliament and the Inns of Court were popular educational institutions with the sons of gentry eager to make a name for themselves in the practice of law. In the countryside, members of the gentry who served as the king's unpaid Justices of the Peace needed some legal knowledge in order to carry out their duties effectively, and those gentleman who had at least a modicum of training in the law were apt to claim wide authority for what was the dominant language of politics at the time: the ancient, unwritten, common law tradition.

The belief in the existence of an ancient constitution based on common law owed a good deal to the antiquarian interests of lawyers who studied the historical records for evidence of rights and liberties enjoyed by Englishmen over the centuries and well before the emergence of the dynastic state in the early modern period.[69] In fact the entire enterprise of history at this time was geared not so much to discovering truths about the past as it was to illustrating by example truths already known. According to common law theorists, the state could not abrogate a legitimate inheritance consisting of rights and liberties whose origins in an ancient community had evinced their soundness for all ages. One of the most respected methods of legitimizing political arrangements in the seventeenth century was the appeal to custom, placing a positive value upon patterns established and tested by generations far removed from contemporary debate, and the doctrine of the ancient constitution fitted flawlessly with this widespread intellectual habit.[70] It was doctrine which also complemented the model of stasis and hierarchy so familiar to contemporaries and which informed everything from the cosmic structure to the humble world of the animal kingdom.

The fifteenth-century jurist Sir John Fortescue claimed that the unwritten customary law of England had remained essentially unchanged since the days of the ancient Britons, thus a king 'can not alter nor change the laws of his realm at his pleasure'.[71] His view was given new voice in the early seventeenth century by the prominent parliamentary leader Sir Edward Coke, who agreed that no subsequent conqueror of the island had altered these basic Saxon standards. Coke, who enjoyed a long and distinguished career which included service as Speaker of the House during Elizabeth's reign, Chief Justice of Common Pleas and King's Bench under James I, and finally as parliamentary critic of royal prerogative, published a series of law cases titled *Reports* (1600–15) and authored a legal text, *Institutes of the Laws of England* (1628–44), which influenced generations of law students.[72]

Another view of the English common law, contemporary with Coke's, was offered by the distinguished antiquarian John Selden, who claimed that while customs changed, evolving imperceptibly over the centuries according to circumstances, they remained perfect at any given moment and were always anchored in the original tradition. Both perspectives agreed that the customary law, originating in practice and separate from royal input, constituted the chief law of the kingdom, since the wisdom (unaltered or evolved) of earlier generations had served the community well for centuries. Under this reading formal documents such as Magna Carta merely declared old unwritten law; the great charter – and indeed all statute law – simply confirmed in writing what had been the rights of Englishmen for centuries. In this respect the common law was the basic law of the kingdom. Among other notable accomplishments, the ancient laws protected person and property, thereby setting the principal task of secular government.

Seventeenth-century lawyers enamoured of the notion of an ancient constitution sometimes suggested that the common law was akin to reason itself, although perhaps not surprisingly, it was also implied that the dictate of reason was best left to the lawyers to interpret. Indeed it was judges who declared traditional law, determining which ordinances were prescriptive by virtue of their having been in place before time out of memory. It was similarly maintained that the customary law was anchored in the law of God, although years of study were required before one could master the former.[73] Thus the common law stood alongside the laws of God and nature, superior to man made statute and informing all proceedings of king in parliament. Because of this correspondence, the common lawyers felt little burden to resort to natural law arguments; the 'artificial reason' of the common law was sufficient to address all questions of political right in a particular situation.[74]

For Fortesque, the kings of England ruled over free subjects whose representatives in parliament participated in the lawmaking process, and in particular in all decisions respecting taxation.[75] The common law lawyers maintained that the House of Commons represented the interests of the politically active members of the general population on all questions concerning property rights and the correlate liberties embodied in Magna Carta. The ancient constitution, it was believed, continued to inform practice because it was characterized by balance, an equilibrium between the prerogative of the crown and the liberties of the subject where each respected and preserved the other's ancient privileges.

Richard Hooker incorporated this concept of equilibrium into the eighth book of his *Laws of Ecclesiastical Polity*, where he maintained that the queen derived her supreme authority from the commonwealth and that this authority was limited by the laws of the land. Subjection could occur in three ways: conquest, where kings 'set their own terms'; divine appointment, enjoying 'the power God assigns'; and human discretion or choice, where the king's power over his subjects is set by 'the articles of the compact between them'. England's monarchy, he believed, belonged to the last category.[76] It is no coincidence that this portion of Hooker's work remained in manuscript until parliament had triumphed over Charles I in 1648.[77] Hooker drew a sharp distinction between the domestic authority of the father and the political authority of the king. The latter authority was granted upon condition by the king's subjects, who, living in a state of nature and recognizing the conditions of strife that exist there, have the rational presence of mind to subject themselves to some form of government.[78]

The Beginnings of Popular Sovereignty

Throughout the first half of the seventeenth century, resistance theorists, when referring to the right of the people to depose a king, thought almost exclusively in terms of the people's representatives, the estates of the realm, the higher magistrates and nobles, as the political agents whose standing fitted them for such action. None of the writers believed that the multitude should play an active role in politics, and the thought of allowing individuals or the people at large to engage in resistance was tantamount to a call for anarchy. But in the context of the English Civil Wars (1642–48), where both King Charles I and his opponents in the parliament were claiming constitutional authority for their respective actions in the conflict, a settlement of the dispute in terms of sorting out the legitimate powers of each respective estate appeared hopeless, and in such a climate new appeals to a broader constituency began to surface.

One of these appeals was contained in George Lawson's major work, *Politica Sacra et Civilis*. The book was first published in 1660 and reissued in 1689, two pivotal moments in the English experience when the shape of the national polity was in the process of being constructed anew. At both junctures monarchs awaited the outcome of constitutional debate and military alignment in the expectation that the power of the executive would be restored to its pre-Civil War competence. Lawson claimed to be writing for ordinary people, offering insights into the origins, generation, and appropriate structure of government of both church and state to a people weary of the instability, conflict and uncertainty brought on by the wars and subsequent Interregnum (1649–60).[79]

Although an ordained member of the Church of England under the strongly Royalist Archbishop of Canterbury William Laud, Lawson had not been opposed to accommodating with the Presbyterian system of church government created by the Long Parliament in 1643. Nor did he reject the friendship of religious Independents, and while he conformed to the re-established Church of England after 1660 and managed to keep his modest living in the little village of More, south of the town of Shrewsbury, his *Politica* reflects a willingness for continued compromise, forgiveness and accommodation with opponents that was by no means typical of Church of England politics after the Restoration. His was a call not for a perfect political order, but for some fixed institutional forms that would comport with England's traditions and current troubled circumstances; more than anything else his was an irenic voice in an age of sectarian bitterness.[80]

Lawson's chief contribution to constitutional debate in the seventeenth century, as Julian Franklin and, more recently, Conal Condren have pointed out, was to shift the right to resistance away from constituted bodies which were presumed to represent all subjects and to settle that right, together with the source of all sovereignty, on the general community as a whole. Thus he made a basic and fundamental distinction between government as a set of agreed institutions, and a united people whose shared community and status as a distinct legal entity remained in place even though a government gone awry might be dissolved. Personal majesty or *use* of sovereignty involved the legislative, judicial and executive powers of the government, although the particular form that a government takes could vary.[81] This personal majesty might inhere in the ruler who exercised sovereignty as a form of usufruct or delegation, but 'real majesty' or fundamental sovereignty was the property of the people. Lawson insisted that real majesty cannot be lost or alienated by the community, 'whilst the community remains a community; and subjection to this is due till it be destroyed'. On the other hand subjection to personal majesty was due only as long as the king lived and governed according to law, 'but upon his death, or upon tyranny in exercise, or acting to the dissolution of the fundamental constitution, he ceaseth to be a sovereign, and the obligation as to him ceaseth'.[82]

The pre-political community was in Lawson's understanding a legal entity quite distinct from the formal institutions of parliament or the church. Informal associations of families and neighbours had first volunteered to come together as a single corporate entity for their mutual 'safety, help, comfort', while always respecting 'propriety of goods, liberty of persons, equality of the members'.[83] Communities were associations composed of free and equal individuals joined together under natural law and lacking nothing but the hierarchical order imposed by a formal political structure with coercive power. When next instituting a civil government in order to better secure the ends of peace and security, every male member of the community assented and this unanimous sanction then bound all inhabitants. Chosen representatives decided on the proper form of government to be adopted, and once established all became subjects under a 'personal majesty'. Their status as subjects did not mean, however, that they forfeited their identity as members of the community, for this could never be dissolved by the government. Even governments which established themselves by conquest could not claim legitimacy until they had obtained the consent of the community; all 'personal majesty' was subject to forfeiture on conditions set by the underlying and inalienable 'real majesty' held by the people.

In Lawson's view the community was free to establish any form of government that it desired, but if power were to be conferred on more than one person, as in the case of England's formula of King, Lords and Commons, it had to be understood that sovereignty could not be divided. In other words such a plural government formed a single moral entity, combining judicial, legislative and executive functions, just as the pre-political community was something more than the sum of the individual members.[84] Thus if the constituent parts of the English sovereign fell into conflict, as was very much the case after 1642, the government would be dissolved and the power to institute a new government would revert to the original community.

Lawson rejected the idea that members of parliament could assert a superiority over the king, what had in fact occurred in 1642, and still remain true to the arrangements of power established by the ancient constitution. The two houses cannot 'exercise the ordinary powers of the king, though they might use his name and did so contrary to his consent. If they allege that his power was forfeited and did devolve on them, that would be hard to prove.'[85] Neither king nor legislature, according to the constitution, could act without the other. But since government had dissolved at that juncture, individuals were justified in complying with the present powers, although in office through usurpation, if in fact this new government had set itself to improving the public good. Yet even in this case, the personal majesty of the usurping authority could not claim legitimacy until it secured the tacit or express consent of the community.

Real majesty could never be alienated to representative assemblies or to
monarchs, even though in the normal course of affairs the community
relies upon its officials to change the course of government when problems arise.

Locke's Christian Contractualism

The defence of 'bounded' government with which we opened this chapter found one of its strongest and most influential voices in a former
political exile, philosopher and physician, the Englishman John Locke
(1632–1704). As an Oxford-trained scholar he was more than familiar
with the ancient and medieval inheritance, the rich and varied body of
ideas respecting consultation and consent which we have introduced
above. And during a period of frenetic activity between 1679 and 1681,
he had read widely in contemporary political theory. In fact, Locke tells
us that he had read 'Lawsons book of the English Government' in 1679,
and the discussion of popular sovereignty in *Two Treatises of Government*
(1688) echoed the radical view put forward by Locke's little-known
predecessor.[86]

In the final chapter of the 'Second Treatise' entitled 'Of the dissolution of Governments', Locke indicated, much like Lawson before him,
that 'when the Government is dissolved, the People are at liberty to provide for themselves, by erecting a new legislature, differing from the
other, by the change of Persons, or Form, or both as they shall find it
most for their safety and good'.[87] But while it is important for us to situate *Two Treatises* in the political culture of Restoration politics, Locke
firmly believed that he was addressing general principles and providing
universal solutions to the problems associated with seventeenth-century
political culture in the widest sense. *Two Treatises* can thus be read both
as a tract for the times written by someone deeply engaged in a struggle
of immediate personal import to the author and his associates, and as a
more detached set of reflections published in the aftermath of a particular revolution but anchored in reflections about human nature and
divine purposes for mankind outside of Paradise.[88]

It might not be amiss to begin our treatment of Locke by indicating
that his mature political views, the views expressed in *Two Treatises*, were
antipodal to the position outlined in his earliest polemical statements
composed in the early 1660s, while he was a fellow and lecturer at Christ

Church, Oxford. At the time of the Restoration of the Stuart monarchy in 1660 Locke was a staunch royalist who declaimed against dissent and disobedience, who opposed religious toleration for non-Anglican Protestants, and who refused to concede any inherent right to property or to a legislative assembly on the part of the subject. Locke shared these political assumptions with the majority of English royalists in the aftermath of civil war and a failed republican experiment.[89]

Indeed there was nothing in Locke's intellectual make-up that suggested his thinking on political matters was at variance with the majority of the politically active population. But when, in 1666, the young scholar accepted an invitation to move to London as a member of Anthony Ashley Cooper's household and quickly assumed the multiple roles of personal physician, political adviser, and confidential secretary to one of the most powerful Restoration politicians, his views began to change. Shaftesbury, who had served King Charles II as Chancellor of the Exchequer and Lord Chancellor before becoming a prominent leader of the opposition to the Stuart Court, was a strong advocate of toleration, the rights of parliament, and individual civil freedoms before he met Locke.[90] The intellectual atmosphere in Shaftesbury's household, the practical business which engaged the day-to-day attention of Locke's employer and friend, was certainly conducive to the reception of ideas which the Oxford don had never before found practicable, or even marginally desirable.

By the late 1660s, then, Locke began to abandon his earlier positions both on the danger of allowing religious toleration and on the obligation of subjects to practise unquestioning obedience to the will of the magistrate. He now claimed that no one, including clerical leaders or indeed the monarch, enjoyed superior access to religious truth and the accompanying obligations. Not surprisingly, it was at this time that Locke would begin his investigation into the roots and character of knowledge that would emerge in print almost twenty years later as *An Essay Concerning Human Understanding*. After 1673 his patron the Earl of Shaftesbury began to take the lead in a developing effort to prevent the succession of King Charles II's Catholic brother, James duke of York. Throughout the 1670s fear of Roman Catholic influence at Court, of the crown's alignment with Louis XIV's France and the perceived connection between 'papist' theology and political absolutism, fuelled opposition measures to discredit James.

When, in 1678, allegations of a 'popish plot' to assassinate the king were made public, Shaftesbury and his supporters undertook a more concerted effort to use parliament as a mechanism to dislodge the heir apparent. In three consecutive parliaments held between 1679 and 1681, the Whig or opposition forces in the House of Commons passed bills to exclude James, only to be thwarted by royal prorogations and dissolutions of the assembly. And as it became apparent to opposition members that the legal, parliamentary avenue to constitutional change would prove ineffectual, more extreme measures were discussed in meetings and in print. Locke's unpublished *Two Treatises of Government*, written sometime after the appearance in print of Sir Robert Filmer's *Patriarcha* (1680), was one of a handful of tracts justifying resistance to the government on the basis of a radical reappraisal of the nature of political obligation and the roots of sovereignty.[91]

The Whig effort to exclude James, and subsequent plans by radical Whig elements to stage a three-pronged uprising in London, the West Country, and in Scotland, all failed to reach the point at which the duke of York's position was seriously endangered, and after 1682 anyone who was suspected of having participated in plans to alter the succession by force – or of having written in support of such plans – found themselves in an untenable position. Locke left for Holland in the summer of 1683, destined to spend the next five years in exile while events in England turned very much against the Whig cause. James assumed the throne without challenge upon his brother's death in 1685 and immediately began a campaign to Catholicize the country in a manner both feared and anticipated by his harshest critics. When he was removed in a revolution led by William of Orange in November 1688, Locke returned to England and published his decade-old manuscript in the hope that the new ruler would recognize the importance of anchoring his title on the consent of a sovereign people.

John Locke's main task in the first book of the *Two Treatises* was to discredit the divine right patriarchal theory of Robert Filmer, and it is important to remind ourselves that Locke was not attacking a convenient straw man for purposes of placing his own alternative theory into sharper relief. Rather his work of demolition was directed at a position which enjoyed the widespread endorsement of Tory politicians and churchmen in late Stuart England. Locke was not exaggerating when he stated in the preface to his book that he would not have devoted so much space to refuting Filmer's ideas 'had not the Pulpit, of late Years, publicly owned his Doctrine, and made it the Current Divinity of the Times'. As we have already seen, patriarchal political ideas comported very well with contemporary social theory, especially in its elevation of the role of the father as the unimpeachable head of household. If he was to be successful, Locke would be obliged to demonstrate how political obligation was both separate and distinct from family government.

Before considering his dispute with Filmer, however, it is important that we separate Locke's ideas from later ascriptions of intention offered by commentators who no longer share the commonplace assumptions of seventeenth-century theology and who conclude that Locke's was the first truly secular political philosophy. God's existence and His firm but ultimately benevolent character were axioms of thought simply assumed by the seventeenth-century author and his audience, while a set of specific intentions for humankind, together with a knowable divine law designed to facilitate adherence to these intentions, provided reference points for one's satisfactory completion of the earthly journey. For Locke there was one science 'incomparably above all the rest... I mean theology', and he believed that theology was 'the comprehension of all other knowledge directed to its true end, i.e., the honour and veneration of the Creator, and the happiness of mankind'.[92]

As early as 1664 Locke wrote that 'there will be no one to deny the existence of God, provided he recognizes either the necessity for some rational account of our life, or that there is a thing that deserves to be called virtue or vice'.[93] Moral duty and rules of action were, for Locke and for most of his contemporaries, unthinkable without a belief in God's existence and engagement in human affairs. Having created them as rational beings for a specific, knowable purpose, God had provided natural law in order that humans might conform themselves to divine intentions, and realize their true nature as a preliminary to eternal reward in the only state of permanency.

Political society, then, must be committed above all else to enforcing this law of nature, the duty of subordinate beings to the prescriptions set by an unquestioned superior. Locke's belief, that while laws must be rational their obligatory force rests upon the command of a legitimate lawmaker, placed his political theory squarely within a traditional Christian theological framework, one where the autonomy and utility associated with later theories had no place. In fact his understanding of the law of nature was not entirely dissimilar from the picture formulated by the Thomist philosophers of the late sixteenth-century Catholic counter-reformation, a picture ultimately derived from Aquinas' model of a universe created by God and ruled by a fixed hierarchy of laws.

Locke agreed with his opponent Filmer that, historically speaking, the first political ruler was probably also a head of household, that familial society was over time, 'by an insensible change', transformed into formal political society.[94] It was easy 'for the Father of the family to become the Prince of it' since children had grown up under paternal rule from infancy. But Locke insisted that when the issue of political authority became pressing, children either expressly or tacitly consented to the transfer of this new power into the hands of their male head of household, a person who was both familiar and, under normal circumstances 'fittest to be trusted'.[95] For if princes have their title to govern as a consequence of their God-ordained rights as fathers; if, as Filmer had maintained, origins dictate duty, then 'it will as strongly prove that all Princes, nay Princes only, ought to be Priests, since 'tis as certain, that in the Beginning, the Father of the Family was Priest, as that he was Ruler in his own Household'.[96] Church of England clerics who embraced patriarchalism could not have been comfortable with this striking analogy. In the words of the leading student of patriarchal theory, Locke was intent upon making history 'a descriptive and politically neutral anthropology'; the past was a useful reservoir of information, but it could not produce values or prescribe obligations.[97]

Locke not only distinguished between political and paternal power by emphasizing that the origins and ends of the father's authority were unique and not to be conflated with the jurisdiction of the magistrate, but he defined paternal power in a manner that made the male parent something less than the absolute and unlimited sovereign over his own household common to patriarchal theory. His overriding concern with humankind's subordination to the divine superior compelled him to place fatherly authority securely within the hierarchical structure which informed all creation. Thus for Locke God, not man, was the maker of children; procreation establishes no claim to paternal command. 'They who say the Father gives Life to his Children, are so dazzled with the thoughts of Monarchy, that they do not, as they ought, remember God, who is the Author and Giver of Life: 'Tis in him alone we live, move, and have our Being. How can he be thought to give Life to another, that knows not wherein his own Life consists?' Parents who desire children are, according to this analysis, 'but the occasions of their being'.

Throughout the *Two Treatises* the author stressed that humans are the workmanship – and the property – of God alone. Parental power over children had nothing to do with conception, nothing to do with blood ties or biology. The law of nature, God's law, has placed all parents 'under an obligation to preserve, nourish, and educate the Children' because these young people are the workmanship of God 'to whom they were to be held accountable for them'.[98] Foster parents are every bit as entitled as biological parents to the obedience of those under their supervision and care because each parent is doing the work charged to them by the Supreme Author of their being. Fulfilling a duty enjoined by a superior was, for Locke, fundamentally at odds with the Filmerian and patriarchalist attribution of unlimited and arbitrary authority in the household setting. The latter bespoke an autonomy, a freedom from fixed norms altogether out of keeping with Christian notions of purpose and dependency.

In two additional breaks with patriarchal theory, Locke accorded equal familial authority to father and mother, a position he argued was dictated by both reason and revelation. Parental power, not simply paternal power, was essential to the overall well-being of the child, and once this fact is recognized, apologists for the absolute political control of the father will recognize the absurdity of their position. Secondly, Locke did not accept the patriarchalist claim that the father's authority over his children continued uninterrupted into adulthood. Parents are to direct their children during the period of 'their yet ignorant nonage', but when reason and understanding are developed in accordance with God's ordinance, the young adult becomes a free individual and the equal of his father. Parents are not even entitled to bind their offspring to the existing political order; each person must accept political obligation on their own, although parental control over a potential inheritance is an important factor in shaping conformity to the existing political system.[99]

Locke's opposition to the permanent inferior status of children to their parents has been interpreted as one manifestation of his larger effort to emancipate the individual from non-consensual structures of authority. There is no denying that Locke's concern for self-direction was key to his voluntarist, conventional political theory, for without establishing the freedom of the rational individual, there would be little point to a contractual political order where institutional and legal limits on the magistrate are defined by the people for their own protection. Yet it is also possible to view Locke's emphasis on the autonomy of the rational individual as an essential prerequisite to the type of personal, action-oriented reformed Christianity central to his view of human purpose. Each person, upon reaching the age where reason guides our thoughts and decisions, must establish his own personal relationship with God. More to the point, each person must be held fully accountable for behaviour in this life, each must be willing to acknowledge complete responsibility for actions (or inaction) in a universe where duty and obligation were clearly understood.

Locke's seriousness about the primacy of individual accountability before a God who rewards and punishes on the basis of conduct in this world informs his picture of the pre-political state of human association. Here again his views reflected the position established a century earlier by Catholic Thomist writers, whose main purpose, we may recall, was to overturn the Lutheran contention that political society was a direct command of God. Locke utilized the Thomist contention that in the state of nature each person enjoys that measure of freedom and independence congruent with his status as a rational being. In claiming that natural freedom meant 'that no one person has political jurisdiction over any other just as no one person can be said to have dominion over anyone else', Suárez set a standard that was eagerly adopted by Locke.[100] For the state of nature to provide an acceptable level of existence, however, each person must exercise their freedom within the bounds of the law of nature. This early society is characterized by human equality where all are, without distinction, 'Servants of one Sovereign Master, sent into the world by his order and about his business'. All who hope to thrive in the state of nature must commit themselves to live by rules of common equity and reason 'that measure God has set to the actions of Men, for their mutual security'.[101]

But Locke also agreed with the Thomists in their conviction that pre-political social relations were uncertain and often troublesome because some people refused to adhere to this universal standard. For Locke the decision to leave the state of nature is a rational one made in the wake of disputes occasioned by population expansion and pressure on available land, together with the introduction of money as a means of exchange. An increasingly complex society provided numerous flashpoints whereby the application of natural law solutions became clouded by human partiality, passion, and in some cases by revenge. Unhappily in the state of nature 'all being Kings as much as he, every Man his Equal, and the greater part no strict Observers of Equity and Justice, the enjoyment of the property he has in this state is very unsafe, very unsecure'.[102] Locke later noted that, practically speaking, the state of nature lacked 'an establish'd, settled, known law, received and allowed by common consent to be the standard of right and wrong'. The law of nature, which would normally be consulted here, was obscured by men's biased interests and general ignorance. In addition, society in the state of nature was without 'a known and indifferent Judge, with Authority to determine all

differences according to the established law'. Again, men's natural partiality would lead them to evaluate and punish the actions of others un-
fairly. Finally, the state of nature affords no 'Power to back and support
the Sentence when right, and to give it due Execution'.[103]

While offering great freedom and opportunity for self-control, Locke
confessed that the pre-political state 'is full of fears and continual dangers' and that men quickly enter into a more formal relationship for
their personal and collective well-being, an arrangement where a consistent and impartial enforcement of the law of nature would be the
highest priority. Locke was making a point, informed by traditional
Christian anthropology, about human nature here, for he had earlier
concluded that the individual who fails to adhere to the law of nature,
'the right rule of reason', repudiates his humanity, 'so far becomes
degenerate, and declares himself to quit the Principles of Human
Nature'.[104] Locke's pre-political society was not, to be sure, akin to
Hobbes's or, after him, Bossuet's, anarchic war of all against all, but
neither was it a situation especially flattering to man's highest claims
about himself as a rational being, claims which Locke himself had
insisted, like the Thomists who preceded him, were the defining qualities of God's special creation.

By insisting that political power in the state of nature rests in the
hands of equal individuals, Locke was claiming that the authority exercised by institutional, formal governments is derived from the original
powers enjoyed by autonomous persons in the state of nature. He stated
that 'this will seem a very strange Doctrine to some Men' but in fact his
entire theory of political origins finds its place in the 'natural freedom'
tradition of thought which holds that, at least in terms of political relations, people in the pre-civil state are not subject to the will of another
individual.[105] Here they may protect themselves and their possessions
from attack without reference to any external lawgiver.

The claim that all legitimate political subjection must originate in consent or agreement would be used by some of the better known absolutists of the late sixteenth and seventeenth centuries, including Barclay,
Grotius and Hobbes, but for Locke the legitimate exercise of power once
conferred takes place exclusively when the magistrate stays within the
bounds set by the original contract. In other words power is first defined
and then delegated, not alienated as it was in absolutist theory. No one
was permitted to transfer absolute authority over his person to another
because the individual does not have 'liberty to destroy himself' nor to
grant another the liberty to do so; only God has a right to dispose of a

person's life. Natural law, together with Scripture (Genesis 1.28; 9.1), ordains the preservation of life and absolutism entails the power to destroy it, the power to overturn God's supreme design. According to Locke absolutism is invalid because people are not permitted to make themselves slaves. God requires of each person conduct incompatible with an unconditional surrender of their freedom.[106]

Just as parental authority was a God-ordained trust, so too political authority, rather than being unlimited and above the known laws, was also a trust, but one with two foci. The magistrate is entrusted by the subject to rule within the limits set in the initial contract, while also respecting the trust conferred by God to respect the principles of natural law and reason. In Locke's state of nature each person was judge and executioner of the law of nature. Anyone who transgressed the law placed themselves in a 'state of war' with their neighbours. And it was this same right to preserve the law of nature which gave persons in civil society the right to resist magistrates who violate this unchanging standard, an 'appeal to heaven' in the interest of preserving the integrity of God's rule for humankind's multifarious activities. In according politically active persons the right to resist the magistrate, then, Locke argued that rebellion could be interpreted as a defensive, conservative action designed to preserve God-given natural rights. Rebels were doing the work of God, not plunging society into anarchy and chaos in order to forward their own particular group fanaticism. Governments which exceeded their trust by attempting to destroy or take away the property of the subjects 'put themselves into a state of War with the people', and under these conditions one was obliged to defend the law of nature.

There are different levels of consent in Locke's theory of political society, and it is these tiers which set his work apart from the more democratic models to be treated in the next chapter. Locke's individuals, recognizing the problems associated with life in the state of nature, first agree to join in a political community with their fellows. Here popular sovereignty, a genuinely democratic impulse, establishes the foundations of the state. Next comes the agreement of the majority of this community to establish a particular form of government, and Locke, while not opposed to monarchy, believes that any durable form must include a representative assembly. But representation in this assembly is to be weighted in favour of property and wealth; a simple numerical majority in choosing representatives would open the way to the possible populist redistribution of property by the poor.

Locke's representative government, then, is an oligarchic structure, one where property-owning elites continue to hold exclusive access to political power. *Two Treatises of Government* called for a fundamental relocation of sovereignty, but Locke was not eager to extend control over the political state to anything approaching the majority population. He was interested in setting clearly defined limits to the power of the modern state, and those limits centred around the protection of the individual citizen's right to his property, his physical security, and his intellectual and spiritual freedom. For Locke, the purview of the state now ran no further than these minimum exigencies; the liberation of the individual and the well-being of the collective whole were no longer antithetical. The state was a human founding, a volitional artifact whose only remaining link with the divine order of things was in its operational comportment with the law of nature, what was for Locke God's law. With *Two Treatises*, with Locke's Christian contractualism, a powerful alternative to absolutist theory was introduced, a theory which could claim filiation with an older theological world view. Religion continued to have its place in this defence of popular sovereignty. But it was religion stripped of its confessional agenda, its persecutory past. The God of the early Enlightenment had enjoined upon men a responsibility to follow the rule of reason, and the civil order was obliged to reflect that knowable rule. Failing that simple objective, no government could count itself legitimate.

Transitions

As we have seen, most seventeenth-century constitutionalist thinking presumed the importance of monarchy to the well-being of civil society. But implicit in the theory was the understanding that the prerogatives of the monarch were subordinate to the responsibilities of power before a wider community of consenting members within the borders of a territorial state. Indeed the slow transition from subject to citizen, a process whose origins have been traced to the late medieval period by Walter Ullmann, had during the seventeenth century undergone a rapid acceleration.[107] Constitutional theory continued to express the central duty of obedience to civil authority, but the subject who formerly obeyed the law as given was, in a few states, replaced by the citizen who conformed to the law as it was made by him or by his representatives. Between 1600

and 1700 what Ullmann called the 'ascending conception of Government', where law and government power rise from 'from the broad base
in the shape of a pyramid', found new energy and new support.[108]

Most of this support – the broad base – came from elements of the
propertied elite, men who gave no thought to the possibility of extending the representative system to the labouring poor. The lives of 'the
ruled' were not to be changed by the sort of expansion of political rights
entertained by the constitutionalist writers discussed here. Nor were
these writers prepared to envision the possibility of government without
a role for the prince. Least of all did they allow for the possibility of a politics disengaged from theological concerns. Those genuinely radical
proposals, republicanism and a profane politics, deserve separate treatment, not only because of their innovative quality, but also for their
unlikely rise to a central status in the politics of the modern age.

4

REPUBLICANISM REKINDLED

For Roman jurists like Cicero, the rendering of the Greek word *politeia* into Latin as *res publica* was intended simply to describe the state or public affairs. It was in this sense of any legitimate political community that Bodin understood *re publica*, or *la chose publique* when he published *Six Books of the Republic*. In English the word best translates as common weal or commonwealth, and similarly refers to the common business, and to the state as the arena of this public business. By the seventeenth century, two additional meanings came to be associated with republic or republicanism: a form of state distinguished from hereditary sovereign monarchy, and a style of political conduct where civic equality, public participation, and public spiritedness were deemed essential to the health of the state.[1] Both of these associations, inasmuch as they were embraced by seventeenth-century theorists, found their most immediate historical roots in the Italian city-republics of the Renaissance. And during our period, they would find their most compelling application in mid-century England, where the Civil War created a temporary power vacuum and a free press, both of which facilitated the emergence of radical new views on public authority.

In the 11 centuries between the principate of Octavian (31 BC–AD 14) and the pontificate of Gregory VII (1073–85), republican theory – and practice – was simply non-existent. It was against this unpropitious backdrop, not a little informed by Christian views of right forms of rule, that the emergence of new republics on Italian soil took place in the High Middle Ages. In fact the earliest of the Italian city-republics emerged in the midst of the investiture controversy between emperor and pope which began in 1085. First in Pisa (1085), then at Genoa, Milan and Arezzo by 1100, and next in Bologna, Padua and Siena by the mid twelfth century, elective and self-governing systems, each with a written constitution defining the form and power of government, took the stage as unsettling alternatives to hereditary monarchy. And while access to citizenship – and thus political rights – was severely limited, these city governments were remarkable accomplishments in an age when feudal, personal monarchy was thought to be the only form of legitimate rule.[2] Defenders of these Italian republics (the best known of whom was Machiavelli) were convinced that only under this unique model of political organization, only by adopting the principle of popular sovereignty, could an organized community hope to achieve its highest goals. The emphasis here was on the moral dimensions of self-government and its practical outcomes. When individual citizens are empowered and obliged to take an active role in public affairs, when equality and personal liberty are secured, then the state can hope to realize its greatness. Healthy republics depended on the willingness of an enlightened citizenry to take on the common business, the *res publica*, through a diffusion of power within various institutions. Courage and public spirit, a rejection of luxury and corruption, a sense of liberty which did not preclude the sacrifice of private interest for public good; all were deemed essential to the healthy republic. According to Machiavelli, 'it is not the well-being of individuals that makes cities great, but the well-being of the community; and it is beyond question that it is only in republics that the common good is looked to properly...'[3] In such a community of free and equal citizens, it was thought that the cultivation of individual talents inevitably led to increased wealth, agricultural and commercial development, public prosperity. Hereditary monarchy, on the other hand, destroys this individual aspiration to greatness, this human drive to succeed, to innovate, to improve. The result in a monarchical regime is stagnation and oppression, the decline of state power and the erosion of civic virtue.

In seventeenth-century Europe, few serious thinkers took these Italian city-states as anything other than brief aberrations from the monarchical norm. And with the exception of Florence and Venice, brief they were, with factional quarrels and party rivalries dooming the bold experiments to chronic instability and an ignominious return to the hereditary principle by the fourteenth century. Florence managed to carry on until the early 1500s before succumbing to the Medici family, while the Venetian state persisted until the dawn of the Napoleonic era (1797). All in all the message was pretty unambiguous: republics were notoriously flawed mechanisms for managing civil affairs. In France, for example, Catholic political theorists used republicanism throughout the century as a term of derision against what was taken to be the inherent disloyalty of the Huguenot minority. Anti-republican language was utilized in order to point up the selfless virtues of monarchical rule, while decrying alleged Huguenot attempts to create a state within a state based upon the model of the Dutch Republic and dominated by a dissident nobility.[4] The fact that today 'the modern constitutional republic stands virtually unchallenged as the sole surviving candidate for a model of political authority in the modern world', should not blind us to the suspect quality of the system just 300 years ago.[5] As with the ancient world of Greece and Rome, and with Renaissance Italy, seventeenth-century European republics were exceptional organizations of public power, both in the ideological and in the more institutional sense, and like their predecessors, these republics were always threatened with destruction by internal division and the selfishness of party.

There were, nonetheless, three outstanding examples of successful republics in the seventeenth century: Venice, Switzerland, and the United Provinces of the Netherlands. All shared the common feature that their geographical and demographic sweep was small; the population of the seven constituent provinces of the Netherlands, for example, was only some 600 000 in 1600. In addition to these success stories, there was one significant failed experiment, and this was undertaken in England during an 11-year period between 1649 and 1660. Ironically, the largest and most diverse output of republican writing originated in the Island Kingdom, where the application of theory to practice clumsily misfired. Despite this high level of intellectual production, however, the collapse of the new English order was not as extraordinary an event as the elimination of the monarchy had been in 1649. This is due to the fact that Republican forms of government stood as peculiar aberrations to the dominant trend towards personal Christian monarchism during the seventeenth century. Despite the examples of Italian city-state prosperity during the Renaissance, the stubborn independence of the Swiss cantons, and the commercial prowess of the United Provinces, the very idea of nation-state sovereignty without the person of the hereditary monarch was uncongenial to most Europeans across the status hierarchy. In France, Spain and in the Habsburg lands, opposition to central authority tended to be particularist, not republican, in character.[6] As late as the start of the nineteenth century, according to one recent scholar, it was still a matter of debate, 'how much a modern constitutional republic could indeed hope to provide a compelling recipe for political legitimacy of any real durability'.[7]

Sixteenth- and seventeenth-century antiquarians and classicists who studied republicanism realized that the principal models for government where power flowed up from the citizenry instead of downwards from God – the Greek city-states and Rome before the imperial era – were pre-Christian in origin. These writers also understood that the ancient practitioners of republican rule were unenthusiastic about other-worldly concerns.[8] The very existence of republics, like Copernican cosmology's reordering of the heavens, seemed for the supporters of the dominant model of Christian monarchy to impugn the integrity of the divinely ordered great chain of being. Republics did this by disallowing political superiors any claim to supernatural commission, by reducing the magistrate to the status of temporary representative of wider, community-defined or even individual interests.

Republican theory began with the assumption, very much at odds with the internationalist and directive traditions of the church, that civil authority originated with the people, that civic activity was essential to the health of the state, and that sovereignty was delegated to the magistrates upon conditions set by a virtuous and disciplined public. And although citizenship might be restricted to a small minority of the overall population, as was certainly the case in pre-Christian Greece and Rome, the very notion that temporal authority might be disengaged from immediate celestial ordinance – and from a divinely commissioned king – was of revolutionary potential. Republicanism implied a vision of reality which did not include a hierarchical system of cosmic order, but instead an order – often transient – shaped by man himself and responding to the flux of circumstance. Reality was open and malleable, not static and closed, not allied to medieval theocracy.[9] Wise constitutional systems were human inventions, not eternal ordinances.

Unintended Republic

Of the three successful republics, it was the Dutch that was the latest to emerge on the political map. While many observers viewed these northerly provinces of the Low Countries as the home of personal liberty, self-government without a monarch, religious toleration and the rule of law, in fact the revolt against the rule of Philip II which began in 1566 was not designed at the outset to jettison the institution of monarchy. Indeed the Dutch Republic was an unintended birth, for few of the leading political figures in the provinces of Holland and Zeeland thought in terms of complete independence when the revolt against Spain began. Even after 1581, when the States General had declared their independence from the empire of Philip II of Spain, there was little consideration given to the precise nature of the new state. As E. H. Kossmann has recently observed, 'people in the Netherlands had no experience with republican government and tended to look upon it as something alien or even unnatural'.[10]

In fact it was not until the middle of the seventeenth century, and then only in Holland, that a republican theory was accepted as a desirable form of polity for the federation of member provinces.[11] The Calvinist leaders of the Dutch state were by no means eager to introduce a general toleration for Lutheran, Catholic, Socinian, and Anabaptist inhabitants. Had the leader of the rebels, the prince of Orange, William the Silent, not been assassinated in 1584, it is unlikely that a republic would have been established at all. William, who held the position of stadtholder (governor) of the two most influential provinces of Holland and Zeeland, was about to receive the title of count at the time of his death. The same offer was not extended to his son and successor Maurice, however, and by 1587 the rebellious Protestants of the Netherlands had abandoned the idea of securing a crowned head and instead emerged as a republic where sovereignty was held by the 'States' or representative assemblies of the seven member provinces.[12]

At a time when none of the countries of Europe had achieved a great deal of centralization, the constitutional arrangements in the Netherlands were arguably the most decentralized on the Continent. Each of the seven provinces enjoyed a high degree of independence under its own government, and within the provinces each town conducted its affairs with a remarkable degree of autonomy. Delegates from these urban oligarchies met together in legislative bodies known as 'States' in order to formulate and implement common provincial policies, and in turn the 'States' sent representatives to the unified States General in the city of Utrecht, there to deliberate issues of concern to the good of the country as a whole, in particular military action and foreign relations.

As we have seen in the previous chapter, Althusius was familiar with this structure and applauded the virtues of federalism. Philip II's desire to make the provinces pay for their government by raising taxes had initiated the dispute between crown and States General, where all new taxes had to receive approval. But the 1579 Union of Utrecht which constituted the foundation of the Republic had never clearly defined the relationship between the States General and the individual provinces.[13] The individual state assemblies, heavily influenced by town councils and local nobility, could continue to claim sovereignty by virtue of the fact that decisions made by the States General required the approval of each province and because prince Maurice had been elected stadtholder by the individual 'States'. His father had been appointed stadtholder by Philip II, and his position was recognized by the rebels in 1572. After 1585, the leader of the republic, the person responsible for setting and carrying out policy, and who held supreme military command, was an elected official who headed a dynamic commercial state which lacked a written constitution. During the course of the seventeenth century, two power bases were locked in competition, one centred around the stadtholder princes of Orange and the other focused on the mercantile leaders of Holland, the wealthiest province in the Union. Economic dynamism was advanced by practical arguments in favour of freedom of conscience for those who could not accept the Reformed Calvinist Church, and while legislation was in place proscribing dissidence, none of the political authorities enforced it. Authors found exceptional opportunities to publish their works unhindered by the authorities, even though restrictive measures did pass into legislation.

In the early seventeenth century those Dutch writers who were sympathetic to the republican model often looked to the city of Venice with some appreciation, incorporating idealized references to the Italian republic as an analogy for what the Dutch were hoping to achieve in northern Europe. Still, in the first half of the seventeenth century, neither Dutch statesmen nor Dutch intellectuals offered a theoretical basis for the republican government under which they lived.[14] In the universities, teachers tended to describe the Dutch Republic in terms of a limited monarchy, with the stadtholder enjoying executive functions, an aristocratic element located in the provincial States, and a popular democratic element represented by urban administrations.[15]

Such a perspective should not surprise us. Most republican theorists, while not invariably opposed to monarchy, were consistent in lamenting the tendency of individual monarchs, hereditary or elective, to place their own private interests before the good of their subject population. Philip II, it was believed, had succumbed to this particular sickness. As students of Aristotle and Polybius, republicans by and large acknowledged that truly durable states combined the monarchical, aristocratic, and democratic principles, and they were usually willing to concede the value of 'mixed' or 'limited' monarchy where the rule of law was honoured by all parties. Most writers were interested primarily in the proper redistribution of power among existing institutions; they did not believe that a broader redistribution of that power among social groups would advance either virtue or material well-being. Power could originate with the people themselves, the democratic element in society, but it was best administered by selfless and public-minded delegated authorities.

There were important connections between the Dutch rebels and the Protestant resistance theorists in France. William of Orange had spent time in France, while the probable author of the *Vindiciae*, Philippe du Plessis-Mornay, visited the Netherlands and contributed to the Dutch effort against Philip II.[16] The parallels between French resistance theory and Dutch thinking are significant, especially their emphasis on popular sovereignty and contract where the prince is described as the servant of the people and where lesser magistrates are charged with the power to resist should the prince violate his trust. But Dutch thought, in the end, was largely the product of unique circumstances unlike those facing the French, where resistance theorists ceased their campaign after the Protestant Henry of Navarre emerged as the strongest claimant to the throne.

Perhaps the most important result of the revolt against Spanish authority in the Netherlands was the emergence of an ideology which stressed liberty, popular sovereignty, constitutional guarantees, representative institutions and the importance of a virtuous citizenry.[17] The commercial prosperity of the Netherlands was associated with personal liberty and self-government from the beginning of the revolt against the administration of Philip II, and the maintenance of this liberty was made the chief end of politics. By the time that the States General of the United Provinces passed a resolution declaring Philip II in forfeit of his sovereignty over the provinces (26 July 1581), ideologies of disobedience had been succeeded by ideologies of resistance and popular sovereignty, where the representatives of the people, the States, were claiming a legitimate resumption of the power that they had earlier granted to the prince under the terms of a unwritten covenant. Sovereignty was now said to reside with the people, but the administration of sovereignty was in the hands of the States. Resistance was consistently pictured as the obligation of men who had inherited from their forebears a political order dedicated to the protection of liberty. The constitutional framework, the laws and the charters of the various cities and provinces, all products themselves of struggles for power between late medieval towns, provinces and lords, together with the institutional duties of the States, were the bedrocks of Dutch liberty. These States possessed sovereign power and utilized their position in order to check the ambitions of the prince. As the revolt proceeded, an emphasis upon civic responsibility and patriotism gradually extended one's allegiance to town and province to a broader affiliation with the United Provinces as a whole.[18]

England's Experiment

Republicanism, as we have seen, was variously defined, but in England a set of common working assumptions were embraced by all seventeenth-century republican writers. First and foremost, these writers believed that their own age was one afflicted by a pattern of deep and disturbing political corruption, where particular interests superseded the overall good of the community, where the rule of law was replaced with the rule of men. Linked with this was a deep anticlericalism, a conviction that clerical interference in the political life of the state had contributed nothing but ill to the life of the citizenry. Secondly, it was thought that this corruption could only be redressed if leaders studied and emulated the wisdom of the ancient, pre-Christian republics. Finally it was believed that only a genuinely republican politics, where private interests were subordinated to public ones, would be effective in securing lasting virtue and liberty.[19]

The years of the English Civil Wars and Interregnum (1642–60) represent one of the key periods in the development of modern republican thought, not least due to the fact that new men of humbler origins – artisans, tradesmen and soldiers – entered into the field of political discourse in an effort to shape events, to translate thought into action, at a moment when traditional political practice was under enormous strain. Nothing comparable to the diversity of intellectual output during this revolutionary period, the pamphlets, petitions, formal treatises, constitutional formulae, is to be found during the Italian Renaissance, an era which one modern scholar has called the first decisive stage in the formation of modern republicanism.[20]

The republican thought of the middle decades of the seventeenth century in England would continue to provide instruction for radical movements in Europe and in America for the next 150 years. The critique of monarchy as an outmoded and counterproductive model of executive authority fit only for slaves; the extension of the franchise and its implications for the empowerment of groups whose interests were not parallel to those of the traditional minoritarian elite; the challenge to age-old property relations represented by members of religious communities seeking to restore one version of primitive Christianity; written constitutions adopted by free and equal citizens: these and other innovative notions published and debated in the years between the outbreak of hostilities and the return of Charles II altered the intellectual landscape of Europe forever.

We should in fairness preface our discussion with the reminder that genuinely republican sentiments were rarely embraced in England before the 1640s, this despite the fact that anyone with university training had studied the political culture of the ancient city-states. Indeed works by Italian republicans and about Italian republics were being translated into English at the end of the sixteenth century, and found a readership with the type of person who would sit in parliament.[21] Still all sides in the emerging dispute between parliament and the crown assumed that monarchy was an essential part of any stable constitution. Monarchy represented the capstone of the social order, the pre-eminent symbol of a hierarchical society that most opponents of the king had no interest in undermining. As we have seen, the entire fabric of historical consciousness, common law, and constitutional precedent assumed the inviolability of the king's person and the sanctity of his royal office. The intensity with which most parliamentarians sought an accommodation with the king up until 1648 is testimony to the importance of the institution in the constitutional thinking of the vast majority of the political elite. And with crown control over the press inhibiting the expression of whatever republican rumblings might be present at the subterranean plane, the historic place of the monarchy in the English constitution was accepted as the starting point for all discussion relating to the exercise of civil authority.

Even sixteenth-century Englishmen understood that *res publica* could include monarchy, because the commonwealth placed the rule of law and the public interest before individual ambition.[22] During the first two years of the Long Parliament, before the outbreak of Civil War in 1642, the king and his opponents shared a host of political assumptions. Even after the first test of arms in 1642 members of parliament believed that their resistance was made necessary solely because an otherwise good king was relying upon evil counsel with the result that accepted rules of

governance, and the fundamental laws, were being abused. The main
issues of contention between king and parliament involved not the
nature of authority but its proper employment.[23] Later, more radical
proposals regarding the origin and nature of political power may have
been the by-product of the military conflict, but they did not contribute
to the start of the disagreement. Even the future Leveller John Lilburne
could before 1640 endorse the time-tested standards of non-resistance
and passive obedience.[24]

Thus when a small minority of MPs, backed by those in the army who
saw themselves as the instruments of God's providential purpose,
ignored the widespread popular yearning for a settlement with Charles
I and instead tried the king for treason and executed him as a criminal
on 30 January 1649, it was the illegitimacy of a military regime, not the
exuberance of republican imagination, which gripped the sensibilities of
the nation. The army leadership may have defined themselves as mere
vehicles carrying out the judgement of God against a 'man of blood' who
refused to concede that heaven had spoken in giving parliamentary
forces a decisive victory in 1646. But for the majority of citizens the
judgement of the divine was just as clearly indicated in the disastrous
harvest of 1648 and in the ongoing conflict in Ireland, The English
republic had been born without the consent of the English people and
against the pattern of shared political experience. Republican political
thought, absent from the stage of constitutional debate during the first
half of the century, was, as in the case of the Netherlands, the child of an
unexpected and largely unwanted republic.[25]

From a wider European perspective, England had played host to a
genuine revolution in the months between December 1648 and March
1649, a revolution with implications well beyond the political arena. The
House of Commons had been purged of two-thirds of its members by an
army convinced that the politicians had betrayed them, the aristocratic
House of Lords was abolished, the divine-right monarchy was annulled,
and the confessional state church destroyed. With their passing one
familiar set of correspondences in the hierarchically organized structure
of creation disappeared from the intellectual stage. A mere remnant of
the Long Parliament, the so-called 'Rump', now claimed to represent
the interests of the nation as a whole; a claim most republicans found
hard to digest by the time that this body was sent packing by Cromwell in
1653.

These dramatic changes had been preceded by the breakdown of censorship during the years of the Civil War, the disintegration of church

courts, and the cessation of normal judicial processes in the countryside. Many preachers sympathetic to the parliamentary cause during the Civil War had linked the king's government with the Roman Antichrist, and some had gone so far as to speak in millennial terms, seeing the war in England, together with the Thirty Years War on the Continent, as the cataclysmic conclusion to the temporal experience, the end of time and the promised return of Christ. Indeed the execution of the king was interpreted by some as essentially clearing the way for King Jesus and his 1000-year rule in communion with the saints.[26] Not the least disturbing result of the regicide for those among the political elite was the proliferation of radical groups whose appeal was to the common folk and their allegedly infallible inner light. If regicide were permissible, if the ancient constitution could be jettisoned, then perhaps other voices might merit attention, perhaps the disenfranchised majority might have a place in the rebuilding of Zion.

The leaders of the republic, and Cromwell especially, did not govern the nation by consent any more than the king had. There were no genuinely free elections before the Restoration in 1660; an army half of whose officers were drawn from the middle and lower ranks of society was the sole guarantor of the new regime as the civilian parliaments of the 1650s, closely controlled by Cromwell, failed to secure solid, lasting stability independent of their military masters. By the summer of 1655, frustrated with the uncooperative nature of the legislative branch, Cromwell opted for direct military rule. Despite the republic's military successes in Ireland, Scotland, and against the Dutch, it is generally agreed that had a free election taken place at any time between 1649 and 1660, the monarchy would have been restored and the army cashiered.[27] Republican theory during the Interregnum was thus often composed within the context of advocacy, obliged to defend the propriety of a political system which was deeply unpopular.

Initial Expedients

Needing to secure at least the acquiescence of former royalists and Presbyterians if the republic were to survive over the long term, the earliest efforts of republican writers were concerned with what Quentin Skinner has called *de facto* theory, where the current regime's ability to maintain security and rights to property (and conversely Charles I's demonstrated failure to do so) was enough to command the allegiance of the citizenry. Avoiding any discussion of moral right or origins and focusing instead on the existing government's competence in protecting the entire population and its estates, the obligation to obey was rooted solely in the practical benefits to be gained for all members of a otherwise violent society.

Marchamont Nedham, a former royalist who won a pardon for plotting against the parliamentary side by turning his considerable editorial skills to the cause of advancing an unpopular republic, made the *de facto* defence repeatedly in the government's weekly journal *Mercurius Politicus*. In his editorials, many of which were drawn from his *The Case of the Commonwealth of England Stated* (1650), Nedham laboured to vindicate the actions of the army and the Rump Parliament by stressing that every government could trace its roots to acts of violence. Anthony Ascham, another early defender of the republic, cautioned that the effort to establish one party's legal right was both futile and counterproductive. 'As for the point of right', he stated in *Of the Confusions and Revolutions of Governments* (1649), 'it is a thing always doubtful, and would ever be disputable in all kingdoms if those governors who are in possession should freely permit all men to examine their title *ab origine*.'[28] The Rump Parliament's decision to oblige all adult males to subscribe an 'Engagement' to be faithful to the new commonwealth made the work of *de facto* theorists like Nedham and Ascham especially apposite.

Thomas Hobbes would bring *de factoism* to its full secular conclusions in *Leviathan*, a book written with clear reference to the 'Engagement' debate, when he insisted that it was the military defeat of Charles I, not his execution, that rendered him incapable of carrying out his essential constitutional function as protector of the people. Republican propagandists also stressed the purported material benefits to be secured in a commonwealth without a prince. In a declaration issued by the Rump on 22 March 1649 and printed in Latin, French and Dutch, the unicameral legislature pointed to the prosperity of Venice and Switzerland. Referring to the Dutch Republic's recent hard fought victory for independence from Spain, the manifesto claimed that: 'Our neighbours in the United Provinces, since their change of government have wonderfully increased in wealth, freedom, trade, and strength, both by sea and land.'[29] Only in republics, it was maintained, was justice administered fairly, dynastic ambitions removed, freedom of conscience defended, and the poor protected from oppression.

Milton's Contribution

Throughout the course of the 1640s John Milton was an unqualified supporter of the parliamentary cause, and he eagerly endorsed the call to arms and the military conflict against the king beginning in 1642. He shared with many Puritans the belief that England had a special role to play in history, that the English people had been charged to oppose God's enemies and forward the work of godly rule upon earth. A key to that work was the promotion of free expression. In *Areopagitica* (1644), Milton charged that papists and crypto-papists within the Church of England sought to bury the truth and vilify the God-given gift of reason by practising censorship. Coupling episcopacy with devotion to absolutism, Milton was convinced that tyranny in England had both a civil and a religious face, and that by 1649 both forms merited elimination if civil and religious liberty were to be secured.[30]

To the disdain for prelacy and monarchy he added a contempt for many members of the Long Parliament when that body hesitated to forward the Reformation after the defeat of the duplicitous Charles I in the second Civil War (1648). With the rout of the king's army in 1648, the parliamentary coalition of Independents and Presbyterians collapsed. The latter represented a majority in the House of Commons and remained committed to trying to reach a settlement with the king, while the Independents, and especially members of the army, felt that the king could no longer be trusted and wished to bring him to justice. The stalemate was broken only when the army staged a coup (known as Pride's Purge) on 6 December 1648, forcing compromising MPs out of the House and leaving only a remnant or Rump to carry on the task of dealing with the defeated king.[31] Royalists joined with Presbyterians in protest at this and at the trial of the king, prompting Milton to write on behalf of the army's actions. He wrote the bulk of *The Tenure of Kings and Magistrates* after Colonel Pride had removed the Presbyterian conciliators from the House of Commons, and during the extra-legal trial of Charles. In the wake of this defence of regicide, Milton was appointed Secretary for Foreign Tongues by the republic's Council of State. He therefore became the official propagandist of the new regime, authoring official works between 1649 and 1651 for the faction that had shattered the historic union of king in parliament.[32]

The Tenure repeatedly makes reference to the inconsistency of Presbyterians on the question of resistance, pointing to sixteenth-century predecessors such as John Knox and George Buchanan who made resistance the cornerstone of Presbyterian political theory. Presbyterians who deplored the army's action, for their part, raised the distinction in resistance theory between inferior magistrates who were permitted the right to resist, and private individuals who were forever disabled from such action. The army, as the instrument of parliament in the first instance, was associated with private persons by Presbyterians seeking compromise.[33] The only instance in which individuals were thought to possess a right to political initiative in Lutheran and Calvinist tracts was when a foreign usurper became a tyrant. In the estimates of Peter Martyr, Theodore Beza, and the author of the *Vindiciae*, native institutions could be protected by individuals when faced with the force brought to bear by an invader. Milton's innovation was to deny that the distinction between an invader and a domestic tyrant was legitimate.[34] If the king of Spain coming in person 'to subdue us or to destroy us, might lawfully by the people of England either be slain in fight, or put to death in captivity, what have a native king to plead, bound by so many Covenants, benefits and honours to the welfare of the people, why he through the contempt of all Laws and Parliament, the only tie of our obedience to him' should be excused his tyrannical conduct?[35]

As the most recent editor of Milton's political writings has argued, the great poet of the Puritan cause was breaking with the Protestant tradition of voluntarism here, the notion that God's will constitutes what can be considered just. Replacing this notion with the contention that lawfulness originates in what is intrinsically reasonable allowed Milton to posit the adoption of ethical judgements independent of God's revealed word.[36] 'Against whom what the people lawfully may doe, as against a common pest, and destroyer of mankind, I suppose no man of clear judgement need go further to be guided than by the very principles of nature in him.'[37] Individual political action was now deemed tenable; if the inferior magistrates refused to take action in the face of tyranny, then it was lawful for any who had sufficient power to do so.

Milton's discussion of the origin of political society began with a state of nature where 'all men naturally were borne free'.[38] Unfortunately, the violence of men in the wake of the historic Fall leads to a collective decision to associate for mutual protection against external threats. As Locke would later do, Milton preferred to argue that men left this state of nature 'for ease, for order, and lest each man should be his own partial judge'.[39] A second agreement is necessary, however, before formal political institutions are created, and the purpose of these structures is to restrain and punish internal malefactors. Unique in this transfer of power, however, was Milton's insistence that in the state of nature each person enjoyed the right to punish anyone who violated the laws of nature. Transferring this common right to punish to one or more magistrates does not mean that 'Deputies and Commissioners', become 'Lords and Masters' who rule outside the law and directly under God's appointment. Civil magistrates wield no new powers which were not at first in the charge of free and equal individuals; no one can alienate their essential liberty to the magistrate and to attempt to do so would be 'extreme madness'.[40]

Milton constantly referred to the agreement between the people and their ruler as a trust instead of a contract. This was an important distinction to make at the time because a contract implied that the ruler had certain rights as well as responsibilities, while on the other hand parties to a trust have a right to dissolve the arrangement without the ruler having been guilty of any offence. The ruler cannot be wronged by such a dissolution because he had no rights granted to him in the first place.[41] If the people's understanding of the public good should change, then they are free to make whatever alterations in the structure of political power they deem appropriate. Human liberty, he wrote in *A Defense of the People of England* (1651) 'is not Caesar's, but is a birthday gift to us from God himself'. In claiming that 'we belong to God, that is, we are truly free and on that account to be rendered to God alone', Milton established a position respecting the sanctity of human freedom that Locke would adopt in his *Second Treatise of Government.*[42]

Milton always harboured reservations as to whether his countrymen were in fact fit for republicanism, and during the course of the Interregnum he always supported the prevailing power. In *A Defense* he referred to the members of the Rump as 'the better and sounder part' of the Senate which now governed the country, and he continued to expect that a moral elite would best guide the nation. By 1653 it was apparent that the Rump was not to be the agent of reform that he expected, and the same was true for the succeeding 'Barebones' Parliament. The elite of virtue was thus reduced to Cromwell and his army associates. After the abrupt dismissal of the Barebones Parliament he announced that 'We all willingly yield the palm of sovereignty to your [Cromwell's] unrivalled ability and virtue, except a few amongst us ... '[43]

The few doubtless included those whom Milton called 'the blockish vulgar' in *Eikonoklastes*, men whose habits of deference and slavishness to those in power made the work of reform so difficult. Only in 1660, when the Restoration was imminent, did he embrace a republicanism that was truly free of the monarchical trappings of the Protectorate. In *The Ready and Easy Way to Establish a Free Commonwealth* he insisted the crisis brought about by the death of the Lord Protector offered an opportunity for the virtuous minority to create a 'free commonwealth' where the servants of the state are self-effacing 'drudges to the public at their own cost and charges; neglect their own affairs; yet are not elevated above their brethren, live soberly in their families, walk the streets as other men, may be spoken to freely, familiarly, without adoration'.[44] To fail in such a holy experiment was for Milton the worst disaster, moral and political, that could befall the elect.

Seventeenth-century Democracy

Seventeenth century people outside the politically active elite did not claim any 'right' to participate in the process whereby members of representative assemblies were chosen, nor were men like Milton eager to afford them such a right. The very notion of voting for political leaders simply was not part of their everyday community experience. In this respect, perhaps more than most, our assumptions are fundamentally different from our pre-twentieth-century predecessors. We tend to associate democracy with political systems which find their legitimacy in the will of a universal electorate, where all members of that electorate are eligible to serve in lawmaking bodies. Things were very different 300 years ago. According to David Wootton, a 'democracy' in the plainest sense was 'any government where power was distributed more broadly than in an aristocracy'.[45] It was thought that any arrangement more inclusive than this, any concession to the labouring male population, invited anarchy and the worst possible abuses of the duties associated with magistery in the wake of the Fall. Any purported 'right' to revolt against one's political superiors, to move beyond the position of an original and irrevocable transfer of authority from the people to chosen rulers (a position, we will recall, endorsed by a number of absolutists), entailed a belief that the transfer had been made conditionally, that rulers had agreed to exercise their delegated authority in a manner consistent with the terms of the initial grant. Power could be reclaimed by the people – or by their delegated representatives – if and when the magistrate exceeded his trust. To this protean notion, to the proposition that a magistrate does not enjoy 'the right to command simply by virtue of his office' the Levellers gave first voice.[46]

The Leveller movement lasted almost four years, from 1645 until 1649. These were years when there was a dangerous power vacuum in England due to the Civil War, when neither king nor parliament had established clear-cut authority. In this setting a wide variety of new voices emerged in print calling for a fundamental reordering of the state. Writers such as William Walwyn, John Wildman, Richard Overton, and John Lilburne, using broadsheets and pamphlets, addressed themselves to common people – craftsmen, soldiers, urban labourers – even though the bulk of their intended audience was illiterate. The popular appeals contained in these occasional pieces were intended to be read aloud in public places.[47] The authors were termed 'Levellers' by their enemies, who incorrectly interpreted their programme as a threat to existing property relationships, but recent scholars writing in a revisionist framework have sought to reduce the importance of the Levellers as a force in the debates over the constitution of the 1640s. Although the movement was once held up in the literature as the champion of democratic, working-class interests, many scholars now question the breadth of the Levellers' support and the overall impact of their main ideas.

Even with this re-evaluation, however, it is hard to deny that the cluster of ideas set out by the Leveller movement in the mid 1640s, unlike most other political ideologies of the seventeenth century, advanced a set of beliefs and a practical programme that was unfamiliar to an early modern sensibility. Calling for universal manhood suffrage without property requirements, for a written constitution reflecting the direct input of the people as a whole, plus a representative assembly which enjoyed a popularly delegated lawmaking and executive power, equality before the law, cessation of arbitrary arrest and the right to legal representation, freedom of religion and expression, the end to military conscription, and the right of resistance if the magistrates ignored their trust, the Levellers were setting aside virtually every convention associated with the dynastic state in favour of a unprecedented reordering of formal human association. Indeed not a single one of their demands was recognized by any European government.[48] At Putney in November 1647, members of the army rank and file met with their officers in order to debate objectives now that the king had been defeated and the majority in parliament wished to disband the army without paying arrears. It was here that Colonel Rainsborough made his well-known appeal for government by consent. His position is representative of the movement as a whole:

I think that the poorest he that is in England has a life to live as the greatest he; and therefore truly, sir, I think it's clear, that every man that is to live under a government ought first by his own consent to put himself under that government; and I think that the poorest man in England is not at all bound in a strict sense to that government that he has not had a voice to put himself under.

With the Levellers a Copernican revolution in the centuries-old hierarchies of the social and political microcosm was undertaken, with the result being a new set of correspondences between the heliocentric heavens and the equalitarian polity. Not simply the politics of restoration common to so much 'revolution' in seventeenth-century Europe, the freedoms demanded in the first 'Agreement of the People' (3 November 1647) placed the leaders of the Leveller movement well outside the boundaries of conventional political discourse. For behind the Agreement of the People was the radical assumption that an unrepresentative parliament was no more entitled to the people's allegiance than a hereditary monarch. The laws enacted by such parliaments, the many precedents of the common law, had no legitimacy if they did not flow from powers authorized by the free consent of the people. The Agreement was a statement of rights and of fundamental written law, analogous to reason, and was to be approved by all freemen. This fundamental law contained only those natural rights which the people had agreed to transfer to the state. The bulwarks of the *ancien régime*: a prescriptive and persecutory state church, a deferential and asymmetric social order designated by legal status, an unassailable hereditary ruling monarch, economic monopolies and trade restrictions; these features of European life were to be supplanted by a new order designed, quite simply, with the past out of mind, with late and present practice, law and custom, cleanly removed from the formulation.

Controlling a party treasury and requiring payment of dues from their membership, capable of raising thousands of signatures for petitions to parliament, the Levellers were the first formal political party in seventeenth-century England.[49] In fact much of their support was centred in London, a city of immigrants from the countryside, in a sense new 'masterless men'. These Londoners were members of an increasingly fluid society, where principles of deference and obedience were no longer instinctual. Another important source of support was in the parliamentary army, an organization made up of volunteers who were used to electing their own officers.[50] And for the first time in English politics

the leaders of a political movement were in many cases drawn from the
ranks of the lower orders and lesser gentry.

Authors such as Lilburne, Walwyn, and Overton – the principal voices
within the ranks of the leadership – were familiar with tradesmen and
wage labourers and expressed their grievances brought about by sky-
rocketing taxes, disrupted trade, unemployment and flat wages during
the war years. Lilburne saw his own personal sufferings – at the hands of
a church establishment which refused him toleration, and of economic
monopolies like the Merchant Adventurers who denied him the right to
engage in the cloth trade in which he had been an apprentice; by the
House of Commons which sent him to Newgate on a charge of slander
against the Speaker, and by the House of Lords who again incarcerated
him in 1646 for refusing to recognize their competence over the affairs
of a commoner – as emblematic of the sufferings endured by all common
people.[51] These authors eschewed Latin and the time-tested recourse to
learned authorities, writing in a plain style to newly literate groups of
mainly urban dwellers, and setting an agenda which had little in common with the political status quo of king, Lords, and Commons.

Their goal, in the end, was to establish a new political culture with the
support of the disenfranchised, particularly the rank and file in the
army, the hard-pressed craftsmen, artisans and labourers of London,
together with the members of religious sects worried lest a new official
church take the place of the discredited episcopal establishment.[52] The
collapse of effective press censorship in the 1640s gave these men a
broad opportunity to extend a propagandistic message of fundamental
political change in the midst of Civil War upheaval. The human equality
promoted by the Levellers, the abandonment of social gradation, doubtless played its role in the eventual elimination of the king, the abolition
of the House of Lords, and the formation of a unique commonwealth
after 1649, but before that date the leadership was focused on effecting
change through peaceful persuasion. Calls for the abolition of the monarchy and the House of Lords were made on the basis of a conviction
that these two institutions had benefited the most from the continuation
of the oppressive Norman legacy. These republican voices in the Leveller movement were coupled with others which were willing to allow the
continuation of king and Lords provided that they did not have a veto
over parliamentary legislation. Frequent elections, the exclusion of lawyers from the Commons, a redistribution of seats, and a salary for MPs in
order that they might be free of the influence of rich patrons were all
component parts of the overall programme.

For Levellers such as Lilburne and Overton, the king, and not simply his wicked counsellors, must be held accountable for actions against a sovereign people whose representatives in the Commons had been repeatedly frustrated in their work of reform. Finding no place for the House of Lords in a society founded on the equality of all men, attacking the whole ramshackle structure of the common law as little more than the self-serving brainchild of the Norman conquerors, and convinced that the impositions of one's predecessors had no claim on the present age, the Levellers insisted that legitimate obligation to law could only find its roots in a reformed House of Commons, one representing the interests of the majority population. Theirs was a struggle to restore the golden age of Anglo-Saxon individual liberties, liberties based on natural right and the law of reason.[53]

Leveller hostility to the abuse of power by self-interested elites at the national level led them to address the matter of reform at the local level. Officeholders and judicial personnel in the communities (including justices of the peace) would be elected directly by those whom they served, not appointed at the centre; decentralization of government functions, especially the law courts, and the replacement of a national army with locally recruited militia, would help to ensure the honesty and integrity of public decision-making at every level. The emerging bureaucratic state, swelling enormously during the years of civil war and insatiable in its tax demands, was to be dismantled and power returned to its authentic home at the local level.[54] In this respect the Levellers, whose views were echoed by John Milton in his *The Ready and Easy Way to Establish a Free Commonwealth* (1660), were part of that larger Europe-wide movement to resist the expansion of the impersonal nation-state, a movement bound, in the end, to ignominious failure.

The Levellers maintained that religious liberty was the firm confederate of civil liberty. Indeed it has been argued that the roots of Leveller popular sovereignty and individual rights are to be found in the culture of the English Protestant sects. Lilburne's church views certainly emphasized the voluntary and contractual nature of membership, and he resigned his own commission in the parliamentary army in 1645 rather than take the Presbyterian-mandated Covenant.[55] The covenant theology of the separatist congregations, and their democratic church organization where leaders were held accountable for their work, encouraged a similar conception of the civil authority.

The Leveller call for toleration and freedom of conscience in the wake of the abolition of episcopacy acquired added urgency in 1646 as parliament took steps to erect a Presbyterian form of church government. Central to Leveller social and political thinking was a radical Calvinist tradition which stressed the spiritual equality of Christ's elect and a sense of strict individual accountability before God without the interposition of spiritual elites. Together with a puritan emphasis on the duty of the elect to act out God's purposes on earth, the religious underpinnings of the movement contributed to the formation of a more inclusive political outlook where persons equal before their Creator would call for greater control over their temporal civil condition. 'All and every particular and individual man and woman, that ever breathed in the world, are by nature all equal and alike in their power, dignity, authority and majesty' was how Lilburne summed up the implications of this theological framework for seventeenth-century government.[56] The democratic experience of sectarian congregations had provided ample experience of self-government at the church level, and the message from the pulpit had emphasized the importance of independence and social action for the good of the community.

In the end the Levellers were defeated by soldiers loyal to Cromwell. There were a number of weaknesses in the movement which prevented the translation of radical ideas into programmatic action. David Wootton has placed the failure of the Leveller leadership to retain the support of the sectaries, whose chief concern was toleration, and of the army rank and file, whose main worry was pay and legal protection for acts committed during wartime, as the first crucial miscalculation. By 1649 Cromwell was able to satisfy the demands of both groups, thereby undermining key numerical support for the Levellers.

It must be said that the Levellers were not advocates of organized violence or armed rebellion, nor did any of their members ever stand for elective office; they believed that the force of reason would be sufficient to effect fundamental change in an oppressive political system. Appealing to the public in and around the capital city, securing thousands of signatures for their many petitions to parliament, the leadership hoped to secure the support of the broadest possible sweep of artisans, tradesmen, and common labourers. Additionally, the egalitarian rhetoric and constitutional proposals of the Levellers had scant appeal amongst the officers of the parliamentary army, and the rank and file who were sympathetic were not prepared to organize enough military strength on their own to realize their goals by force.[57] There was no ruthlessly committed Leveller party willing to secure its agenda through whatever means necessary. Lilburne was a brilliant propagandist, supremely

effective in making his personal autobiography of mistreatment at the
hands of the government the story of oppression against all free-born
Englishmen, but he was not a pragmatic political operative willing to
push his ideas by any means to hand.

Religion and 'True Levellers'

The breakdown in the authority of church and state occasioned by the
Civil Wars, the failure of the parliamentarians to agree on an appropriate substitute for the discredited Church of England, and the extension
of toleration under the Instrument of Government in December 1653,
led to a wide-ranging expansion of religious perspectives and the growth
of independent 'gathered' churches all opposed to a state-supported
and obligatory clerical establishment. The membership of Anabaptist,
Quaker, Ranter, Seeker, and Muggletonian groups was both fluid and
migratory, as new ideas and personal insight were given encouragement
by the lack of any effective coercive machinery. Theological views
and unstructured practices once confined to underground status now
surfaced to map alternative paths to salvation. Hostility to tithes and
to ordained clerical elites, together with the growth of lay preaching
and popular participation in the life of the voluntary church, particularly
in the cities, emboldened large numbers of people to consider again
the implications of voluntary association, spiritual equality and popular
participation in worship for every aspect of political life, but especially
for traditional notions of deference and unyielding allegiance to the
powers in place.[58] The unlettered lay preacher put to the test the
idea that special training, always the perquisite of the well-to-do, was
essential to leadership and authority. Something of the impact of theological innovation on politics can be seen in the communitarian commitments of a small group of self-described 'True Levellers' whose leader
was Gerrard Winstanley.

Under the direction of the one-time Baptist Winstanley, a man who
had come to London as a clothing apprentice in 1630 but whose career
as a freeman of the Merchant Tailors' Company was cut short in 1643 by
economic depression, the Diggers or self-anointed 'True Levellers' began
in early 1649 to move beyond the political programme of Lilburne,
Walwyn and Overton to address what they saw as the fundamental link
between economic inequality and the distribution of political power in

English society. Winstanley had been reduced to work as an agricultural day labourer in rural Surrey during the Civil Wars, and there his religious commitments evolved from Anabaptism to Antinomianism, where personal inward illumination, the mysterious work of the spirit, overrules the precepts of the written Word. For Winstanley, the divine intelligence was synonymous with this inner light, and God was in the world, not separate from it, as the principle of reason controlling all creation. 'Though men speak the very words of Scripture, but speak not with the mind of Him that gives life', he wrote in *The Saints Paradise* (1648), 'they may be strangers or even enemies to the God of the Scriptures. But if the same anointing dwell in you as in the Apostles, you can see into the mystery of Scripture, though you should never hear the Scripture from men.'[59] By following reason or the principle of God within, free from the oppressive culture of formal religious, legal and political systems, humans could find perfection on earth.

After the execution of the king, the Rump Parliament had adopted the word 'commonwealth' to describe the new political reality in England. The emphasis on the good of the entire community implicit in the acceptance of a word in common use since the early sixteenth century was transformed by Winstanley into an attack against the manifold evils of covetousness. Believing that human redemption would take place on earth once the law of reason had been established as the rule by which men governed their lives, in April 1649 Winstanley joined with William Everard, a former soldier and lay preacher, to take up a form of primitive communism with about 30 other like-minded souls on St George's Hill, waste-land in the parish of Walton-on-Thames located well south of the centre of political activity in London. The little 'Digger' squatter community was soon replicated at nine other locations near London and as far away as Gloucestershire and Nottinghamshire, although the total number of followers never exceeded a few hundred men and women.[60]

According to Winstanley, reason and Christian living would only find their full flowering in a society where the earth was owned in common; private possessions, he was convinced, led to sin, to conduct inimical to the life of the spirit. The existence of bondmen and beggars in a society where vast disparities of wealth were common was testimony to the current sinfulness of mankind. With private property 'some are lifted up into the chair of tyranny, and others trod under the foot-stool of misery, as if the earth were made for a few, not for all men'.[61] Only an unquestioned right to use the earth will guarantee individual freedom and put a close to the cause of all conflict and injustice.

Convinced that true equality was impossible so long as private property and the legal system that supported it were maintained, the Diggers struggled for a return to the prelapsarian condition of common ownership and production, where, in Winstanley's estimation, God was reason, the afterlife a myth, and redemption a prospect to be realized within the temporal sphere. For the Diggers, common ownership and shared labour were the clearest signs of the redemption of mankind on earth, a restoration of humankind's rational nature to its original state. Not surprisingly, by April 1650 irate local villagers had destroyed Winstanley's settlement in Surrey, unwilling to draw any distinction between religious utopians and troublesome vagrants. The other remaining outposts soon suffered much the same fate.

In the aftermath of this debacle, Winstanley began to recognize that his ideals for a world restored to its prelapsarian condition required a more formal statement of social organization once the present order was extinguished. In *The Law of Freedom in a Platform* (1652), dedicated to Cromwell, Winstanley described an overwhelmingly agrarian society where land and resources for production were jointly held, and where a parliament elected by all adult males would facilitate the transition to common ownership. Rotation in all public offices was coupled with a firm emphasis on decentralized power, securing local community control over the militia, the production of food and goods, the administration of law, and the provision of free and universal public education for the young. There would be no clergy or religious establishment in this communitarian society, but issues of public interest would be discussed by elected leaders. Not surprisingly, *The Law of Freedom in a Platform* had no appreciable impact on members of the Rump, on Cromwell, or even on the Levellers, all of whom distanced themselves from the radical economic proposals embraced by Winstanley. While his ideas were taken up again much later in a world of industrial hardship, the vision was peremptorily dismissed in mid seventeenth-century England, and the author ended his days quite out of character with his earlier forays, working as a tithe collector, church warden and parish constable.[62]

Harrington's Determinism

The Commonwealth of Oceana (1656), James Harrington's fictional account of the good society, was written at a time of great popular disillusionment with the Protectorate of Oliver Cromwell. Republican theorists, by and large, had accepted the improvised Commonwealth in 1649, but after the expulsion of the Rump in 1653 a number of authors came forward to register their dissatisfaction with the troublesome turn of events.[63] Most likely begun in 1654, just as Cromwell moved towards monarchy in all but name, the work alludes repeatedly to conditions under the Protectorate. Yet there is no evidence to suggest that Harrington was in favour of republican ideas before 1649; in fact he had been appointed a gentleman of the bedchamber to Charles I beginning in 1647, and probably remained with the king until just before Charles was executed.[64] John Aubrey later wrote of Harrington's deep respect and personal affection for the king. The work was composed at a time when Cromwell was moving from failure to failure in his efforts to secure a parliament whose ideals of godly reform comported with his own.

Like his contemporary, Nedham, Harrington rejected what he termed 'modern prudence' – those constitutional arrangements of the medieval or 'Gothic' period, the cavils of the common law which promoted the interests of a minority – and called instead for a return to republican political principles, the wisdom, virtue, and martial discipline of classical antiquity. But unlike *de facto* theorists such as Nedham, Harrington sought to make sense of the English Civil War from the perspective of larger patterns of social change. His overriding goal in what was essentially a work of counsel, a plan for the reconstruction of the English state at a moment of deep crisis, was to escape the very process of historical change and master time itself, to found a political order and a set of institutions immune from the corruptibility that had heretofore attended all existing governmental systems. It was an objective, or delusion, taken up again by Marx in the nineteenth century, and in Harrington's day it constituted nothing less than a profound rejection of the medieval penchant for seeing all forms of human endeavour as undergoing excess and decay, for the stroke of fortune to unsettle things terrestrial. He was convinced that laws shaped history; *Oceana* would point the way to a scientific understanding of these laws.[65]

Harrington's efforts to transcend the whirl and tumble of historical change were anchored in a rigorous study of the European past, an inquiry whose purpose was to discover beneath the variety of systems a causal nexus, a universal rule, an underlying force within the social order guiding all political life.[66] 'No man can be a Politician except he be first an Historian or a Traveller', he contended, 'for except he can see what Must be, or May be, he is no Politician.'[67] His study of the ancient republics – especially Sparta and Israel – and of modern Venice (which he had visited in the 1630s), informed all of his proposals for constitutional reform in England. Like his predecessor Machiavelli, whom he greatly admired, Harrington's interest in history was devoid of all theological assumptions; although he believed that the movement of history was guided by divine providence, *Oceana* was a model state whose stability was based upon the crucial fact that government reflects the prevailing economic, not religious, structure of society. The function of religion for Machiavelli, for Nedham, and for Harrington, was not to inculcate doctrinal truth but to mould men into good citizens.

At its most fundamental level, Harrington insisted that a stable and respected government could only be secured so long as the political structure continued to reflect the distribution of economic power in the nation. When the institutions of government, what Harrington called the 'superstructure', failed to reflect the balance of property and power in society, what he termed the 'foundation', instability was the result.[68] Monarchy was most appropriate where the bulk of property in the kingdom was owned and regulated by the prince. Controlling this land enabled the king to maintain the loyalty of the military class. Power-sharing between the king and the aristocracy is imperative when a significant portion of the land is owned by a privileged minority. Under the rule of monarchs and aristocrats, armies of loyal followers guaranteed that organized violence was at the disposal of landed elites. Similarly, a commonwealth where power is shared with a broad section of property owners is most appropriate where landholding, and consequently the power of the sword, is widely dispersed, amongst freemen who are also citizen soldiers.[69] Thus the proper form of government is always dictated by a power arrangement founded in the balance of property ownership at a particular moment, and the study of history provides the student with a knowledge of those factors leading to shifts in the distribution of property which always precede political conflict. One studies political history, quite simply, in order to bring it to a close.

Harrington would escape the process of historical change, transcend the errors of the past and secure political incorruptibility by erecting a constitutional order where economic relationships ceased to evolve to the point where enormous disparities in property ownership upset the established balance. Specifically in the case of his own country, he proposed the enactment of an agrarian law which would prevent the concentration of property – and military force – in the hands of the few.

'This kind of law', citing Old Testament precedent, 'fixing the balance in lands is called agrarian, and was first introduced by God himself, who divided the land of Canaan unto his people by lots, and is of such virtue that, wherever it hath held, that government hath not altered, except by consent.'[70] Permanent political stability could be achieved in mid seventeenth-century England through the deliberate regulation of property relations whereby extremes of wealth and poverty would be avoided.

According to his ideal formula, no man would own land worth more than £2000 per annum in England and Ireland, or more than £500 in Scotland, thus ensuring the preservation of a large landowning population throughout the British archipelago. Political rights, while reflecting one's economic standing in the community, would be widely extended, with freemen whose annual incomes were below £100 per annum permitted to vote and to serve in the lower house of a bicameral legislature, while those earning over £100 had the option of serving in the upper house. This latter body (called the Senate) would frame all laws for the republic while the more representative lower house reserved the right to approve or reject the legislation without amending or debating its provisions.

Addressing the reasons for these respective functions, Harrington suggested that while the wisdom of the commonwealth may be in the aristocracy, the interest is in the entire body of the people. 'The wisdom of the few may be the light of mankind, but the interest of the few is not the profit of mankind, nor of a commonwealth.'[71] Mandatory rotation in office for all elected members of the sovereign legislature would guarantee equal access to the magistracy and frustrate the formation of faction. Here the unhappy experience of the Long Parliament and the unicameral experience of the little-loved Rump Parliament were doubtless factors shaping his ideas. Executive functions of the government – military, financial, foreign relations – would be carried out, again on a rotating basis, by individuals elected to their respective posts by the Senate. The political process was to be opened up to new groups under his plan; the £100 requirement to serve in the Senate, for example, was half the figure needed simply to vote under Cromwell's Instrument of Government. Excluded from active citizenship were 'servants' and the propertyless in general, that overwhelming majority of the population who laboured on lands owned by others for very little recompense. An official church under state regulation was to be permitted, but toleration (excluding Catholics, Jews and 'idolaters') was to be allowed those

Protestants who could not bring themselves to conform to the parliamentary prescribed form of worship.

Given the changing status of property ownership in England over the previous century, where, beginning in the reign of Henry VIII, a financially hard-pressed Crown had been alienating land to ambitious commoners, where the post-feudal nobility, stripped of their military retinues by Henry VII, now shared wealth and land with untitled men, and where the Civil War itself was not unconnected with an effort by new groups to share in political sovereignty, the only political model fit to address new economic realities was the republican one. According to Harrington's materialist history, absolute monarchy had lost its exclusive title to sovereign authority as the diffusion of property proceeded apace from the Reformation forward. It is worth recalling here the words of Harrington's most recent editor, J. G. A. Pocock, who states that *Oceana* was written 'less to justify the fall of the English monarchy than to explain it, and this is why the work is important'.[72] Historical necessity, the decline of one political structure and the emergence of another, not any theory of abstract natural rights, made all alternatives to republicanism unworkable, unreasonable, and unjust.[73]

Harrington believed that in the republican model being proposed, human nature itself might be improved, and virtue promoted, provided of course that government were established to reflect the economic conditions of the people it represented. He subscribed to a position on the relationship between the individual and the state which emphasized the salutary effects of healthy institutions on character. This was in opposition to the view, held by Machiavelli and Milton amongst others, that even the best institutions cannot operate effectively where those in positions of power are corrupt, where the public spirit of those holding office is wanting. For Harrington, whatever corruption of manners marked contemporary England, the fault lay principally with a political structure out of harmony with the economic realities of the day.[74] Corruption was a result of political instability, not the cause of political malaise, 'for as man is sinful, but yet the world is perfect, so may the citizen be sinful and yet the commonwealth perfect'.[75] One can structure individual interests so that even bad men will act as though they were virtuous.

Cromwell having disappointed him by an unwillingness to retire the Protectorate, between 1656 and the Restoration in 1660 Harrington was tireless in promoting his vision of a rational and incorruptible republic to a wider audience. After the Lord Protector's death in 1658, the author of *Oceana* and others sympathetic to his ideas produced a large number of pamphlets in the hope that members of the restored Long Parliament might seize the opportunity to erect a durable republic before the penchant for a return to the discredited monarchical form, the harmful myth of the ancient constitution, became overwhelming. The ideas were discussed and debated by members of the Rota Club in the autumn of 1659, a meeting founded by Harrington with the goal of influencing those active in the government at all levels.[76] Few of those in positions of power during this fluid and dangerous period were much enamoured of Harrington's attempt to instal a perfect and timeless republican order; few shared his belief that man, in suggesting the possibility of perfection without change, might be like God. Deeply earnest to transform the constitutional programme of the fictional Oceana into reality, Harrington's model for a better world was sadly lumped by his critics with those earlier fictional accounts of no place, More's *Utopia* and Bacon's *The New Atlantis*.

Some Sequels

Harrington's claim that a powerful monarchy was out of step with the economic realities of mid seventeenth-century England seemed to ring true both during the 25-year reign of Charles II, who was restored to power amidst much popular rejoicing in May 1660, and during the brief 3-year tenure of his brother James II. Embarrassed in war by the Dutch in the 1660s, shaken by attempts by opponents of the Court to alter the terms of the succession in 1679–81, and finally, in 1688, collapsing when James was driven from the throne, the Stuarts had not succeeded in establishing the type of lasting political stability promised by a resumption of the ancient constitutional forms.

By the middle 1670s, Harrington's ideas, albeit altered in consideration of changed political circumstances, were once again championed by men who were fearful lest the monarchy attempt to follow the pattern of intolerance and absolutism set by Louis XIV across the Channel. The 1673 marriage of James to the Catholic Princess Mary of Modena appeared to lend credence to these apprehensions. Described by Professor Pocock as 'Neo-Harringtonians', writers such as Henry Neville and Algernon Sydney attempted to assimilate the anti-monarchical ideas of Harrington with the Whig notion of a balanced constitution where a monarch whose powers were limited by law governed in conjunction with an aristocratic and a popular interest. These 'Neo-Harringtonians' would bring the wisdom of *Oceana* up-to-date by recognizing the importance of the ancient constitution to English political experience, while at the same time adjusting power relations within the tripartite system to reflect those underlying economic shifts analysed with such precision by Harrington.

In the midst of the Exclusion Crisis, when it appeared to some that the Whig party's parliamentary stalemate with Charles II over the issue of succession might lead to another civil war, Henry Neville published *Plato Redivivus* (1680) in the hope of influencing the outcome of the immediate dispute, while also pointing the way towards structural changes designed to avoid similar crises in the future. Neville had been active trying to promote Harrington's ideas in the restored Rump in 1659 and, after his arrest in 1663, left for a self-imposed exile in Italy. Returning in 1669, he supported the emerging Whig party in their opposition to standing armies, their call for annual parliaments, and their insistence upon parliamentary control over patronage appointments, but he viewed the effort to exclude James duke of York as merely a treatment of one of the symptoms of misgovernment, not a root cause.[77]

Claiming to contain 'A repetition of a great many principles and positions out of *Oceana*', Neville's *Plato Redivivus* declared that the ancient constitution could not be revived when changes in the balance of land had made it imperative that greater political power be accorded the gentry, whom Neville linked with the commons.[78] The ancient framework of king, Lords, and Commons could be preserved, he believed, but only if the prerogative powers of the executive or 'principal magistrate' were transferred to the House of Commons. In *Plato Redivivus* these prerogative powers would be exercised by councils with a rotating membership elected by and accountable to parliament. In a similar expression of power-shifting designed to reflect the economic strength of members in the democratic body, the historic House of Lords would be preserved, but new peers would be chosen by the Commons, thereby preventing the elevation to noble status of mere sycophants of the crown.

In the end Charles II prevailed in his struggle against the Whigs in 1681, inaugurating a policy of rooting out opponents to the government and ensuring the peaceful transfer of executive power to James II in 1685. In fact, Harrington's and Neville's basic conviction that unalterable historical forces were pointing to the disintegration of personal monarchy seemed strikingly at odds with what appeared to members of the Whig opposition as a Europe-wide movement towards absolute monarchy, even tyranny, with its ultimate accompaniment of luxury, idleness and corruption. In 1694 the republican Robert Molesworth published *An Account of Denmark* in which he recounted the unhappy results of the 1660 monarchical coup in Denmark.[79] And in 1697, when King William attempted to keep a standing army intact after the conclusion of the Peace of Ryswick with France, a flurry of pamphlets and books appeared, warning of the potential danger of this precedent. Unlike Neville, republican theorists during the latter part of the seventeenth century began to revisit the whole concept of an ancient constitution and the liberties which it stood for against the encroachments of the executive.[80] Not only the members of the House of Commons, but even the historic peerage, so much disparaged by Harrington, now had a role to play in republican efforts to prevent what appeared to be a growing assault upon the liberties of the subject.

Like Neville, Algernon Sydney had served the Rump Parliament in 1652–3, and again in 1659. After the Restoration he too left for Italy, and he remained in exile on the Continent until 1677.[81] Soon after returning to England he stood, unsuccessfully, for the three consecutive parliaments which were called during the Exclusion Crisis, and between the failure of the final Parliament at Oxford in 1681 and his execution for alleged complicity in a plot (Rye House) to kill the king and the duke of York, Sydney composed his most famous work, not published until 1696: *Discourses Concerning Government*. Like John Locke's *Two Treatises of Government*, a work also written in the midst of the Exclusion Crisis and only published in 1689, Sydney's manuscript was both a reply to the Tory publication of Sir Robert Filmer's *Patriarcha* and a call to action against kings who had violated the trust reposed in them by their subjects. Following Harrington and Neville, Sydney saw the factions and disorders of the day as a result of the 'rupture' of the balance of property, but unlike Neville he thought that a healthy nobility whose essential characteristic was virtue, not just birth or royal favour, was essential to the establishment of a lasting balance in his own day.[82] Virtue is the end of government, and while he did not share in Harrington's belief that good men were not essential for the proper functioning of good institutions, he was, like his republican predecessor John Milton, confident that fallen men were capable of pursuing a virtuous course.

Sydney did not provide much in the way of a positive outline of the form of government most likely to secure the ancient liberties, but his trial and execution turned him into a martyr and hero for later eighteenth-century republicans.[83] Indeed the publication of the

Discourses in 1698 was but a part of a wider effort to disseminate the ideas of earlier republican theorists to a new generation. Joined by the appearance of Milton's *Historical and Political Works* (1698), the republication of Neville's *Plato Redivivus* (1698), and the works of Harrington, the commonwealth authors of the eighteenth century enjoyed easy access to an earlier ferment of ideas regarding republican civil order. The inheritance, so rich in potential although untested in practice, would not be squandered.

5

THE EMERGENCE OF THE MODERN STATE

Seventeenth-century political theorists were addressing the inhabitants of a continent where the unity symbolized by the papacy and the Holy Roman Empire had vanished, where the myth of a universal Christendom had been replaced by separate and sovereign states whose claims to power were derived from inside the political community, not from an external and transnational authority. These emerging states increasingly wielded their territorial power with a monopoly over the use of physical coercion and with a moral authority separate from either divine sanction on the one hand, or mere brute force on the other. And by the end of the century, these same sovereign states would anchor their existence not in the person of an individual ruler or rulers, but in a set of institutional structures whose public power continued even as individual magistrates passed from the scene. By 1700 neither the people nor the prince defined states which had become impersonal and theoretical entities, higher communities whose existence transcended the imprint of individuals and even status groups.[1] By 1700 sovereignty inhered not in the prince, as had been the case at the opening of the century, nor in the popular will, as evidenced in some countries towards the end of the century, but in a particular order of continuous public authority, a final and absolute judicial entity divorced from the flesh and allied to the realm of abstraction.

At the start of the century, most men continued to believe that political society had been organized in response to the will of God, to the datum of sinful human nature, and to the precepts of the natural law as set by an ultimately benevolent Father. The earthly king remained the essential personification of the body politic, and few thought of this body as a distinct and abstract personality, one which absorbed both people and prince into a larger fabric and whose higher purpose was no longer the fulfilment of divine ordinance, but merely the continuous material advancement of the territory and its people. Hobbes was the first to abandon the dualism of people and ruler, reducing the people to the will of the state which they had created, and substituting the abstract notion of the nation for the person of the ruler.[2] The sovereign state, in Hobbes' view, was unlimited and omnipotent; it alone determined law and it alone set collective goals which had nothing to do with discharging divine obligations. It is his radical contribution, so foundational to all modern conceptions of civil authority, which stands at the centre of our examination in this chapter.

Four key developments in the realm of political thought marked the emergence of the modern state in Europe during the course of the seventeenth century, developments which range across the entire period under discussion. Early in the century a daring new understanding of natural law was put forward by the Dutch jurist Hugo Grotius, one which divorced that law from its centuries-old theological underpinnings and shifted its foundations to an entirely earthly setting. This naturalistic view would be further developed by Samuel Pufendorf and by Thomas Hobbes later in the century. In addition, a new call for the withdrawal of the state from the business of enforcing religious orthodoxy was heard in a number of countries. Linked to the rise of individualism but also at the root of the original Protestant call for autonomy and integrity in spiritual discourse, the prescription of religious regimes by temporal authorities was deprecated by critics as inimical to the interests of state security and to individual prospects for salvation. A third development involved the emergence of a new view of rights, rights no longer associated with the well-being of the community as a whole but instead linked with the autonomy of the individual and his freedom against the encroachments of the state. Finally, assumptions concerning human nature and the nature of the state itself began to be disconnected from overtly religious paradigms. In their place new theories began to locate the origins of sovereignty and the scope of legitimate power in the practical, mundane needs of society as a self-contained, non-teleological project. We will address each of these developments separately, keeping in mind that their leading exponents were writing against what was still a powerful and influential set of more traditional assumptions, older postulates that continued to inform working governments even as late as 1700.

Natural Law without Divinity

In the midst of the turmoil and upheaval caused by the Thirty Years War, where relations between states and between religious opponents within states had descended into near anarchy, the first fundamentally secular understanding of the law of nature was presented by the Dutch jurist and diplomat Hugo Grotius in 1625 with his publication of *De jure belle ac pacis* (Of the Law of War and Peace). A large part of his motivation for this work can be attributed to his desire to establish rules which might lessen or perhaps even prevent the worst excesses of religious warfare. Earlier Catholic natural law theorists, from Aquinas to Bellarmine, had been predisposed to integrate pagan learning and Christian theology in their accounts of the transcendent law, while most Protestant reformers preferred to rely solely upon Scripture for their directions concerning civil society and politics, disparaging the convoluted pathways of 'papist' scholastic reasoning. Opponents whose respective sources of authority appeared to be nothing more than mistaken conventions by the other side, had done little to bring about an end to Europe's destructive penchants. For Grotius, a divided Christendom appeared incompetent to heal the wounds that it had inflicted on itself since the middle of the previous century.

The *De jure* won an immediate audience throughout Europe. There were at least 14 editions of Grotius' book by 1680 (despite its being placed on the Papal Index, where it would remain until the early twentieth century), and after 1654 English translations began to appear.[3] In addition to freeing natural law theory from its scholastic ancestry, Grotius was keen to formulate a moral and political philosophy that would answer the objections of late sixteenth-century sceptics who saw little basis for belief in universals, and who instead found the source of law, both within and between states, in changeable human custom. The sceptics found their most important allies among the ancient Greek sophists, writers who tended to hold that all law is but convention, contingent and variable, possessing no more moral content other than the group habits which are so varied amongst people. The Sophist Antiphon went so far as to insist that law was nothing but violence done to human nature, which at its core was designed to dominate others in the interests of oneself. Thus there was no moral component to the law, only the need to control and to inhibit what was natural to the human constitution.[4]

Grotius was born in 1583 in the city of Delft, Holland, just two years after the Spanish king, Philip II, had been officially deposed by the rebel government of the Netherlands. The military leader of the aspiring republic, William of Orange, established his residence in the city at this crucial time, and was assassinated in Delft when Grotius was one year old.[5] Jan De Groot, Grotius' lawyer father, was a regent of the city and thus an important figure in the patrician oligarchy which controlled local political affairs and sent delegates to the provincial governing body, the States of Holland. After studying at Leiden University, where he had been admitted at the age of eleven, Grotius was chosen by Johan van Oldenbarnevelt to accompany him on a diplomatic mission to France in 1598. At the time Oldenbarnevelt held the position of Advocate of the States of Holland, which was equivalent to chief minister of the most powerful province and thus in effect chief minister of the entire United Provinces. Grotius would remain allied to his patron, serving as adviser, writing papers and speeches, and receiving a number of official paid appointments from him, until 1619 when Oldenbarnevelt was charged with high treason and executed, a fate narrowly avoided by Grotius, who instead was sentenced to a life term of imprisonment.

The cause of this personal disaster is to be found in a religious dispute which reached new heights in Holland after 1610.[6] In addition to the officially supported Calvinist churches, a *de facto* toleration had been in place since the early days of the rebellion against Spanish authorities, and Jews, Mennonite Baptists, Lutherans, and even Catholics had been permitted to worship as they chose. Increasingly Dutch Calvinists, locked as they were in a life and death struggle against the forces of Counter-Reformation Spain, came to reject this unique toleration, and more particularly feared the growing impact of the anti-Calvinist teachings of Jacob Arminius, a professor of theology at Leiden from 1603 until his death in 1609. Arminius rejected the predestinarian theology of Dutch Calvinists, teaching instead the importance of works, and the freedom of sinners to choose God's saving grace.[7]

Followers of Arminius turned to the States of Holland for protection from their critics amongst the Calvinist majority, and found supporters in Oldenbarnevelt and Grotius. For Grotius, as manuscripts from this period reveal, a common core of belief united all Christians, and agreement on an ethically oriented minimalist faith was the only means of ending religious strife.[8] In a manner later adopted by Locke and Spinoza at the end of the century, Grotius insisted that the remedy for the disease of religious violence involved 'limiting the number of necessary articles of faith to those few which are self-evident, and to inquire into the other doctrinal points which lead to the perfection of pious wisdom without prejudice, preserving charity and under the guidance of the Holy Scriptures'.[9] Grotius preferred that a strong state enforce this ecumenism; in his view neither clerics nor ecclesiastical establishments should be allowed to dictate orthodoxy. By 1617 the Calvinist position had gained the upper hand over ecumenists like Grotius, winning the support of the stadtholder, Maurice of Nassau, who in turn used his influence over members of the States General of the union.[10] When Oldenbarnevelt attempted to shift control of the army away from the stadtholder and into the hands of the more amenable States of Holland, his gambit failed. Both he and Grotius paid the penalty for championing unacceptable ideas. After serving two years of his life sentence, Grotius escaped to France and lived the remainder of his life in exile, largely in France but also in Sweden, where he won appointment as Queen Christina's resident ambassador in Paris.[11]

Grotius began to detail the principles of a desacralized law of nature free from transcendent attachments in a manuscript begun in 1604 but not published until the nineteenth century. His starting point was the Aristotelian conviction that man is by nature a rational and a social animal, but he also acknowledged that the basic force shaping all human affairs was the desire for self-preservation, that 'by nature's ordinance each individual should be desirous of his own good fortune in preference to that of another'. Grotius defined as the first two principles of an observable law of nature the right to defend oneself and the right to secure those things from the earth which were necessary for the preservation of life.[12] These principles, so essential to social existence, Grotius believed even sceptics had to accept.

Agreeing with Aristotle's conviction that humans were by nature social beings who were neither physically equipped nor temperamentally disposed for isolated existence, and whose full nature was to live as rational beings, Grotius was led to conclude two further laws of nature, both proceeding from the first two: people should not inflict injury upon their fellows, nor should they seize that which has been taken into possession by another – 'The former is the law of inoffensiveness; the latter is the law of abstinence.'[13] Men act justly when they behave in conformity to their natural longing for society.[14] Before they organize themselves into a formal civil society, they need not necessarily help their neighbour, but neither should they harm them on any pretext. When individuals contract to enter into a formal civil life and to take up issues of general utility, the state and the government which is erected can enjoy no right exceeding that belonging to individuals in a state of nature. According to

Grotius, the basic laws of nature are not abrogated when life shifts to the
civil state. Even the most dread power – the right to punish offenders
against the laws of nature with death – was enjoyed by individuals in the
pre-political era and transferred to the magistrate in order to secure 'a
more dependable means of protection', another idea taken up again by
Locke at the end of the century.

The law of nature when uncoupled from its traditional theological
moorings was, for Grotius, a universal rule for individual and collective
conduct, both within and between nations, accessible to all humans
through the use of 'right reason' and without reference to any positive
law contained in Scripture. Later in the century, Locke would attempt to
equate the law of nature with 'reason, which is that law', but in the end
he saw Revelation as a more accessible emanation of natural law for the
majority of men.[15] According to Grotius, it is simply and exclusively 'a
dictate of right reason which points out that an act, according as it is or is
not in conformity with rational nature, has in it a quality of moral base-
ness or moral necessity; and that in consequence, such an act is either
forbidden or enjoined by the author of nature, God'.[16] The commands
contained in the Decalogue had routinely been taken as containing the
essence of the law of nature, but Grotius maintained that these directives, which had not even been given to the Gentiles, were positive laws,
and as such were alterable by God. 'A Law obliges, only those, to whom it
is given', he stated in reference to the laws given to the ancient Jews.
Similarly the injunctions contained in the New Testament indicate 'what
is lawful for Christians to do'.[17]

In an infamous passage designed to stress the unalterable character of
laws fitted to a specific human nature, Grotius claimed that even without
a God, or with one who 'for whom the affairs of men are of no concern',
the rules governing conduct would still apply, given our innate nature.
Knowledge and application of unchanging natural law, which pre-
scribes few beliefs beyond that there is a deity who has care of human
affairs, can alone free men from the conflicts and inhumanity associated
with contemporary religious debate. To release morality and politics
from Scripture was thus an indispensable preliminary to a peaceful society. With the controversy between Dutch Calvinists and their Arminian
Remonstrant counterparts, together with the opening stages of the brutal Thirty Years War as a discouraging empirical backdrop, Grotius
struggled to anchor the law of nature in 'notions so certain that no one
can deny them without doing violence to himself'.[18] Searching for Cartesian certainty in politics akin to the truths of mathematics, a renewed

natural law theory was sure to appeal to anyone wearied by religious controversy and its violent military manifestations. Hobbes certainly met these criteria. Writing in the midst of the English Civil Wars, the author of *Leviathan* (1651) sought a solution to the elusive problem of sovereignty in a nation torn apart by political disputes anchored in religious premises. Hobbes was the first to insist that the laws of nature are those behaviours necessary for beings who are equal in their passions and abilities to coexist without continuous conflict. These rules were as immutable as Galileo's laws, and the proper understanding of them was 'the true and only moral philosophy'. Reason permits men to see rules which transcend the subjectivity of individual passion in the state of nature, and while he gives a somewhat varied list of the laws of nature in *Elements of Law*, *De cive* and *Leviathan*, each list is reducible to the Old Testament imperative of placing oneself in the position of another and acting accordingly.[19]

The laws of nature were not for Hobbes, as they continued to be for Locke, the dictates of a superior, the transcendent injunctions of the divine deduced by human reason. In *De cive* he had taken pains to illustrate how Scripture in fact endorsed the natural law, but only the former had issued directly from God. Natural laws were conclusions reached by men through the application of reason in the wake of the experience of conditions in the state of nature. A law of nature is 'a Precept, or general Rule, found out by Reason, by which a man is forbidden to do, that, which is destructive of his life, or taketh away the means of preserving the same; and to omit, that, by which he thinketh it may be best preserved'.[20] And without a universal adherence to this formula, without reasonable deductions from the principle of self-preservation, there was little long-term hope for the maintenance of mankind. Beginning with this cardinal law of nature, the law of self-preservation, reason led men to enter into agreements in order to curb the excesses of behaviour when guided by the private right of self-determination. Political obligation – and justice – emerged when men agreed to a common superior who could enforce covenants and compel obedience to specific rules of conduct that were conducive to peace and security. Simple covenants between equals will not preserve society; only the appointment of an agreed authority who has the power to make law and force obedience, only someone who can operate on the fears of men, will guarantee the ends prescribed by the law of nature.

Forty years after the death of Grotius, the son of a Lutheran pastor from rural Saxony – a land not immune from the many depredations associated with the Thirty Years War – continued the effort to anchor natural law in non-theological soil. But Samuel Pufendorf published his most important work, *On the Law of Nature and Nations* (1672) in new conditions brought about by the eclipse of Europe's religious struggles at mid century. The 1648 Peace of Westphalia effectively subordinated war to political and commercial, not religious, considerations, and ushered in a period of international conflicts which earlier seventeenth-century theorists had not experienced. Gone after the conclusion of the Thirty Years War was the practical power of pan-European authorities such as the papacy and the Holy Roman Empire, for the Treaty had provided that individual territorial rulers in the Empire would now decide the form of religious worship within their respective dominions. The sovereign states which emerged from this mid-century peace became the political foundation of the modern West, each one struggling to achieve economic and military superiority over their neighbours.[21]

Like Grotius, Pufendorf wished to free his philosophy of society, law and history from all sacred underpinnings and to build them anew exclusively on the twin foundations of reason and observation. In particular, he wished to employ the methodology of the physical and natural sciences in the study of human relations.[22] He accepted that Europe's religious differences were irreconcilable and hoped to anchor a universal morality on new premises that men of all faiths could accept as empirically valid. His natural law theory was thus free from the influences of orthodoxy and Aristotelian traditionalism. Nature was no longer to be seen as a purposeful realm governed by specific teleological dispositions, nor was natural law a set of internal dispositions native to humankind. Instead the new view of nature, espoused by theorists as diverse as Galileo, Bacon, Descartes, Pierre Gassendi, and Hobbes, had God imposing motion and order on an otherwise non-purposive host of atoms, thereby creating a natural order of regularities which could be studied and known by man with a certainty approaching the mathematical.[23]

Born in the same year as Benedict Spinoza and John Locke (1632), Pufendorf was a student at Leipzig from 1650 to 1656, and in 1658 he took a post as tutor to the family of the Swedish minister in Denmark. The outbreak of war between Sweden and Denmark in that year landed the unsuspecting tutor in a Danish prison, where he kept himself busy completing the text of his first work on political theory, *Elements of Universal Jurisprudence*, first published in 1660. In 1661 Pufendorf was appointed to the philosophy faculty at Heidelberg, and nine years later he accepted a faculty position at the University of Lund in Sweden. It was here in 1672 that he finished the text of *On the Law of Nature and of Nations*. The following year a compendium of this work titled *On the Duty of Man and Citizen According to Natural Law* was published as a text for students of the law, and this book, appearing in over 60 editions and in numerous languages, remained a popular exposition of Pufendorf's moral and political philosophy throughout the course of the next century.[24] During the years from 1658 to 1677, then, Pufendorf devoted most of his intellectual energy to the task of building a political and moral philosophy based on a novel vision of natural law, and addressing new conditions brought about by the end of Europe's religious wars and the subsequent rise of the autonomous dynastic state system.

The starting point of Pufendorf's political philosophy envisioned a primordial state of nature where the basic equality of all men was affirmed against the traditional doctrines of hierarchy and natural authority forwarded by contemporary thinkers such as Filmer and Bossuet. Pufendorf described the state of nature as one of sociability and common peaceful intercourse where reason played some role in guiding men in the precepts of natural law.[25] Following Grotius, man's sociability was to be discovered in the observed facts of human nature, where each person recognized that his own preservation is best served by uniting with others to secure the necessities of life. 'Man, it is clearly apparent, is an animal most eager to preserve himself, essentially in need, ill-equipped to maintain himself without the aid of those who are like him, and very well suited for the mutual promotion of advantages.' At the same time, however, and in conformity with the Hobbesian picture of the state of nature, Pufendorf asserted that men are also 'often malicious, insolent, easily annoyed, and both ready and able to inflict harm'. For this type of rational but easily irascible being to be safe and secure 'it is necessary that he be sociable'. Thus the fundamental law of nature dictated that each person must 'cultivate and maintain toward others a peaceable sociality that is consistent with the native character and end of mankind in general'.[26]

Unfortunately, the state of nature lacked an unbiased mediator or judge who was empowered to settle disputes which arose between individuals, making such an existence less likely to advance the common good than would otherwise be the case in a civil state. Hobbes was wrong to condemn the whole of humankind for its unmediated perversity, but it was nonetheless true that most men would not conform themselves to the duties of natural law in a state of nature, a position iterated by Locke in his *Two Treatises* only a few years after the appearance of Pufendorf's work. Aristotle's conviction that men entered civil society out of a natural desire to associate with others was not shared by Pufendorf, who believed that for 'an animal that loves himself and his own advantage in the highest degree', concrete motives had to be in operation at the moment of the contract.[27] Nonetheless, sacrificing one's natural liberty and accepting the jurisdiction of another authority was the product of rational deliberation alone.

In dramatic fashion, Pufendorf sharply distinguished the boundaries of natural law or the law of nature from civil law on the one hand, and, more controversially, moral theology or divine law on the other. He did this directly in the Preface to *On the Duty of Man and Citizen According to Natural Law*, the short work that was destined to find its way into the curriculum of Protestant universities across Europe. The subject matter of natural law, according to the author, was nothing more than a set of social duties which made it possible for men to live with one another in a peaceful and productive manner. Divinity and civil law might also properly outline aspects of duty in this life, but the former was restricted to the obligations of man as a Christian while the latter covered one's obligations as a member of a particular state. Divine law was gleaned from Revelation and was concerned most immediately with salvation, while civil law came to us as the will of a particular sovereign in a single state. Only the natural law was applicable to every nation and people, to every culture and condition, and only its rules were established exclusively by the faculty of reason, a faculty which indicated those behaviours key to 'sociality among men'.[28] The natural law regulated external actions, directed men in their daily lives, and unflinchingly evaluated man in terms of his present condition in the wake of the historic Fall, 'as one whose nature has been corrupted and thus as an animal seething with evil desires'.[29]

For Pufendorf, study of the natural law as he defined it offered the best hope for realizing a moral order or 'sociality' capable of transcending the confessional and ideological hatreds bred by the moral exclusiveness of different peoples and churches in seventeenth-century Europe.[30] His version of natural law morality was thus what we might call a social theory designed to transform selfish individuals into cooperative members of a unified society. A host of rules drawn from divinity, together with the provincial standards of individual states, had all failed dismally in this life-saving enterprise, and it was now time to employ a different and certainly more irenic standard. Pufendorf's insistence on the natural equality of all men, that we treat other men as our equals, was put forward as one of the duties of sociality inasmuch as it does enormous service in assuaging corrupt man's acute sense of self-esteem. But as Richard Tuck has recently pointed out, Pufendorf's position here represented a direct challenge to the 'feudal and Renaissance honour ethic based on inequality'.[31] Men are altogether unsocial, and thus uncaring about the good of society and ultimately themselves, 'who suppose themselves superior to others, demand total license for themselves alone and claim honour above others and a special share of the world's goods, when they have no special right above others'.[32] Honest humility is always called for when interacting with others, a prescription both simple and revolutionary within the context of late seventeenth-century European culture.

States without Confessions

The law of nature decrying injury and harm to others stood in stark contrast to the widespread contemporary efforts of churches and magistrates to impose particular brands of Christianity on their fellows. 'I saw throughout the Christian world a license in waging war that would shame barbarous nations' was how Grotius set the issue in *De jure*.[33] And since states and churches did not enjoy any rights that were not available to individuals in a state of nature, persecution and forced conversion were in violation of the eternal law. A minimalist morality and theology were to be found in the only law which was applicable to humans everywhere. Beyond adherence to these few rules 'there are several Ways of Living, some better than others, and every one may choose what he pleases of all those sorts'.[34] Here were views unlikely to influence the men for whom the promotion of 'orthodoxy' justified any and all measures against the heretic, but in his efforts to free politics from Scripture and to base the former exclusively on fundamental rules which applied across borders, Grotius' contribution would not be ignored by those seeking an exit from the disaster of sectarian bigotry, an escape from the bloodstained dominion of the arbitrary.

Locke was clearly one such seeker. He was deeply concerned with the nature of religion in public life and the relationship between ecclesiastical and political power. He wrote in 1660 that religious disputes, and the intervention of government in these disputes, were the primary cause of war, 'all those flames that have made such havoc and desolation in

Europe' since the Reformation. The root of the problem, to his mind, was that clerical leaders, Protestant and Catholic alike, had pressed the erroneous ideas that (1) the path to heaven is singular and narrow and (2) it was the duty of governments to use whatever means come to hand in order to suppress nonconformity. Given the diversity of religious perspectives in post-Reformation Europe, these tenets were bound to result in violent conflict. Locke did not think that the clerical establishment was sincerely interested in the salvation of souls with its advocacy of these ideas. Rather clergy sought political power for themselves, the power to control the mass of the subject population and the lives and property of those whose view of the eternal was judged aberrant. This was a very harsh position to hold for a man who counted amongst his closest friends some of the leading latitudinarian divines in the Church of England.

Locke's *Letter Concerning Toleration* was composed in 1685 while the author was in exile in Holland, and in the immediate aftermath of Louis XIV's revocation of the Edict of Nantes. The persecution of the Protestant minority in France, together with the French king's military ambitions against the Netherlands, struck fear into the hearts of all Protestants in Northern Europe, men and women who would have been very surprised indeed by the efforts of modern historians to assign 1648 as the date which signalled the close of the wars of religion in Europe. The right to toleration was, for Locke, a religious right based upon each individual's obligation to establish a personal, unmediated relationship with his Maker. Echoes of Luther's priesthood of all believers can be heard in this radical appeal, radical because, as we have seen, no seventeenth-century state disclaimed its right to come between its subjects and God.

Locke maintained, in what may seem like a commonplace to us, that belief must be sincere for it to inform our chances for salvation. For the state to prescribe religious belief and practice, even if that belief and practice turns out to be appropriate in God's eyes, is inefficacious in the quest for salvation because it is formulated and enjoined by another. And for Locke the claim that one man or clerical institution can know for another, can of right come between the individual and the Deity, is the epitome of arrogance, an unconscionable attempt to take the place of God. It was not the responsibility of the state to take charge for the salvation of its subjects. That is too important an undertaking to be left to an institution whose proper goal is securing the temporal well-being of its population. The importance of building and maintaining a personal relationship with God was indicated by Locke's exclusion of atheists from his call for toleration, an exclusion predicated on the assumption that atheists have no rational grounds for acting morally in this life. Without God and the prospect of reward and punishment after this life, there could be no moral order, no law of nature independent of human appetite and desire. In Locke's view, we had a right to religious freedom solely because God existed and required of us a personal faith unencumbered by the pretensions of organized church and state.

Locke's advocacy of toleration may not have extended to an Amsterdam Jew who shared with him the same year of birth, but whose death at the age of 44 was lamented by few. The liberal Dutch theologian and close friend of Locke, Philipp van Limborch, could not recall ever having read 'so pestilential a book' as Baruch Spinoza's 1670 *Tractatus theologico politicus* (A Treatise on Religion and Politics). Across Europe a sense of shock in intellectual circles at the book's elision of traditional theological precepts and regulatory guideposts was commonplace. The Cambridge Platonists Ralph Cudworth and Henry More expressed dismay at the alleged 'atheism' of the book. A former correspondent of Spinoza's, Willem van Blijenbergh, wrote that: 'Every Christian, nay every man of sense, ought to abhor such a book.'

And the advice was acted upon. The *Tractatus theologico politicus* was quickly condemned by the Synod of the Reformed Calvinist Church, and formally banned in 1674. At the close of the century Pierre Bayle's article on Spinoza in the *Historical and Critical Dictionary* (1697) called the work 'a pernicious and detestable book in which he slips in all the seeds of atheism'.[35] Spinoza's bold historical and philological criticism of the Bible, his effort to settle political society on a lasting and peaceful foundation by abandoning the contentiousness of biblical interpretation and divine law as set by the churches for the more promising touchstone of universal reason or natural understanding, had been soundly rejected. So too had his modern, secular notion that religious figures should have no institutional influence or official role in shaping state policy. But that the point had been made so openly spoke volumes for the shifting intellectual climate during the final quarter of the century.

Spinoza's political thought, and in particular his position on the place of institutional religion in the life of the state, is inseparable from the broader cultural and political developments in the United Provinces of the Netherlands during the mid seventeenth century. His merchant parents were descendants of Portuguese Marranos, Jews from the

Iberian peninsula who had left their inquisitorial homeland and joined a thriving community in the more tolerant setting of late sixteenth-century Holland. Raised and educated in an intellectually vibrant urban Jewish community, he was rejected by that community and excommunicated from the synagogue before he had reached the age of 24. Charged with holding heretical opinions and cast out of the synagogue on 27 July 1656, it is likely that the young man had come under the influence of other Jews of heterodox tendencies, with the sceptical work of Descartes, and with a radical critique of the Bible published by the Frenchman Isaac La Peyrere in 1655.[36] Whatever the specifics of the case, he managed to remain in the city for the next four years, supporting himself as a lens grinder and making contacts with members of unorthodox Christian groups such as the Quakers, the Mennonites and the Collegiants (an anticlerical group outside the Calvinist majority). Attracted by the simple beliefs of these groups, so different from the dominant and largely intolerant Calvinism of Holland and the Judaism of his youth, Spinoza (who now Latinized 'Baruch' to 'Benedict') began to associate with a wide range of liberal religious thinkers. In 1660, the year of the Restoration in England, he left Amsterdam under pressure from city authorities who in turn were responding to the appeals of the rabbis, and for the next ten years Spinoza lived a quiet and austere life in two small villages before settling in The Hague in 1670. It was here in 1677 that he died and was buried at the age of 44.

The leading political figure during the third quarter of the century, the period of Spinoza's intellectual development and first appearance in print, was Councillor Pensionary of Holland, Johan de Witt. Entering the political limelight in the aftermath of a serious conflict between the stadtholder, Prince William III, and the regents of Holland over reductions in the size of the army once independence had been achieved from Spain in 1648, de Witt sought to reconcile Calvinist supporters of the House of Orange with the more tolerant mercantile deputies in the States of Holland.[37] But his policy of combining official condemnation of dissent with inaction against the Catholics, liberal Arminians, and other non-Calvinist sects won him few supporters amongst those who wished to enforce the prohibition against dissent adopted back in 1619 at the Synod of Dordrecht, when the Arminians or 'Remonstrants' (amongst whose numbers Grotius is to be counted) failed in their effort to secure government protection against the Calvinist majority.[38] It is possible that Spinoza may have known de Witt personally through his association with Johan Hudde, Burgomaster of Amsterdam. At any rate, Spinoza heartily endorsed de Witt's enlightened policy of tolerance and the free exchange of ideas in a state where refugees from an otherwise persecuting Europe had sought asylum.[39]

In addition, after the death of William II in 1650, the office of stadtholder, traditionally held by the princes of Orange, was not filled, with the result that the seven Dutch provinces now governed themselves in a truly republican fashion. A republican propaganda campaign designed to encourage the provinces to abolish the office of stadtholder altogether was begun, and leading the way were two brothers whose ideas would resonate in the thought of Spinoza: Johan and Pieter de la Court.[40] Accepting Hobbes's picture of a violent state of nature where partial individuals seek to satisfy their passions at the expense of their fellows, they proposed constitutional structures which would regulate the selfish wills of both rulers and ruled. In their view all monarchs were despotic. In *The True Interest and Political Maxims of the Republic of Holland* (1662), Pieter de la Court accused the princes of Orange of advancing their own interests at the expense of the Republic, especially its commercial prosperity. And at the heart of Dutch commercial prowess, according to the author, was the steadfast unwillingness of government to impose religious beliefs or institutional requirements on the general population. To now allow the Calvinist majority to impose its confession and practice on others would be to sap the strength and security of the Republic. Here the de la Courts adopted another component of Hobbes's thought – the unitary nature of sovereign power – for they were convinced that the state must have control over all public acts, including acts of worship, and must set policy in this area pursuant to the material well-being of the community.

Spinoza began work on his major political statement, the *Tractatus* in 1665, at a time when the Dutch Republic was engaged in the second naval war with England in as many decades, and against an opponent (Charles II) who was the uncle of the young William III of the House of Orange, the darling of the Dutch orthodox Calvinists, and the man who would be stadtholder. The prospect of the return to power of men committed to enforcing Calvinist orthodoxy could not have pleased Spinoza. His political thought in the *Tractatus*, although deeply informed by his overall first principles of metaphysics, was, like the work of Hobbes and Pufendorf, exceptional in that it was entirely removed from all considerations stemming from revealed religion, a universal touchstone for his contemporaries which in Spinoza's mind was inextricably linked with controversy and intolerance.

In the preface to the work, he alleged that what now passed for piety and religion 'take the form of ridiculous mysteries, and men who utterly despise reason, who reject and turn away from the intellect as corrupt – these are the men (and this is of all things the most iniquitous) who are believed to possess the divine light!'[41] The ethical claims of Scripture were not discredited by Spinoza, but he insisted that Revelation was designed solely to instil obedience in weak minds, not to cultivate understanding in autonomous ones. The first six chapters of the *Tractatus* critiqued the Bible with the intention of removing its varied 'superstitions' from their central place in political theory and practice. His sole authority on all matters was the purified religion of reason, what in Cartesian terms were ideas clear and distinct to the human intellect, and he identified as his chief goal the authentic well-being of the individual, the discovery of the best way to live.[42] It is in this sense that he was, in the view of one recent scholar, 'the first European to avow the secularization of intellectual life as an ideal, and to live it'.[43] In fact in his early work, probably composed in 1662 and unpublished during his lifetime, Spinoza explained that he had first come to philosophy through a painful recognition that most humans follow paths largely bereft of meaning and joy, even when their lives were distinguished by social position, material wealth and honour. Our true end and the antidote to the anxiety fomented by our pursuit of perishable goods is to employ philosophy in order to seek and secure a higher human nature, and he associated this nature with 'the knowledge of the union that the mind has with the whole of nature'.[44]

Politics and ethics, then, were not to be distinguished, for the purpose of civil society and political institutions was to provide the conditions whereby the rational individual might pursue the highest good, a notion antipodal to the politics of Augustinianism with its concern for curbing sinful humanity from its worst natural penchants. And Spinoza's metaphysics is at one with ethics as well, inasmuch as knowledge of ourselves as part of a larger system of nature helps us to determine the best course of action in this life. For Spinoza, all of existence was the unitary manifestation of God or nature. All truth was a single and coherent body of knowledge, a part of a unitary reality called Substance or Nature or God. This God was the sole object of real worth in our lives, the one source of understanding guaranteed to provide us with lasting rewards. We perfect ourselves to the extent that we purify our intellects from confusion and achieve unity with the intellect of God.[45]

Peace and security were the only licit ends of the non-confessional state, and liberty, defined as a life lived in accordance with reason, was the inalienable right of each individual under formal government. Government's charge was to enable men 'to develop their mental and physical faculties in safety, to use their reason without restraint and to refrain from the strife and the vicious mutual abuse that are prompted by hatred, anger or deceit. Thus the purpose of the state is, in reality, freedom.'[46] Against the rising demands of the Calvinist clergy who called for the imposition of the majority religion on the entire population (and recalling his own treatment at the hands of the Jewish community in Amsterdam), Spinoza believed that only government could preserve the free thought and expression that were essential to human well-being.

For Spinoza, magistrates undermined their own power when they denied freedom of thought and expression. 'It is true that sovereigns can by their right treat as enemies all who do not absolutely agree with them on all matters, but the point at issue is not what is their right, but what is to their interest.'[47] Citizens may abrogate their right to action without restraint when the state is formed, and they should comply with laws even if they do not agree with them, but they can never surrender their right to independent thought. Unlike formal religious systems which depend upon a prophetic revelation for their institutional legitimacy, and where non-subscription to the revealed truths marks one out as an apostate, the true political order finds its strength in allowing men to pursue their personal goals in a manner where disagreements are settled by reasoned discussion and known law. Ironically, Spinoza pointed to the prosperous city of Amsterdam as an illustration of the potential for good inherent in a diversity of views. There religion or sect 'is of no account' in determining a man's legal rights and private station. Recalling his own unfortunate experience in that city, he concluded that 'the real schismatics are those who condemn the writings of others and seditiously incite the quarrelsome mob against the writers, rather than the writers themselves, who usually write only for scholars and appeal to reason alone'.[48]

Spinoza did concede that traditional religion with its anthropomorphic understanding of God was necessary in the life of the state because it brought the unreflective masses into proper obedience. This is one of the reasons that Spinoza emphasized biblical interpretation in the *Tractatus*. Distinctions between the various churches simply represent differences in imagination, and these differences should be regulated by the state when they become the cause of physical conflict. The imaginings and superstitions of the multitude cannot be eradicated so long as God is presented through the medium of inadequate ideas, a being in bodily form with the same passions, loves and dislikes as his creatures. The eternal truths of reason, on the other hand, can only be perceived through the intellect, which few are capable of exercising in the requisite degree.

Given this reality, the state should be allowed to determine the rites and outward observances of religion using the criterion of public peace as the only touchstone. Inner religion or belief, on the other hand, should be left to the individual.[49] Like Hobbes, who insisted in *Leviathan* that the sovereign must hold the exclusive right to set the canons of Scripture, Spinoza held that the variant claims of tradition, scholarship and the inner spirit to determine the meaning of God's word had to be rejected. Since the sovereign is charged with preserving the welfare of the state, 'and to command what it judges to be thus necessary, it follows that it is also the duty of the sovereign alone to decide what form piety towards one's neighbour should take, that is, in what way every man is required to obey God'.[50] Mandating the form of outward worship, as long as personal belief was not abridged, was for Spinoza a responsible exercise of civil power.

Individual Rights

The theory of universal natural rights, owned by each individual without exception and whose moral force is independent of all systems of positive law and social practice, has often been identified by scholars as first emerging in the seventeenth century, and more specifically in the writings of Hobbes and Locke. The concept has subsequently had additional adjectives attached to it: human, inalienable, inherent, imprescriptible, but the essential core meaning has remained fixed over the past 350 years. Natural rights, at least as embodied in the great written declarations of the late eighteenth century in America and in France, did not take into consideration one's status in the family, in the workplace, or in the state when setting its bold standards. These declarations maintained that government was a human, not a divine, artifice whose primary purpose was rights-protection. Rights preceded government; they are more original, being derived from the Creator and therefore preemptive of the duties which had been stressed under earlier theories of divinely originated government.[51]

In the nineteenth century Jeremy Bentham would pour ridicule on the whole notion of entitlements independent of human ordinance, urging that all right 'is the child of law' and actually exercised by people, while: 'Natural rights is simply nonsense, natural and imprescriptible rights rhetorical nonsense, nonsense upon stilts.'[52] Declarations of natural rights, Bentham believed, distracted men from the hard work of legislating for the public good. Notwithstanding such criticism the theory has become in our own day central to the charge of the United Nations and the modern liberal state alike, and the watchword of most political practitioners in these states. It has even been extended from the original cluster of civil and personal freedoms to include an ever-widening range of social and economic prerogatives, with varying degrees of success since the end of the Second World War.

The articulation of individual natural rights in the seventeenth century was in good measure an outgrowth of a larger body of medieval natural law theory.[53] But while the natural law implied both duties and rights, the medieval world was more concerned, by and large, with the former. For Aquinas, right was taken to mean 'the fair' in human relations, while the Spaniard Suarez described it as 'a kind of moral power which every man has, either over his own property or with respect to that which is due to him'. In an important respect rights had always been central to the natural law tradition, in the sense that it required specific forms of behaviour towards another, behaviour which thereby conferred a moral right on everyone to be treated in an appropriate fashion. But otherwise rights were not viewed as a key social value. In defining a host of religious 'others', for example, the medieval church had done its utmost to forget its own minority status before the age of Constantine and instead worked to ensure that the Muslim, the Jew, the heretic, the leper and the witch were excluded from considerations of what would later be called natural rights.

Indeed no writer in the sweep of persecuting centuries that separated Aquinas and Suarez made anything approaching the definitive transition from the idea of right as a standard of conduct to the concept of right as a possession, a subjective and personal property separate from and antecedent to government, one that applies to all men in the same way.[54] It could perhaps be claimed that rights were enjoyed collectively by members of formal groups – physicians, clergymen, university graduates, attorneys – but these rights had been won from established governments and served merely to distinguish the privileged from the bulk of their earthly peers. Before the seventeenth century, then, universal rights were associated overwhelmingly with conformity to higher law, and violation of that law (however defined) normally earned one an appointment with judicial torture and death. Only subsequently did rights come to be linked with an individual ownership and dominion over self and property that could not be infringed by government. And it was this gradual acceptance of man as an autonomous individual, rational, inherently dignified, and capable of moral choice and action, which pointed the way towards a new view of politics in the seventeenth century. This shift away from duties to the state and the submergence of the individual into an appropriate corporate status group, took place within a variety of contexts, not the least of which was the long-term influence of spiritual individualism at the heart of the Reformation and the scepticism informing natural philosophy. But it would be unwise to claim too much for the Reformation in this area, since the warring camps of the rival churches did little to advance the autonomy of the individual between 1520 and 1700.[55] Saving souls always took precedence over respect for any supposed rights associated solely with the life of the flesh, and this was true whether the work was conducted against the uncivilized Amerindians or the stubborn north Germans.

Still the Protestant emphasis on authenticating one's personal relationship with God without the direction of layered superiors had its place in enhancing the integrity of the person within a larger godly community. The notion that each person, simply by virtue of his humanity and basic equality, enjoys specific rights of nature against his fellows and against the state, and in particular specific economic, religious and political rights, had by the closing decades of the century come to play an important role in political debate. At the end of our century, then, positive law tended to originate from the notion that certain basic rights, separate from human dictate, had to be protected.[56]

In the seventeenth century as today, the most vocal proponents of natural rights more often than not emerged from the ranks of the oppressed, for as theorists of human rights inform us, rights are normally defined only as they are denied or abused.[57] The rights claims of the English Levellers, for example, included economic and social, as well as political elements. In the late sixteenth century, a number of Spanish jurists had begun to defend the native peoples of Spanish-controlled America by asserting that all humans enjoyed the natural right not to be mistreated and destroyed. Vitoria, Molina and de Soto all expressed the view that the indigenous peoples of America were not to be enslaved, plundered, or assaulted because of their refusal to accept Christianity.

They enjoyed a right to their own political orders just as Europeans did.[58] However, it was with Grotius that hints of a modern secular theory of natural rights initially made their appearance, for he was the first to conceptualize a complete legal system in terms of rights rather than laws.[59] Grotius insisted that the entire law of nature, rooted in man's natural sociability and obliging him to preserve social peace, was designed to ensure respect for individual rights. Social life is made possible by observing the rights of each member, and the most basic right is the one of self-preservation.[60] The linkage between natural rights and the law of nature made it possible to claim that the acts of courts and legislatures could not define the status of the subject without regard to a higher touchstone, one which denied the legitimacy, without the free assent of citizens, of the unrestrained and omnicompetent state. Locke owned a copy of the 1650 Latin edition of *De jure*, and acquired another edition during his exile in Holland during the 1680s.[61] After 1654 English editions of the work began to appear, and Grotius became very popular with Whig opponents of absolutism during the second half of the century in England.

Pufendorf also subscribed to elements of a theory of individual natural rights which, although not as extensive as Locke's, has become part of the cluster of ideas known as modern liberalism. In the pre-civil state Pufendorf accorded men the natural right to do 'whatever contributes to their own preservation' provided the rights of others are not violated. Freedom from all human authority is also the birthright of individuals in the natural state, a condition which presupposes natural equality. However, unlike Locke, Pufendorf did not emphasize the centrality of these rights in the civil state, preferring instead the need for obedience to social conventions and arrangements designed to further sociality, assuming always that these conventions are the product of voluntary agreements.

For their part, Hobbes and Spinoza reduced natural rights to liberties which belonged, without exception, to every person in the state of nature. Hobbes argued that individuals owned a right to act to preserve themselves in the state of nature, to do whatever they believed would forward their own prospects for survival. In this state they did not have a right to life, a claim-right imposing duties on another, but merely a right to do those things that in their own judgement would secure their life. 'The Right of Nature', he insisted, 'which Writers commonly call Jus Naturale [which] is the Liberty each man hath, to use his own power, as he will himself, for the preservation of his own Nature; that is to say, of his own Life.'[62] Of course others in this pre-political state may continue to harm or destroy others, if, in their estimation, it will advance their own security. Similarly Spinoza asserted that there can be no wrong-doing in the state of nature, no justice or injustice, no immorality. Because man is part of nature, a finite mode of eternal Substance, his actions in the state of nature are always in harmony with nature and are undertaken by the highest natural right. Whatever a man is able to do by his own power in order to secure his wants in such a state is appropriate.[63]

Unfortunately, outside civil society these unlimited natural rights are of very little benefit to single individuals, most of whom are led by blind passions and emotions which invariably drive them into mutual conflict. With simple survival always in peril, Spinoza concluded that natural rights avail men little in the state of nature.[64] For Hobbes these clashing liberty-rights were apt to increase the chances for mutual conflict and disorder in the pre-civil state, and provided the best argument in favour of erecting an absolutist government.[65] Hobbes also drew a sharp distinction between right and law, the first consisting of all human capacities, 'in liberty to do, or to forebear', while the latter 'determineth, and bindeth to one of them'. Rights in the state of nature are limited only by the individual's capacity to enforce his desires, and for Hobbes these rights had to be renounced once the contract to erect a common sovereign was agreed by all. Rights in this sense provided a key background to the formation of civil society; it is the transfer of these rights which leads to political obligation. They in no respect limited the scope and the power of the government thus created.[66]

On the status of natural rights, the case with Locke was very different from the views offered by Hobbes and Spinoza. Locke believed that the first and foremost task of any legitimate government was to preserve and protect the natural rights of individuals, rights derived from the God-mandated natural law and operative even in the state of nature. Locke never engaged in a detailed discussion of the concept of rights, but there are references to a range of specific rights, and to natural rights, in his writings and principally in *Two Treatises of Government*.[67] In the preface to that work he speaks of the recently concluded Revolution of 1688 as an illustration of Englishmen's 'love of their Just and Natural Rights' and the subsequent references to specific rights are always linked to the law of nature. Each person had a right, by this natural law, to life or 'the right man has to subsist and enjoy the conveniences of life'. Thus men have a right to preserve themselves, a right to the creatures and the produce of the earth that are necessary to existence and, in the state of nature, a right to punish those who violate natural law. We have a right to destroy anything or any person who threatens our lives, and children have a right to be nourished and maintained by their parents. Men also enjoyed a right to freedom, which Locke defined as a liberty 'to order their Actions, and dispose of their Possessions and Persons as they think fit, within the bounds of the Law of Nature, without asking leave, or depending upon the Will of any other Man'. Finally, each person has a right to his property, both property in his person, and 'the labour of his body, and the work of his hands'.[68] If the government were to abridge these natural rights in any respect, or fail to protect them when infringed by other individuals, then it would no longer remain a licit entity. Taken together, natural rights are identical with power, and these powers set limits on the types of laws that a government may enact.

As we know, Locke published his *Two Treatises of Government* in the immediate aftermath of the Glorious Revolution, and according to the preface, the author intended 'to establish the throne of our great re-storer, our present King William, to make good his title'. But the political doctrine of natural rights contained in the work was directly at odds with the official theory contained in the Bill of Rights. After a hastily arranged Convention Parliament had offered the crown to William and Mary in 1689, the same body issued a Declaration of Rights. A few months later, both king and parliament adopted a more formal Bill of Rights. The rights described there were not natural rights bestowed by God prior to the formation of organized political life. They were, instead, the 'ancient rights and liberties' as provided in 'the known laws and statutes and freedoms of this realm'.[69] They were rights that belonged not to all human beings but to the inhabitants of the Island Kingdom alone, and in some cases the 'rights' enumerated in the document are no more than particular restraints on the king and conditions respecting the meeting of parliament. Nowhere in the document is it stated that the govern-ment of England exists for the sake of securing individual inalienable rights. Ancient rights are not natural ones; the former post-date the formation of government and are the creations of a particular legal system; they have no independent or God-ordained status. Most import-antly, the Bill of Rights does not provide for a natural right of revolution against authorities who violate or who attempt to abridge universal rights. Locke's innovative natural rights theory transformed the rhetoric of historic rights into the department of universal and imprescriptible powers enjoyed by each citizen and guaranteed by a benevolent Creator. The transformation would have an enormous impact on the thought of the eighteenth century, and not least in Britain's North American colonial empire.

The State as Human Artifact

Prior to the middle of the seventeenth century, when Thomas Hobbes made the abstract notion of the impersonal state the focus of attention with respect to the individual's rights and duties, it was thought by most writers that political allegiance was owed to the person of the ruler, local as well as national, ecclesiastical no less than temporal. Hobbes's enormous project thus marked an important transition, signalling the end of a centuries-long season when public power was treated as personal prerogative. The concept of state as the apparatus of government separate from the person or persons who happen at any moment to have control over it, remained very much an alien notion throughout the course of the medieval and early modern periods. Even though republican theorists in Renaissance Italy emphasized the need to place tight restrictions on rulers and magistrates, and where city-state government was increasingly associated with a structure of laws and institutions simply administered by elected leaders, the individual ruler continued to play a pivotal role in defining the nature of the republic. Yet by the close of our period, personal ascendancy ceased to be as crucial to the idea of the state as it had been formerly. The new model found an increasingly favourable reception in northern Europe, and in particular among Dutch and English republican writers.[70] Not surprisingly, these ideas were emphatically rejected by seventeenth-century absolutist writers for whom personal, proprietary power remained the essence of sovereignty.

Hobbes was the best known, and the most infamous, of absolutist writers who began his discussion of the origin of the state from consensual premises, although, as we shall see, many of his ideas were echoed by Pufendorf. For Hobbes there were no natural superiors whose authority to control the lives of others was set by God and whose position reflected a wider order of correspondences in the universal Great Chain of Being. His facility in combining consensual arguments respecting the origins of sovereign power with traditional absolutist arguments on the scope of that power earned him the enmity of both camps, a considerable feat for someone hoping to anchor his political theory in an all-encompassing system of philosophy.

It is generally agreed today that there were two main impulses behind Hobbes's work on political philosophy. In the largest sense he saw himself as engaged in an effort to redefine and to unify all philosophical endeavours, to demonstrate how natural philosophy or physics, and civil philosophy or politics were to be conducted along the same methodological lines. Man, biological and social, was the object of each undertaking respectively; his proper role in political society proceeded in large measure from his behaviour as a special kind of animal.[71] Political philosophy, then, was but a part of a unified field of knowledge. Secondly, Hobbes was responding in his political writings to a specific crisis in mid seventeenth-century England, a crisis which in his mind was related to the religious conflicts engulfing Europe since the mid sixteenth century. For Hobbes, the English Civil War was not to be divorced from the uninformed fanaticism of religious zealots. A resolution of the dilemma created when religion compels action incompatible with the peaceful pursuit of temporal ends in civil society had to be achieved if the bloodletting were to end.

The famous beginning point of Hobbes's political theory involves his treatment of the state of nature. This pre-political human condition is not a historical fact but a logical postulate drawn from his view of man as a being where selfish passion normally overrides deliberative reason, where sociability is not part of the human endowment. In the state of constant war which is the condition of man in the natural or pre-political society (a view, as we have seen, that was conventional for consent theorists), there is no industry, no science, no cultivation, for none of these undertakings is safe from the predations of others. Most disturbingly, and unlike Locke's theologically framed state of nature, Hobbes held that in the pre-civil state 'notions of right and wrong, justice and injustice have there no place'. Without an agreed common civil power 'there is no law, no injustice' and force and fraud become 'the two cardinal virtues'. Individuals may engage in any action that might ensure their safety and preservation. The result is that life, in Hobbes's best known words, is for everyone 'solitary, poor, nasty, brutish, and short'.[72] Hobbes's royalist contemporary Edward Hyde, earl of Clarendon, expressed the shock of many when he observed that the picture of the state of nature in *Leviathan* made men worse than beasts, worse certainly than conventionally portrayed in the wake of the Fall, where at least they retained a modicum of sociability, and where the law of nature applied even without a common superior.[73] Hobbes's radical position made the requirements of the second table of the Decalogue, Commandments 6–10, respecting conduct towards others, effective only when the sovereign has made laws enforcing biblical directives.

Here was a perspective heartily endorsed by Spinoza, who as we shall see, nonetheless demurred from Hobbes's absolutist solution. In his *Ethics*, a work begun in the 1660s but not published until after his death, Spinoza set out to provide his readers with a knowledge of humans as part of a greater system of nature. And it was the well-ordered state that was key to providing the conditions under which the individual might enjoy the highest good, this union with the one; prior to the creation of the civil state men could not capture this good, for the natural state was one of Hobbesian antagonism. Spinoza agreed with Grotius, with the de la Courts, and with Hobbes, that man passed through a disorderly state of nature before forging a social compact and instituting government. Like Hobbes, Spinoza asserted that there could be no wrongdoing in the state of nature, no justice or injustice, no immorality. Because man is part of nature, a finite mode of eternal Substance, his actions in the state of nature are always in harmony with nature and are undertaken by the highest natural right. Whatever a man is able to do by his own power in order to secure his wants in such a state is appropriate.[74] Unfortunately, outside civil society these unlimited natural rights are of very little benefit to single individuals, most of whom are led by blind passions and emotions which invariably drive them into mutual conflict. With simple survival always in peril, natural rights avail men little in the state of nature.

Indeed Spinoza's naturalistic anthropology, estimating man's nature on the basis of what is observable rather than in Aristotelian and scholastic terms of what it is designed to be, paints an unattractive picture of domineering, vengeful, envious and ambitious beings who, once they begin to squabble, next 'do their utmost to enslave one another'.[75] In the state of nature where passion outweighs the force of reason, rights are coextensive with power; living in constant fear of violence, subjection and annihilation, no one is able to engage in the form of intellectual pursuit needed for an understanding of the greatest good. Reasonable men will recognize the futility and danger of this condition, combine forces, and work to create a common power with rules whose purpose is to promote the common welfare.[76] Government and the power to coerce following known laws are clearly prerequisite to the fruitful exercise of reason. Hobbes hoped for reasonable men to step forward as well. In chapter 15 of *Leviathan* he asserted that men's passions move them to define good and evil on the basis of their own private needs. His view of man here was not unlike that later held by his countryman John Locke, at least to the extent that both men believed that humans have no inborn tendency to prefer what is morally good from that which is evil. 'Good and Evil', according to Hobbes, 'are names that signify our Appetites, and Aversions.'[77] Human passions push man towards that which affords pleasure and away from that which stimulates aversion, with self-preservation being the great end pursued by all. The 'good' is whatever appears to bring personal safety and pleasure to the individual. What distinguishes human beings from other animals is that individuals are capable of deliberation, of pausing and weighing the probable advantages and disadvantages of a particular course of action. Man's curiosity drove him to develop a cognitive capacity – reasoning – that separates him from other animals. For Hobbes, the pursuit of these conflicting desires leads to 'disputes, controversies, and at last war'. There is no agreement in the state of nature on what constitutes the common good, no cooperative efforts to ensure the well-being of each member. In the ongoing struggle for self-preservation and the search for personal felicity, men create the conditions which make that felicity impossible. For Hobbes it was the awful experience of the state of nature which brought man to exercise his most noble faculty, his ability to utilize reason, in order to lift himself out of an impossible condition of his own making. Civil society is not a natural predisposition of mankind, as Aristotle had assumed, but a necessity born of a hard and unpalatable experience.

In erecting the absolutist state, Hobbes was clearly within the contractual tradition which held that political power originated with the people, an artificial and not a natural institution. Even in the case of conquest, the new ruler subsequently concludes an agreement with his subjects. Sovereignty for Hobbes was not the decree of heaven in the Bodinian sense, but the inevitable result of a dispassionate assessment of human nature and the natural proclivities of equal human beings. There could be no obligation on men 'which ariseth not from some act of his own; for all men equally are by nature free'.[78] In agreeing that one man or group of men will execute the common will in the interest of peace and security, men consent to give up their right of nature to do whatever they deem necessary for their own preservation, thereby renouncing the practical anarchy and the evils of insecurity which obtained in the natural state. 'The end of Obedience', he declared, 'is Protection', and when that protection is no longer forthcoming, either because of conquest or the successful rebellion of another party, then our obligation to obey shifts to whoever takes up the job of affording the same protection.[79] When *Leviathan* was published in 1651, just such a case of domestic rebellion had occurred, and the logic of Hobbes's sentiments was not appreciated by royalist sympathizers.

The original covenant creating the Leviathan state is entered into out of fear on the part of the individuals involved, fear that any other alternative will mean the abbreviation of their own lives in the state of nature. The sovereign is to be allowed enormous discretion in securing and maintaining civil peace, making law and doing in effect 'whatsoever he shall think necessary to be done, both beforehand, for the preserving of peace and security...and when peace and security are lost, for the recovery of the same'.[80] Without undivided sovereignty and lawmaking authority, whether in the person of the prince or in a collective body, the self-interested and socially destructive passions of man will press a reversion to the state of nature.

The sovereign's power extended even into religion, determining doctrine to be taught and worship to be observed by all citizens, lest a separate and rival church establishment threaten the well-being of the entire body politic. As for 'rights' to property, again Hobbes insisted that there was no 'mine and thine' before the erection of the sovereign state, thus it was for the Leviathan to determine what is a man's property, and this determination might change upon the will of the lawmaker, whose only obligation is to preserve the peace and security of the parties to the covenant. 'The Kings word', he stated in *Leviathan*, 'is sufficient to take any thing from any Subject.'[81] English parliamentarians who based their struggle against Stuart prerogative on the notion that kings are obliged to govern within the limits set by the political nation, took umbrage at Hobbes's views on property. Royalists, on the other hand, especially those keen to defend such measures as Ship Money, forced loans, and other forms of non-parliamentary taxation, found some comfort in this aspect of his thought.

Only when the first law of nature – the law of self-preservation – was violated by the Leviathan was the subject allowed to resist, a position at odds with royalist sentiment throughout the century, but employed with much vigour by parliamentarians keen to limit the prerogative claims of the Stuart kings. The right to defend oneself by force, insisted Henry Parker in 1642, was permitted by 'the clearest beams of human reason, and the strongest inclinations of nature'.[82] Hobbes contended that all moral principles find their anchor in the primary right of self-preservation. The decision to take up arms against the king in 1642 was, for the opponents of Charles I, an unblemished example of the entire community defending this basic right.

Like Bodin, whom he cited in *Elements of Law*, and like Aquinas, Hobbes accepted the Aristotelian precept that there were three pure forms of government: monarchy, aristocracy, and democracy.[83] The best form was of course monarchy, since firm executive decision-making was crucial in a Europe of hostile and competitive powers, states which Hobbes – and later Locke – thought to be in a state of nature with respect to each other. Mixing any of these forms destroyed the principle of sovereignty because power would then be subject to limitations. He also agreed with these earlier absolutist writers that the main characteristics of sovereign power included the right to shape legislation, make war and conclude peace, appoint all officers of state and act as the supreme judge over the subject population. These convictions were very much in comportment with the ideas of a number of English royalists who defended the prerogative actions of James I and especially Charles I. Hobbes did take exception to the recommendation of some absolutist writers that the subject may practise passive disobedience to the prince, refusing to obey a command but silently accepting the penalty. Instead he insisted that at the moment of the original contract, subjects had freely agreed to accede to all of the sovereign's commands; this was the essence of the agreement freely entered into by all.

Pufendorf's position on the powers of the sovereign state created by contract was similar to the model advanced by Hobbes. In making the transition from the natural to the civil state, Pufendorf envisioned two contracts, the first involving an agreement amongst male heads of families to associate as a corporate people by entering into a perpetual union or community whose purpose is 'to administer the means of their safety and security by common counsel and leadership'. Everyone must consent to this initial agreement, and those who elect to demur are to be left outside any future state, free to fend for themselves as best they can in a state of liberty.[84] The second contract establishes by majority decision the specific type or model of government and entails an agreement to subject oneself to it. The form of government may involve the rule of one man or one assembly, or even an assembly of all, but whatever the form the magistrate pledges to 'bind himself or themselves to provide for the common security and safety' while the subjects 'bind themselves to obedience to him or them' unconditionally.[85] This subjection must be without qualification if the state is to carry out its function in a consistent manner over time. 'The only means by which the wills of many may be united is that each submit his will to the will of one man or one assembly, in such a way that from that time on whatever that man or that assembly wills in what concerns the common security be taken as the will of all and everyone.'[86]

Once the second contract is forged, the state acquires from the free consent of the people a composite moral personhood, what we might now call a legal personality, which no man or group of men may take away from the agreed holder of sovereign power.[87] The state founded in this way is to be 'conceived in the manner of a single person who understands and wills, and performs other, peculiar actions distinct from the actions of single individuals'.[88] According to Pufendorf, all legitimate states are adventitious and conventional entities which, because of their origin in consent or agreement, take on the character of 'composite moral persons' where the public authority, whether constituted as monarchy, aristocracy, or democracy, acts with one voice. This modern notion of the state, with a will independent of individual persons, represented another example of the basic shift in seventeenth-century conceptions of public authority inaugurated by Hobbes. The state's authority was to be distinguished from that of the ruler entrusted with the exercise of power, while this authority was also separate from the community over which it was established. It had become, in the words of one modern theorist, 'an entity with a life of its own; an entity which is at once distinct from both rulers and ruled and is able in consequence to call upon the allegiances of both parties'.[89]

Pufendorf's contractualist theory of the state was combined with an absolutist definition of sovereignty in an effort to provide a secular foundation for the modern polity where notions of divine right and natural hierarchy had no place. He thus freed political thought from theological contexts while justifying the actions of the consolidating independent Westphalian system of sovereign states of the late seventeenth century; transcendental justifications for this state were now replaced by a natural one.[90] It is in this sense that Pufendorf betrayed himself as a defender of established and unlimited political authority, even when that authority violated the spirit and the letter of natural law. As a historian Pufendorf was an exponent of reason of state, and he was interested in legitimizing the type of state being erected by the people for whom he worked, a strong entity capable of putting an end to the sort of destructive instability witnessed in the war-torn Empire of his youth. Although he had suggested at one point in *On the Law of Nature and Nations* that at the time of the initial contract to establish a sovereign power the people might limit sovereignty by certain laws whose purpose was to preclude tyrannical practices, still the sovereign wields enormous discretion in pursuing what he takes to be the public good.[91]

This is seen clearly in his understanding of sovereign power which, once conferred, is absolute and unlimited, even in religious matters. The sovereign is never obliged to account for its actions to any man, and while the sovereign should conform to law in order to strengthen its overall authority, sovereign authority is superior to human and civil law in the sense that the same power cannot be superior to itself. For Pufendorf, resistance to popularly constituted authority could not be allowed, for it was always wrong to attempt to take back by force what had been granted freely and willingly. Even when the state has wrongly threatened individual citizens 'with the most atrocious injuries', the aggrieved could protect themselves only by flight, and these transgressions on the part of rulers 'must be placed in the class of those evils to which the human condition is exposed in this mortal state'.[92] Should the offended subject remain within the boundaries of the state, then they must of right 'endure any injury or damage rather than draw their swords against one who remains the father of their country, however harsh he may be'.[93] It was not the case that the people have delegated supreme authority to the state and may repossess it should the magistrate fail to satisfy the requirements of the original contract.

The record of civil unrest which history confirms to be the lot of those who remove an unjust prince was, in Pufendorf's estimation, sufficient reason for acquiescence in the face of abuse and even violence. Every duty associated with the supreme authority is part of the central goal of inculcating good citizenship. Ministers of religion, in addition to teaching doctrines related to salvation, must inculcate precepts 'by which the minds of mortals are especially disposed to bear well [the burdens] of civil life'. Public schools must instruct 'about the right of supreme sovereigns and the obligation of citizens corresponding to it'. And the sovereign must caution against laziness, enforce sumptuary laws, and demand military readiness in light of international dangers.[94]

A Late Dissent

One way to appreciate the radical nature of this view of sovereignty is to explore the work of Hobbes through the eyes of one of his most influential and better known critics, the German philosopher Gottfried Wilhelm Leibniz. Born in 1646, just two years before the close of the Thirty Years War, and dying just after the close of the War of the Austrian Succession in 1716, Leibniz never reconciled himself to the novel developments in church and state which were erasing the last vestiges of common identity represented by universal Christendom. His was a voice for what had been lost in the struggle to evolve a system of independent states, a longing for a synthesis in knowledge, belief and conduct no longer possible in a hostile world of competing nation-states. Leibniz did not complete a systematic treatise or system on politics, or indeed on any subject of special interest to him. His wide-ranging intellectual interests, in mathematics, science, logic, metaphysics, history, diplomacy, and engineering, coupled with 'an unachievable ambition to excel in every sphere of intellectual activity' made it troublesome for him to finish individual, long-term projects.[95] Despite the fragmentary nature of his writings, however, it is clear that the overall goal of Leibniz' social and political philosophy was the shaping of a universal society which conformed to an ideal provided by God at the Creation.

Leibniz' chief criticism of Hobbes's political theory involved one of the most troublesome and long-standing issues in Christian theology. The problem concerned the nature of heavenly justice and the will of God. Those who believed that a thing is just or good or true simply because God willed it were known as voluntarists or nominalists. This school held that justice is completely contingent on the will of a supreme lawmaker who is absolutely free to change his mind. Justice, then, emerges from an empirical understanding of God's volition in a particular case at a particular moment; beyond the divine will lies an amoral universe. The principal medieval exponent of this voluntarist perspective was William of Ockham, and it was this view that Hobbes adopted in *Leviathan*, where God's sovereign power is highlighted and confirmed.

Hobbes was not hesitant to point out that the appeal to principles of right reason had led men to very different conclusions on almost every subject imaginable. And whereas most might attribute this lack of consensus respecting the dictate of reason to man's frail intellect, Hobbes took the bold step of declaring that there was no underlying voice of reason, no universal and accessible dictate of justice or morality. The nominalist God is a being without superior, the arbitrary God of Abraham and Isaac, the God whose fiat can make the killing of one's son an act of higher devotion to the Creator. Similarly the temporal magistrate must define good and evil in the interests of accomplishing his single charge: the peace and security of his subjects. Before the magistrate does this, there can be no standards of right and wrong in the state of nature. In seventeenth-century theological debate, voluntarism was most often associated with the predestinarian tendencies in orthodox Calvinism, where God elects some to salvation for reasons which elude the grasp of human reason.

The alternative to voluntarism was known as realism or essentialism, and it was this perspective that Leibniz introduced in his attack on the ethical implications of *Leviathan*. The realist school of thought, tracing its origins back to Socrates, Plato, and Aristotle before finding a Christian home in the school of Aquinas, held that justice, goodness and truth have fixed and eternal natures quite distinct from the lawmaker, and that one can understand the content of these concepts through the exercise of reason. The God of the realist tradition acts and commands in conformity to reason and a fixed natural order of creation. God wills something because it is intrinsically and eternally just; as a benevolent ruler He does not exercise an arbitrary will and make justice a mere contingency. Not surprisingly, realism was embraced by those who supported the Thomist belief that human cooperation with grace was essential to the work of salvation. The strength of the realist position lay in its affirmation of a benevolent God whose will can be known through the gift of reason. The weakness, at least for its nominalist critics, was that realism turned God into a metaphor for reason and the natural order of things; the government of the world no longer required a personal deity.[96]

Leibniz, together with a host of like-minded critics before him, was convinced that Hobbes's voluntarism, where the will and power of the lawmaker defined justice, led directly to a political world where tyranny and brutality could claim philosophical legitimacy. Leibniz rejected Hobbes's association of justice with power, for 'to say that "just" is whatever pleases the most powerful is nothing else than saying that there is no certain and determined justice which keeps one from doing whatever he wants to do and can do with impunity, however evil it may be'.[97] If all could agree on a common understanding of justice, then most of the questions of right that arise between sovereigns and people, and between churches, now the cause of endless dispute, would disappear. 'Put yourself in the place of another', he recommended in his 'Meditation on the Common Concept of Justice' (1702), 'and you will have the true point of view of judging what is just or not.'[98]

As we know, most seventeenth-century theorists interpreted human government as a microcosm of divine government; earthly institutions and practices, if properly ordered, would mirror the divine archetype. By drawing a parallel between the voluntarist's God and the temporal magistrate, right and wrong, justice and its opposite, truth and error, were each reduced to the variable will of the sovereign, fracturing all notions of continuity and making impossible any sense of personal security or rational living in a universe of moral absolutes. In the Hobbesian picture, the natural world which men inhabit offers no pre-established set of moral standards which dictate conduct prior to the establishment of a sovereign power. And once that indefeasible and illimitable power is established by equal individuals who fear for their own safety in the state of nature, morality is invented – and can be re-invented indefinitely – as the will and power of the magistrate.

For the many lawyers and divines who were appalled by this Hobbesian version of legal positivism, and for Cavaliers who saw him as an apologist for the usurper Cromwell in the 1650s, Hobbes's contempt for the common law, for the play of right reason, meant that men in such a civil state became little more than the slaves of a capricious master. Not surprisingly the royalist Sir Robert Filmer thought otherwise about Hobbes's overall accomplishment, admitting that 'with no small content I read Mr Hobbes' book *De Cive*, and his *Leviathan*, about the rights of sovereignty, which no man, that I know, hath so amply and judiciously handled'.[99] During the Restoration period royalists were not hesitant about enlisting the support of the philosopher of Malmesbury in their struggle against Whig constitutionalists.[100]

The compromise advocated by Leibniz and a wide range of Christian theologians was to insist that God combines understanding and will when setting standards for human conduct. Through his intellectual nature, what the Presbyterian divine Richard Baxter called 'sapiential excellencies', God knows the eternal good and has the power to turn this good into a moral imperative for humankind.[101] Even some of those who applauded Hobbes's elevation of God's sovereign power were keen to soften the implications of his ethical theory. The Anglican divine Samuel Parker, for instance, thought that Scripture stressed God's power and empire, not his essence, but nonetheless affirmed that divine power was always exercised in a manner 'that will comply with the reputation of his other attributes'.[102] The divine intelligence would not indulge in acts which were irrational to the human mind; eternal goodness would not indulge the arbitrary.

Leibniz was also distressed by the minimal objectives of the state as set by Hobbes, the restriction of government to the bare preservation of peace and individual safety. He was eager to involve the state in a wide range of welfare schemes whose purpose was to improve the quality of life for the entire citizenry, but in particular for the poor and uneducated. He believed that it was the responsibility of those in power not only to prevent misery and secure peace, but to take an activist role in promoting the common welfare through a variety of schemes designed to improve the quality of life. Economic planning, public health and education, the prevention of poverty, sponsorship of academies of arts and sciences – all were within the orbit of the state's legitimate mandate.[103] And if this same charity could be made a part of the international system, then the disputes among nations, and in particular religious divisions, might be brought to an acceptable resolution.

No such scheme for the sort of activist state proposed by Leibniz was about to be embraced by national governments in the late seventeenth century. His essentially Aristotelian picture of the state as an agent in the formation of virtue was dismissed by Hobbes, as was the notion that political society was a natural condition for humankind. Even Locke's minimal state, erected by common consent or convention and sharing in realist assumptions about the created order, sought merely the protection of the individual in order that everyone might more effectively pursue their selfish interests. Never before had the origins and intentions of the civil structure been so dramatically unfastened from transhuman intentions. From the start of the century in the naturalism of Grotius, to the mid-century crisis in England and Hobbes's erection of the unimpeachable, yet freely willed Leviathan, to Spinoza's declaration of the impersonal oneness of creation, the state matured as an entity less the object of divine intention and more the abstract harvest of human needs. The empirical study of human behaviour, not the shouldering of Aristotelian and Christian teleology, increasingly set the starting point for all discussion about the parameters and the possibilities of social interaction. Unobserved in political praxis for another century, the state as idea, as a set of principles and ends determined by fallible citizens, had become part of the vocabulary of political life.

CONCLUSION: EXIT DIVINITY

If one ecumenical trend in political practice can be distinguished over the course of the seventeenth century, it must be associated with the enhancement of the authority of the prince at the expense of rival power arrangements, including clerical ones, in the territorial community. Reason of state, indeed the very continuation of the state as an autonomous entity in the face of enormous commercial, colonial, religious and military rivalries, pointed in the direction of a greater arrogation of power at the centre, at the diminution and in some cases the elimination of regional autonomy and cultural particularism, and at increased financial and service burdens being borne by the population at large.[1] While all rulers had to be responsive to the interests of noble supporters, and although these same rulers had to cooperate skilfully with representative bodies, on the whole crown efforts were successful, and the encroachment of central power into many aspects of life was both quantitatively and qualitatively different from the type of power enjoyed by earlier Renaissance-style princes. Importantly, as Marc Raeff has pointed out, 'Centralization had the paradoxical result of fostering greater separation and division within Europe' after the Reformation, which in turn forwarded the drive towards self-sufficient and mutually hostile political units, each with its own public-relations machinery in the state church and with what amounted to a monopoly over organized violence through an increasingly professionalized military.[2]

What then were the signal contributions of seventeenth-century political thought to the problems of society in an era of emergent nation-states? Which ideas, born and maturing during this century of conflict and state-building, were to have a lasting impact on the shape of modern thought and practice? In what respects can modern secular and constitutional democracy, currently the central claimant to ideological and practical legitimacy around the globe, trace its ancestry to a century where absolute monarchy was thought to be the truly 'modern' model of public authority? It is clear, after all, that the status society, absolutism, confessional and intolerant states – all remained fixtures across most of

171

Europe for another century. It would indeed be rash to claim too much for the more innovative thinkers of the period. Ostracism and contempt were the daily companions of Hobbes, Spinoza, and Winstanley, while Locke and Grotius spent long periods in exile for their political beliefs. As for the Levellers, the first modern democratic theorists, they were put down by Cromwell's loyal military in a manner all too familiar to modern sensibilities.

Those who were alert to the growth of state power at the centre included both individuals and groups whose main concern was with religious issues, and others who thought more in terms of purely secular matters. Absolutism appeared to be the preferred governmental model of writers and practitioners whose pre-eminent worry was territorial coherence and stability in a Europe where the attenuation of conflict on religious grounds after 1648 was supplanted by the quickening and intensification of warfare prompted by more terrestrial, and in particular economic, considerations. But challenges to the more extreme forms of absolutism were to find voice in constitutionalist and, more provocatively, in republican writings. For these groups the locus of sovereignty was to be found in a more complicated fabric where princes, or in the case of republicans, executive authority, shared the burdens of power with a wider community of representative groups. And perhaps most disturbingly for all segments of the traditional ruling elite across Europe, ideas in support of a broadening of access to the empire of politics were heard with increasing frequency, especially in England, by the close of the century. The locus of sovereignty, admission to and control over the expanding capacity of the state, thus became a significant point of departure for political theorists in the universities, in the cabinets, in the Estates, in the army, and, increasingly, in the coffee houses.

Indeed, at least two of the developments that have shaped so much of modern democratic politics had been clearly embraced at Europe's British periphery by the time of John Locke's death in 1704, while something of the impact of these innovations was being felt across much of the Continent west of the Elbe. Whereas at the outset of the century it was widely held that government had as one of its principal charges the creation of a God-fearing community under the direction of a single church, by 1700 political society was thought by some to be the mechanism by which individuals could seek their own material, intellectual, and spiritual well-being and as a result promote the overall prosperity of the state. This first transformation involved the replacement of corporate or status group interests with individual and private ones, where government now anchored its legitimacy in the promotion and protection of the citizens who, regardless of status or association, were to be treated as equals before the law. Obviously this change had proceeded much further in the Netherlands and in Britain than in any other European state. The powerful bonds which linked the nobility and the crown in France, for example, meant that privilege and exemption continued to divide that society into increasingly antithetical interest groups.

The second development, very broadly speaking, involved the gradual abandonment of the notion which associated sovereignty with the person of the monarch and the political order with a divine order, and its replacement first by the idea that sovereignty rested with the people but ultimately in the more abstract idea that sovereignty inhered in the state as a whole, in the constitutional and institutional structures of power which had been erected by the people for ends which had been desacralized, divorced from any theological paradigm. A natural and utility-oriented standard of the state's origin and purpose, one built exclusively upon the natural needs of individuals who were motivated by an unlovely self-interest, was coming to displace a God-ordained and hierarchically organized mandate for human governance where purpose and eternal destiny loomed large. There was, then, an emerging sense that the religious criteria which for centuries had guided the interpretation and the organization of civil affairs were being expropriated by a set of distinctly less transcendent benchmarks.

This latter development was, once again, slow to develop outside Britain and the Dutch Republic. In France, for example, the persistence of specific corporate relationships between the king and the Estates inhibited the formation of an impersonal state which treated all citizens in an evenhanded manner. The proprietary element in the French monarchy, the representation of the state as the special charge of the personal monarch, remained very strong as the privileged nobility offered its support in return for continued tax and legal exemptions. Such a proprietary model had been destroyed by two revolutions in England, where parliament effectively undertook to designate the succession beginning in 1660. The legal equality of citizens in a flourishing commercial economy, the growth of a civil bureaucracy, incipient departmentalization, and cabinet government all contributed to the rise of the abstract sovereign state idea. Central administration employed around 1000 men before the English Civil War, but by 1725 this number had grown to 2700 career officials.[3] 'King and Country' began to take on new meaning in the eighteenth century, with the second object of allegiance emerging as the authentic, albeit abstract, centre of personal reverence and sacrifice.

Larger economic and territorial developments in the second half of the century contributed to the shift whereby the state's role as enforcer of orthodoxy at home and chief proselytizer in the international arena was gradually succeeded by the model of the state as guarantor of national – and by implication individual – prosperity. Colbert's mercant-ilist policies in France, Emperor Leopold's establishment in 1666 of a Council of Commerce, the series of English Navigation Acts and the Anglo-Dutch wars of the 1660s and 1670s, where two Protestant nations were pitted against one another for reasons divorced from all eschato-logical considerations, clashes over shipping rights and colonial hege-mony, the broad alliances formed to curb the territorial ambitions of Louis XIV – all indicated a pragmatic and secularized view of a nation's premier interests. Increasingly the success of trading companies, joint stock concerns, and overseas colonies was viewed by governments as essential to the defence of the state. Commerce and capital were now worth defending at all costs; the fate of one's slave traders, monopoly trading companies, and private exploiters in the East Indies, in the Caribbean, in North America, could not be ignored, or their activities left to take their natural course, lest the wealth – and thus the security – of the homeland be compromised. Economic and social policy had taken its place alongside religious practice at the highest level of government's core responsibilities. Increasing the state's stock of precious metals had become as important to the maintenance of social stability as enlarging the sweep of religious conformity to prescribed forms.

The mercantilist state which emerged over the course of the next cen-tury found itself advancing the very sorts of interests and cultural assumptions which had been condemned by medieval Christian Europe as antithetical to life's spiritual purpose. Administrative and political action no longer restricted itself to negative endeavours: preserving peace, law and order, and religious uniformity. Political decision-making now involved an assumption that society could be shaped, directed into more productive channels through the adoption of policies conceived to forward the material ambitions of the entire citizenry, policies which took no account of expectations for the next life.[4] The 'moral economy' of the citizenry was gradually becoming irrelevant to the state, the entire affair being shuttled over to the churches of a divided Christendom to handle as best they could without the aid of the state's monopoly over coercive power. The grudging Toleration Act of 1689 in England, while officially disbarring Protestant dissenters from the Church of England from any role in the civil and political life of the nation, at least acknowledged the principle of individual choice where it concerned matters of the soul.

In some very important respects, John Locke stood at the threshold of this new world, especially in his focus on the state's obligation to the individual and not to status groups, and in his claim that political power might revert to sovereign people if this delegated authority were repeatedly abused by the magistrate. Locke's insistence that the rights of individuals preceded and must be protected by the state was such an essential core of his thought that he allowed for individuals, and not just the entire community, to resist a tyrant. Moreover, he held that the right owned by individuals in the state of nature to punish a malefactor carried over into the civil state and permitted each person to punish the magistrate who violated the agreed contract establishing civil society. Sovereignty for Locke, as David Wootton has pointed out, was held by morally responsible individuals who were obliged to take immediate care for their own political well-being and the well-being of their fellows.[5] No longer could persons abjure their responsibility for the quality of civil existence in their country; no longer could magistrates claim divine sanction for their 'right' to misgovern.

But in the end, and despite these significant innovations, Locke was unwilling to abandon the sureties of the earlier cosmological and moral paradigm. Like the vast majority of his predecessors and contemporaries, Locke attempted to base all human relations on what he could not demonstrate: the existence of a divinely ordered set of moral obligations, one that God had empowered humankind to know and obey through the exercise of reason.[6] For Locke all persons remained 'the servants of one sovereign master, sent into the world by his order and about his business', and one ignored the requirement of God's pre-established moral code at the cost of forfeiting one's soul. In other words, Locke's picture of moral obligation was based upon a faith in the existence of a providential and ultimately benevolent divine order, the exact nature of which had been the subject of dispute within religious circles for centuries. And political action had to take account of that order, had to make it the starting point of any discussion of sovereignty in a sinful world. In particular, Locke's providential but rational moral order called for the inalienability of fundamental human rights, where liberty of person and property are not the gifts of the state but the inherent defining attributes of humanity as designated by a loving Creator.

Locke's politics, while discovering the individual and making civil society the defender of individual natural rights, continued to view the purpose of the state in terms of an agenda which originated outside the ambit of human affairs.

Hobbes took bolder steps, crossing without hesitation the troublesome religious threshold into a world without external guideposts, into a modern age where value and goodness are designed solely by erring human beings. Unflinchingly, he laboured to establish human relations in terms of desentimentalized and secular self-interest, divorced from any purportedly higher and universally obligatory moral imperatives. In this respect he was advancing the earlier naturalistic conclusions of Grotius. The Dutchman had preceded Hobbes in the construction of a system of morality and political action separate from the type of theological strictures which informed Locke's mind at the close of the century, but Grotius' estimate of human nature began with an assertion of human sociability that was absent from *Leviathan*, thus restoring to prominence a much older Aristotelian premise about man's natural tendencies. The social drive, not the urge to self-preservation motivated by fear of one's neighbours, meant that for Grotius injustice could be defined as anything which detracted from an ordered community of rational beings. Justice then is all that belongs to man's natural instinct to sociability, all that leads to communal satisfaction.[7] It has no connection to divine law; it is not related to the Decalogue or to the Sermon on the Mount, and it would remain in force even if there were no God. The existence and content of the law of nature can be proved a priori – by showing that an act or thing agrees with man's rational nature, or a posteriori – by amassing evidence of what is believed by all peoples and nations.

For the less sanguine Hobbes, obligation emerged from a direct and unsentimental assessment of how men actually conducted themselves in the absence of civil institutions designed to enforce particular behaviours. It was his conviction that there were no theologically based notions of right and wrong, of proper and improper conduct, before the exclusively human artifact called civil society, before the establishment of a sovereign power. Here Hobbes was secularizing the notion of a God-fearing society and replacing it with an empirical set of felt human needs. In other words, it was not the fear of God's wrath that held society together, but the more immediate fear of one's fellows if civil society were to give way to the state of nature.

Spinoza was to confirm Hobbes's picture of natural right in the precivil state by describing individuals subject to nature as justified in pursuing any goal which either reason or passion tells them is useful. Any 'force, fraud, entreaty' was permissible in the quest to satiate desire, and it was appropriate to label anyone an enemy who stood in the way of these unending pursuits. In such a world of chaos the state becomes the highest good, and 'devotion to country is the highest form of piety a man can show'.[8] Hobbes concluded that there was no fixed standard of meritorious human conduct set by a providential superior, only positive law as determined by the Leviathan whose charge was to guarantee the safety and the security of those citizens who had vouchsafed him total authority. The sovereignty enjoyed by this Leviathan was based on power, not divine right or popular consent periodically renewed. It was this naturalistic approach to human social relations, this refusal to begin with any theologically inspired assumptions about man's place in a world informed by special law, which made his approach to politics both as alien to the standards of discourse in his day as they are commonplace in ours.

In the preface to the first edition of his *The Law of Nature and Nations* (1672) Pufendorf identified Hobbes as a successor to Grotius, and the author was himself attacked as a Hobbesian for asserting that human actions do not exhibit any inherent moral qualities, that instead all such qualities are simply imputed to actions by some individual or group. Pufendorf was also rebuked for proposing the notion, again endorsed by Grotius and Hobbes, that the principles of the law of nature can be understood, without theological linkages, as simply a means towards the overall security of individuals in society. For all three writers, the right was that which was crucial to individuals in need of protection from their fellow man. To determine this right conduct, one need not have recourse to any form of special revelation or divine positive law.[9] The desire for self-preservation had become the starting point for a naturalistic understanding of the laws of nature, and this naturalism would contribute significantly to the development of an alternative picture of the function of government in a Europe of competitive nation-states.

Towards the end of the century it was no longer so readily assumed that only in a godly and self-abnegating society could peace and prosperity be assured, or that national well-being was closely tied to enforced orthodoxy lest divine providence visit military defeat, civil war or natural disaster on the recalcitrant polity. A new recognition of the constructive and socially beneficial power of self-interest began to displace the older association of human ambition with the first sin, and hence with the need for coercive, hierarchical government. As we have seen, something of this shift was anticipated by James Harrington in England, who believed that good institutional mechanisms and laws were more important than good men to the effective functioning of civil order.

But it was in the French Jansenist community that a mixture of Augustinian pessimism regarding human motivation and Hobbesian assumptions about conduct outside civil society combined to offer a radically new picture of the mainsprings of improving social life. Jansenism began with a critical understanding of the limits and weakness of reason, the power of the passions and the influence of human pride on conduct.[10] Blaise Pascal, whose larger project was to convince his readers that absorption in the self is the very root of misery, had noted mankind's tendency to serve and to please others from a root desire of self-aggrandizement, defining the unjust as those who 'have not yet found a way of satisfying concupiscence without harming others'.[11] All apparent virtues are nothing more than calculated means to forward our *amour propre*, and Pascal was deeply troubled by the condition. 'We have founded upon and drawn from concupiscence itself admirable rules of civil order, morality, and justice' but the entire edifice is built upon a 'villainous human foundation'. As early as 1675 the French Jansenist Pierre Nicole observed that while the Fall of Adam had introduced a wide array of human vices, the cupidity which has replaced man's charitable instincts was actually a powerful force in the creation of a more comfortable form of earthly existence. 'Where is that charity', he asked, 'which is contented to build a house for you, replenish it with movables, adorn it with tapestry, and put the key thereof into your hands? Cupidity will do it, and cheerfully too.'[12] Rather than curbing such self-love and preaching old-fashioned charity, Nicole advocated the promotion of *amour propre* in the interests of community well-being. Government's role should be to regulate this personal greed, to assure that what can be an enormous force for good does not degenerate into an anarchic free-for-all. 'There is nothing, then, from which one draws greater service than human greed itself. But in order that greed be disposed to render such services, it is necessary that something constrain her to it; for if left to herself she has neither limits nor measure. Instead of serving human society, she would destroy it.'

According to Nicole, who like most Jansenists supported the absolutist model in France, the 'art' which regulates greed is 'the political order which restrains it by fear of punishment, and applies it to things useful to society'.[13] Men's base and sinful nature would lead them to overturn the entire productive order created by self-love if the government did not provide a regulatory function based upon coercive power. Nicole's sentiments were echoed by his countryman Pierre Bayle, who went so far as to explain that even atheists could be good citizens, because they, like believers, were motivated first and foremost by their own material self-interest, and this could be regulated solely by fear of civil punishment and reward without recourse to the threat of divine sanction. Men reacted to short-term pains and pleasures; those at a distance had minimal, if any, claims on their behaviour.

But it was a Dutch physician living in England, Bernard de Mandeville, who forsook the traditional deprecation of the selfish vices and turned them instead to the advantage of the nation in the international arena and to the greater well-being of the citizenry in the domestic sphere. Born in 1670, Mandeville was raised in Rotterdam and, possibly educated at the city's Erasmian school, was familiar with the French Jansenists' emphasis on the role of the passions in human motivation.[14] He agreed entirely that reason was directed by the claims of the individual ego. Where he broke with these important predecessors was in his insistence that virtue could be equated with the social utility, the public benefit, of an action without regard to its intrinsic merits.

The Jansenists had insisted that the unregenerate could never claim the purifying grace which distinguished the saved from the damned, could never claim to be virtuous on the basis of mere social convention. To Mandeville, a trained physician who embraced a completely naturalistic understanding of his subject, such theological assumptions were meaningless. Moral behaviour in his view was nothing more than the compliance of egoistic but necessitous creatures to the opinions of others in light of the fact that these opinions secure everyone's well-being. Fulfilling basic and natural desires leads men to seek the approbation of others who can provide these ends. Like Hobbes, Mandeville held that men had no natural propensity for sociability, and unlike Descartes, he rejected the argument which placed humans in a category distinct from animals by virtue of their possessing a rational faculty. Human and animal passions were akin to one another, while the imposition of moral systems represented the domestication of the human beast by political elites. Man as a self-regarding animal became a tame and sociable creature thanks to the work of lawgivers who successfully manipulated the appetite of pride into constructive and socially beneficial channels.[15]

Absent from Mandeville's *Fable of the Bees* (1714) was the seventeenth-century's preoccupation with the godly personality, with divine intentions respecting duty and service, with the religious structuring of earthly existence for transcendent ends, with the subordination of personal ambition and the need for unblemished moral virtue. Also missing from his analysis of the productive and loyal citizen was the long-standing goal of civic humanism: the creation and nurture of virtuous individuals who eschew private interest in pursuit of the higher public end. Civic humanism commonly associated the decline of healthy political systems with an increase in luxury, pride and personal ambition, the very developments that were celebrated by Mandeville. The *Fable*, the author claimed, was based upon scientific, not theological, principles, and it was this naturalistic foundation which, while seeming to comport with the facts of social behaviour, so disturbed his numerous critics. By denying the need for enforced moral rectitude and instead directing what had always been labelled vice into proper channels, Mandeville claimed that governments could guarantee the security of the nation-state in an age of intensifying commercial and imperial rivalry. Not God or the inculcation of a fixed godly virtue would unite men in society, but mammon and the scramble for economic advancement, so long as the pursuit of the latter was regulated by laws which protected the person and property of all members.

When an enlarged edition of the *Fable* was published in 1723, it was presented by the Grand Jury of Middlesex, England, to the Court of the King's Bench as a public nuisance. The presentment stated that the work was designed 'to run down Religion and Virtue as prejudicial to Society, and detrimental to the State; and to recommend luxury, Avarice, Pride, and all vices, as being necessary to Public Welfare, and not tending to the Destruction of the Constitution...'[16] But as E. J. Hundert has recently pointed out, Mandeville was much more than a spokesperson for the new world of non-landed wealth creation. He was, instead, a self-conscious member of a European Republic of Letters who recast a number of traditions of political discourse, natural philosophy, and Christian moral psychology in an effort to develop a critical science of man upon naturalistic foundations. The task of reducing moral rules to the shrewd manipulation of individual pride, undertaken by cunning politicians whose primary objective was to enhance the quality of earthly existence for the largest number, appeared to many as nothing less than a direct attack upon Christian ethics. The corruption that civic humanists saw in commercial and individualistic society was, for many Christians, the sinfulness of Adam repeated by men destined for damnation. Neither view, however, would prove effective against the new outlook in the eighteenth century. And no political order which did not take account of the individual and his egoistic appetites, his insatiable vanity, would find its position strengthened with respect to its neighbours over the course of the next 300 years.

That such a self-regarding society could cohere, that its atomistic penchants could somehow advance a larger public interest without setting an overriding – and transhuman – moral standard for itself, was difficult for contemporaries to imagine. Now, 300 years later, most citizens in the Western democracies are hard-pressed to envision how the public interest can be served in any other manner. Born in the midst of deep religious divisions in a troubled Christian culture, the natural history of man had confirmed some of the key components of Augustinian anthropology. The idea of government for and by self-regarding people, universally detested throughout most of human history, has today become part of the political vocabulary of most governments around the world, even the most blatantly anti-democratic ones. The modern secular state, whose primary function has become the enhancement of individual security and constitutional freedoms, and which, perhaps ironically, has at its disposal unprecedented powers of coercion over its own citizens, owes not a little to the otherwise unfamiliar and deeply religious intellectual landscape of the seventeenth century.

NOTES AND REFERENCES

Preface

1. In this respect I am following the cautions proposed by Nanerl Keohane, *Philosophy and the State in France* (Princeton, NJ, 1980), p. xii. See also Susan Moller Okin, *Women in Western Political Thought* (Princeton, NJ, 1979), pp. 5–7.
2. Richelieu, *The Political Testament of Cardinal Richelieu*, trans. Henry Bertram Hill (Madison, WI, 1972), p. 75.
3. Brian Tierney, *Religion, Law, and the Growth of Constitutional Thought, 1150–1650* (Cambridge, 1982), p. 81; Alfred North Whitehead, *Science and the Modern World* (New York, 1925). See also the cautions expressed by Iain Hampsher-Monk, *A History of Modern Political Thought* (Oxford, 1992), pp. x–xi.

Introduction

1. Robert Nisbet, *The Social Philosophers: Community and Conflict in Western Thought* (New York, 1973), p. 132; Leslie Green, *The Authority of the State* (Oxford, 1988), pp. 1–2.
2. Joseph Canning, *A History of Medieval Political Thought, 300–1450* (London, 1996), p. xi. See also Hagen Schulze, *States, Nations and Nationalism: From the Middle Ages to the Present*, trans. William E. Yuill (Oxford, 1996), p. 7.
3. Canning, *History of Medieval Political Thought*, pp. 114–25, discusses the revival of Roman Law studies.
4. Schulze, *States, Nations and Nationalism*, pp. 30–1.
5. See, for example, H. R. Trevor-Roper, *The Crisis of the Seventeenth Century* (New York, 1956); Geoffrey Parker and Leslie M. Smith (eds), *The General Crisis of the Seventeenth Century* (London, 1978); Maurice Ashley, *The Golden Century: Europe 1598–1715* (New York, 1969); Frederick L. Nussbaum, *The Triumph of Science and Reason, 1660–1715* (New York, 1953).
6. J. H. Burns, *The Cambridge History of Political Thought, 1450–1700* (Cambridge, 1991), p. 2.
7. Herbert Butterfield, *The Whig Interpretation of History* (New York, 1931, 1965).
8. Peter Burke, *Popular Culture in Early Modern Europe* (New York, 1978), p. 262.

182

9. Thomas Hobbes, *Leviathan*, ed. Richard Tuck (Cambridge, 1991), p. 489.

10. Paul Hazard, *The European Mind, 1680–1715*, trans. J. Lewis May (New York, 1963), p. xv.

1 Civil Authority in an Unfamiliar Setting

1. Charles Tilly, *The Formation of National States in Western Europe* (Princeton, NJ, 1995), p. 24. Tilly, *Coercion, Capital, and European States, AD 990–1990* (Oxford, 1990), pp. 66–95; Joseph R. Strayer, *On the Medieval Origins of the Modern State* (Princeton, NJ, 1970), p. 105.

2. Quoting Wolfgang Reinhard, 'Power Elites, State Servants, Ruling Classes, and the Growth of State Power' in Reinhard (ed.), *Power Elites and State Building* (Oxford, 1996), p. 1.

3. This great variety is discussed by Victor Kiernan, *State and Society in Europe, 1550–1650* (New York, 1980), p. 4.

4. Quentin Skinner, *The Foundations of Modern Political Thought*, 2 vols (Cambridge, 1978), 2:349–54.

5. Marc Raeff, 'The Well-ordered Police State and the Development of Modernity in Seventeenth and Eighteenth-Century Europe', *American Historical Review*, 80, no.3 (1975), 1221–43.

6. Carl J. Friedrich, *The Age of the Baroque, 1600–1660* (New York, 1952), p. 17.

7. Perez Zagorin, *Rebels and Rulers, 1500–1650*, 2 vols (Cambridge, 1982), 1:62–4. Roland Mousnier, *Social Hierarchies, 1450 to the Present*, trans. Peter Evans (New York, 1973), pp. 75–6. See also the discussion in William Beik, *Absolutism and Society in Seventeenth-Century France: State Power and Provincial Aristocracy in Languedoc* (Cambridge, 1985), pp. 6–9, where Mousnier's thesis is challenged.

8. Bodin quoted in J. H. Shennan, *Liberty and Order in Early Modern Europe: the Subject and the State, 1650–1800* (London, 1986), p. 2.

9. Edmund Morgan (ed.), *Puritan Political Ideas, 1558–1754* (Indianapolis, 1965), p. xvii.

10. Tierney, *Constitutional Thought*, p. 43.

11. Robert Eccleshall, *Order and Reason in Politics: Theories of Absolute and Limited Monarchy in England* (Oxford, 1978), p. 51.

12. Hooker, *Laws of Ecclesiastical Polity*, in *The Works of Mr Richard Hooker*, 2 vols (Oxford, 1875), 2:495. See also, more generally, E. M. Tilliard, *The Elizabethan World Picture* (New York, n.d.) and Arthur Lovejoy, *The Great Chain of Being* (Baltimore, MD, 1930).

13. Burns (ed.), *Cambridge History of Political Thought, 1450–1700*, p. 2.

14. E. H. Kossmann, 'The Singularity of Absolutism', in Ragnild Hatton (ed.), *Louis XIV and Absolutism* (Columbus, OH, 1976), p. 9.

15. David Wootton (ed.), *Divine Right and Democracy* (Harmondsworth, 1986), pp. 22–3.

16. J. H. Burns, *The True Law of Kingship: Concepts of Monarchy in Early Modern Scotland* (Oxford, 1996), p. 1.

17. D. H. Pennington, *Europe in the Seventeenth Century* (New York, 1980), p. 40.
18. John Miller (ed.), *Absolutism in Seventeenth-Century Europe* (London, 1990), p. 2.
19. Pensées, quoted in Raymond Birn, *Crisis, Absolutism, Revolution: Europe 1648–1789* (New York, 1992), p. 28.
20. John B. Wolf, *The Emergence of the Great Powers, 1685–1715* (New York, 1951), pp. 3–4; Reinhard, 'Power Elites', pp. 6–7.
21. Brian M. Downing, *The Military Revolution and Political Change: Origins of Democracy and Autocracy in Early Modern Europe* (Princeton, NJ, 1992). See also William McNeill, *The Pursuit of Power: Technology, Armed Forces, and Society since AD 1000* (Chicago, 1982).
22. Parker and Smith (eds), *General Crisis*, p. 14; Theodore Rabb, *The Struggle for Stability in Early Modern Europe* (New York, 1975), p. 60.
23. Fernand Braudel, *The Mediterranean and the Mediterranean World in the Age of Philip II*, 2 vols (New York, 1973), 2:725.
24. Thomas Munck, *Seventeenth-Century Europe 1598–1700 (London, 1990)*, p. 140, Richard Bonney, *The European Dynastic States*, 1494–1660 (Oxford, 1991), p. 376.
25. Munck, *Seventeenth-Century Europe*, p. 140.
26. On the values of the medieval aristocracy, see J. Huizinga, *The Waning of the Middle Ages* (Garden City, NY, 1954), ch. 1.
27. Munck, *Seventeenth-Century Europe*, p. 156.
28. Richard Tuck, *Philosophy and Government, 1598–1700* (Cambridge, 1993), pp. 3–4.
29. Pennington, *Seventeenth Century*, p. 3.
30. Quoting Reinhard, 'Power Elites', p. 8.
31. Richard Dunn, *The Age of Religious Wars, 1559–1715* (New York, 1979), p. 6.
32. Wootton (ed.), *Divine Right and Democracy*, p. 25.
33. Roger Mettam (ed.), *Government and Society in Louis XIV's France* (London, 1970), p. 153.
34. Pennington, *Europe in the Seventeenth Century*, pp. 264–5; Charles Tilly, *European Revolutions, 1492–1992* (Oxford, 1993), p. 158.
35. Parker and Smith (eds), *General Crisis of the Seventeenth Century*, p. 13.
36. Kossmann, 'Singularity of Absolutism', p. 8.
37. Henry Kamen, *European Society, 1500–1700* (London, 1984), p. 278.
38. On the Irish rebellion, see R. F. Foster, *Modern Ireland, 1600–1972* (London, 1989), pp. 85–100; on the peasant uprising in Austria, see Bonney, *Dynastic States*, pp. 289–90.
39. Pennington, *Seventeenth Century*, pp. 265–6.
40. J. H. Plumb, *The Growth of Political Stability in England, 1675–1725* (Atlantic Highlands, NJ, 1967), p. 1. See also Charles Tilly, 'Reflections on the History of European State-Making' in Tilly (ed.), *The Formation of National States in Western Europe*, pp. 21–5.
41. Cary J. Nederman and Kate Langdon Forhan (eds), *Medieval Political Theory – A Reader: The Quest for the Body Politic, 1100–1400* (New York, 1993), p. 14. Also J. H. Shennan, *Government and Society in France,*

1461– 1661 (London, 1969), pp. 13–14, on the traditional duties of the monarch.

42. Richard Baxter, *A Holy Commonwealth*, ed. William Lamont (Cambridge, 1994), pp. 127, 128; Richard Schlatter, *Richard Baxter and Puritan Politics* (Rutgers, NJ, 1957), p. 23.
43. Geoffrey Symcox (ed.), *War, Diplomacy, and Imperialism, 1618–1783* (New York, 1974), p. 3.
44. In Alister McGrath, *The Intellectual Origins of the Protestant Reformation* (Oxford, 1991), pp. 215–16.
45. Bodo Nishen, 'The Political Thought of John Bergius', *Central European History*, 15, no.3 (1982), 203–23.
46. Pennington, *Seventeenth Century*, p. 2.
47. On the Elizabethan Catholic problem, see Peter Holmes, *Resistance and Compromise: The Political Thought of Elizabethan Catholics* (Cambridge, 1982).
48. Munck, *Seventeenth-Century Europe*, p. 25.
49. Kamen, *European Society*, p. 40.
50. Charles Tilly, *European Revolutions*, 1492–1992 (Oxford, 1993), pp. 157–8.
51. Parker and Smith (eds), *General Crisis*, p. 14. Jeremy Black, *European Warfare, 1660–1815* (New Haven, CT, 1994), pp. 7–10, places the major part of the growth of armies and navies to the second half of the century. See also, Geoffrey Parker, *The Military Revolution: Military Innovation and the Rise of the West, 1500–1800* (Cambridge, 1988).
52. Bodin quoted in Bonney, *Dynastic States*, p. 312.
53. Quoted in Wootton (ed.), *Divine Right*, p. 95.
54. Francis Oakley, *The Medieval Experience: Foundations of Western Cultural Singularity* (Toronto, 1988), p. 112.
55. Quoted in G. N. Clark, *The Seventeenth Century* (Oxford, 1947), p. 219. On St Augustine see Herbert H. Deane, *The Political and Social Ideas of St Augustine* (New York, 1963), pp. 116–53. On Luther see W. D. J. Cargill Thompson, *The Political Thought of Martin Luther* (Totawa, NJ, 1984), pp. 91–111.
56. McGrath, *Reformation Thought*, pp. 207–9, 212. Also Wootton, *Divine Right*, p. 27.
57. Hooker quoted in Paul Rahe, 'Antiquity Surpassed: The Repudiation of Classical Republicanism', in David Wootton (ed.), *Republicanism, Liberty and Commercial Society, 1649–1776* (Stanford, CA, 1994), pp. 241–2.
58. Walter Ullmann, *Principles of Government and Politics in the Middle Ages* (London, 1961), pp. 19–26, introduces the ascending and descending theories of government.
59. David Wootton, 'The Levellers', in *Cambridge History of Political Thought, 1450–1700*, p. 420.

2 Contours of Absolute Monarchy

1. Roger Mettam, 'France', in Miller (ed.), *Absolutism*, pp. 43–4; 'Absolutism', in C. D. Kernig (ed.), *Marxism, Communism and Western Society*, 8 vols (New York, 1972), 1:1.

2. Quoting Herbert H. Rowen, 'Louis XIV and Absolutism' in John C. Rule (ed.), *Louis XIV and the Craft of Kingship* (Columbus, OH, 1969), p. 303.
3. J. H. Burns, 'The Idea of Absolutism' in Miller (ed.), *Absolutism*, p. 21.
4. Perry Anderson, *Lineages of the Absolutist State* (London, 1974). See also James Anderson and Stuart Hill, 'Absolutism and Other Ancestors', in Anderson (ed.), *The Rise of the Modern State* (Atlantic Highlands, NJ, 1986), p. 29.
5. Kiernan, *State and Society*, p. 12; Brian Downing, *The Military Revolution*.
6. Hobbes, *Leviathan*, ed. C. B. MacPherson (Harmondsworth, 1968), p. 187.
7. Bodin, *The Six Books of a Commonweal*, trans. Richard Knolles (London, 1606), ed. K. D. McRae (Cambridge, MA, 1962), p. 84.
8. Nanerl Keohane, *Philosophy and the State in France: the Renaissance to the Enlightenment* (Princeton, NJ, 1980), p. 18; Francis Oakley, *Omnipotence, Covenant and Order* (Ithaca, NY, 1984), p. 93.
9. Harrington, *Oceana*, in J. G. A. Pocock (ed.), *The Political Works of James Harrington* (Cambridge, 1977), p. 264.
10. Quoted in Roland Mousnier, *The Institutions of France under the Absolute Monarchy, 1598–1789*, 2 vols, trans. Arthur Goldhammer (Chicago, 1979–84), 2:657.
11. For coverage of these issues, see Richard Bonney, *Political Change in France under Richelieu and Mazarin, 1624–1661* (Oxford, 1978); Geoffrey Treasure, *Cardinal Richelieu and the Development of Absolutism* (New York, 1972).
12. Cardinal de Retz quoted in Schulze, *States, Nations and Nationalism*, p. 48.
13. Miller (ed.), *Absolutism*, p. 17; Bonney, *Political Change*, pp. 420–1.
14. Munck, *Seventeenth Century*, p. 340.
15. Quoted in A. F. Upton, 'Sweden', in Miller (ed.), *Absolutism*, p. 116.
16. Philip Longworth, 'The Emergence of Absolutism in Russia', in Miller (ed.), *Absolutism*, pp. 175–93. See also Longworth, *Alexis, Tsar of all the Russias* (New York, 1984), and Paul Dukes, *The Making of Russian Absolutism, 1613–1801* (New York, 1982), pp. 1–58.
17. G. Durand, 'What is Absolutism', in Ragnhild Hatton (ed.), *Louis XIV and Absolutism* (Columbus, OH, 1976), pp. 19–21; Herbert W. Rowan, 'Kingship and Republicanism in the Seventeenth Century', in Charles H. Carter (ed.), *From the Renaissance to the Counter-Reformation* (New York, 1965), p. 424.
18. Schulze, *States, Nations, Nationalism*, pp. 58–60; Mettam, 'France', in Miller (ed.), *Absolutism*, pp. 43–67.
19. Bonney, *European Dynastic States*, p. 340.
20. Keohane, *Philosophy and the State*, p. 3.
21. Wootton, *Divine Right*, p. 24. For background on this period see, more generally, Derik Hirst, *Authority and Conflict: England, 1603–1658* (New York, 1986) and J. P. Kenyon, *Stuart England* (Harmondsworth, 1978).
22. Kiernan, *State and Society*, p. 30. See also Henry Kamen, *Golden Age Spain* (Atlantic Highlands, NJ, 1988), pp. 37–49.
23. I. A. A. Thompson, 'Castile', in Miller (ed.), *Absolutism*, p. 70.
24. Pennington, *Europe in the Seventeenth-Century*, pp. 383–4.
25. Munck, *Seventeenth Century*, p. 51.

26. For a useful discussion of Spain's position relative to the other great powers at this juncture, see Paul Kennedy, *Rise and Fall of the Great Powers* (New York, 1989), pp. 31–72.

27. Margaret Judson, *The Crisis of the Constitution, 1603–1645* (New York, 1964, first published 1949), p. 138.

28. John Dunster quoted in ibid., p. 184.

29. W. H. Greenleaf, *Order, Empiricism and Politics* (Oxford, 1964), p. 53. See also Glenn Burgess, *The Politics of the Ancient Constitution: An Introduction to English Political Thought, 1603–1642* (London, 1992), p. 132.

30. Burgess, *Ancient Constitution*, p. 134.

31. C. V. Wedgewood, *Strafford, 1593–1641* (London, 1935), p. 75.

32. Robert Eccleshall, *Order and Reason in Politics*, pp. 47–8.

33. Judson, *Crisis*, p. 179.

34. Quoting Antony Black, *Monarchy and Community: Political Ideas in the Later Conciliar Controversy* (Cambridge, 1970), p. 1.

35. Francisco Suarez, *A Defense of the Catholic and Apostolic Faith against the Errors of the Anglican Sect* (1612) in *Selections from Three Works*, 2 vols, trans. G. L. Williams (Oxford, 1944), 2:697.

36. James I, *The Political Works of James I*, ed. Charles H. MacIlwain (New York, 1965, first published 1946), p. 74.

37. Seller quoted in Skinner, *Foundations*, 2:73–4.

38. Skinner, *Foundations*, 2:113.

39. William of Ockham, 'Eight Questions on the Power of the Pope', in Ockham, *A Letter to the Friars Minor and Other Writings*, ed. A. S. McGrade, trans. John Kilcullen (Cambridge, 1995), pp. 303–33.

40. Roland Mousnier, *The Assassination of Henry IV*, trans. Joan Spencer (New York, 1973), pp. 161–2.

41. Nederman and Forham (eds), *Medieval Political Theory*, p. 14.

42. On the anointing of kings, see Roland Mousnier, *The Institutions of France under the Absolute Monarchy*, 2: 654–6.

43. Coke quoted in Judson, *Crisis*, p. 17.

44. Judson, *Crisis*, p. 149. Cf. Glenn Burgess, *Absolute Monarchy and the Stuart Constitution* (New Haven, CT, 1996), esp. ch.2.

45. Quoted in J. H. Shennan, *Government and Society in France, 1461–1661* (New York, 1969), pp. 82–3.

46. Downing, *Military Revolution*, p. 141.

47. John Locke, *Two Treatises of Government*, ed. Peter Laslett (Cambridge, 1965), 1.1.

48. Bucer quoted in McGrath, *Reformation Thought*, p. 214.

49. Bossuet, *Politics Drawn from the Very Word of Holy Scripture*, ed. and trans. Patrick Riley (Cambridge, 1990), p. 61.

50. Romans 10.12.

51. J. M. Kelly, *A Short History of Western Legal Theory* (Oxford, 1992), pp. 57–8.

52. Cicero, *De Legibus*, trans. C. W. Keys (Cambridge, MA, 1961, first published 1928), 1.6.18–19.

53. Ibid., 1.15.42.

54. Kelly, *Western Legal Theory*, p. 103. See also Donald R. Kelley, *The Human Measure: Social Thought in the Western Legal Tradition* (Cambridge, MA, 1990), pp. 68–9.
55. Skinner, *Foundations*, 2:148–9; Suarez, *A Treatise on Laws and God the Lawgiver* in *Selections From Three Works*, 2:41.
56. Bernice Hamilton, *Political Thought in Sixteenth-Century Spain* (Oxford, 1963), pp. 28–9.
57. J. P. Sommerville, *Politics and Ideology in England, 1603–1640* (New York, 1986), pp. 14–15; Friedrich, *Age of the Baroque*, p. 22.
58. Judson, *Crisis*, p. 22.
59. Fleetwood quoted in Sommerville, *Politics and Ideology*, p. 97.
60. Bacon quoted in Judson, *Crisis*, p. 133.
61. Thompson, 'Castile' in Miller (ed.), *Absolutism*, p. 72.
62. Preston King, *The Ideology of Order: a Comparative Analysis of Jean Bodin and Thomas Hobbes* (New York, 1974), p. 73.
63. Kenneth D. McRae (ed.), *The Six Books of a Republic* (Cambridge, MA, 1962), p. A63.
64. King, *Ideology of Order*, pp. 41–3; also Robert Kingdon, 'Calvinism and Resistance Theory', in Burns (ed.), *Cambridge History of Political Thought*, p. 207.
65. Bodin, *Six Books*, ed. McRae, p. 18.
66. Ibid., p. 51.
67. Bodin, *Six Books*, ed. McRae, p. 20.
68. Richard Baxter, *A Holy Commonwealth*, ed. William Lamont (Cambridge, 1994), p. 124.
69. Bodin, *Six Books*, in Julian Franklin (ed.), *Bodin On Sovereignty* (Cambridge, 1992), p. 86.
70. Ibid., pp. 89–90.
71. Julian Franklin (trans. and ed.), *Constitutionalism and Resistance in the Sixteenth Century: Three Treatises by Hotman, Beza, and Mornay* (New York, 1969), pp. 16–17.
72. Locke, *Two Treatises*, 2:200. Robert Zaller, 'The Tyrant in English Revolutionary Thought', *Journal of the History of Ideas*, 54 (1993), 589–590.
73. Johann P. Sommerville, 'James I and the divine right of Kings', in Linda Levy Peck (ed.), *The Mental World of the Jacobean Court* (Cambridge, 1991), pp. 58–9.
74. Corinne C. Weston, 'England, Ancient Constitution and Common Law', in Burns (ed.), *Cambridge History of Political Thought*, p. 374.
75. Johann P. Sommerville (ed.), *King James VI and I: Political Writings* (Cambridge, 1994), pp. xv–xviii.
76. McIlwain (ed.), *The Political Works of James I*, p. 62.
77. *Trew Law*, in Sommerville (ed.), p. 72.
78. *Trew Law*, p. 69.
79. Jenny Wormald, 'James VI and I, Basilikon Doron and the Trew Law of Free Monarchies: the Scottish context and the English translation', in Linda Levy Peck (ed.), *The Mental World of the Jacobean Court*, p. 51.
80. *Basilicon Doron*, in Sommerville (ed.), *Political Writings*, pp. 12, 13.
81. Ibid., p. 20.

82. Ibid., pp. 183,184.
83. *Trew Law*, in ibid., p. 63.
84. Ibid., p. 214.
85. Ibid., pp. xvii, 63.
86. Robert Filmer, *Patriarcha*, in J.P. Sommerville (ed.), *Patriarcha and Other Writings* (Cambridge, 1991), p. 2.
87. William Barclay, *The Kingdom and the Royal Power*, quoted in Bonney, *Dynastic States*, p. 559, n. 13.
88. Gordon Schochet, *Patriarchalism in Political Thought* (New York, 1975), pp. 63, 73; Sommerville, *Politics and Ideology*, p. 27.
89. Schochet, *Patriarchalism*, p. 19; Sommerville, 'Absolutism and Royalism', in Burns (ed.), *Cambridge History*, p. 355.
90. Patrick Riley (ed.), *Politics Drawn from the Very Word of Holy Scripture* (Cambridge, 1991), p. xv.
91. Quoted in Mousnier, *Institutions of France*, 2:671.
92. Riley (ed.), *Politics*, pp. xiv, xxx.
93. Skinner, *Foundations*, 2:113.
94. Quoted in Riley (ed.), *Politics*, p. xxv.
95. Christopher Hill, *The Bible and the Seventeenth-Century Revolution* (Harmondsworth, 1994), p. 20.
96. Ibid., pp. 5, 15.
97. Riley (ed.), *Politics*, p. xlii.
98. Ibid., pp. 45, 47.
99. Ibid., p. 52.
100. Saravia quoted in Johan P. Sommerville, *Thomas Hobbes: Political Ideas in Historical Context* (London, 1992), p. 83.
101. Quoted in Sommerville, *Politics and Ideology*, p. 32.
102. Filmer, *Patriarcha*, p. 11.
103. Sommerville, *Politics and Ideology*, p. 30.
104. Schochet, *Patriarchalism*, pp. 6, 15, 76–81.
105. Kossman, 'Significance of Absolutism', p. 11.

3 Constitutions and Consent

1. William Molyneux, *The Case of Ireland's being Bound by Acts of Parliament in England Stated* (Dublin, 1698), p. 100.
2. James M. Blythe, *Ideal Government and the Mixed Constitution in the Middle Ages* (Princeton, NJ, 1992), p. 3. For the French example, see also Julian H. Franklin, *Jean Bodin and the Rise of Absolutist Theory* (Cambridge, 1973), ch. 1: 'The Persistence of Medieval Constitutionalism'.
3. Hagen Schulze, *States, Nations and Nationalism* (Oxford, 1996), p. 21.
4. Quoting Francis Oakley, *Medieval Experience*, p. 106.

5. Upton, 'Sweden', in Miller (ed.), *Absolutism*, p. 104.
6. Nicholas Henshall, *The Myth of Absolutism: Change and Continuity in early modern European Monarchy* (New York, 1992), pp. 120–1.
7. Wootton, *Divine Right*, p. 37.
8. Tierney, *Constitutional Thought*, p. x.
9. A thorough treatment of this tradition is presented in J. G. A. Pocock, *The Machiavellian Moment: Florentine Political Thought and the Atlantic Republican Tradition* (Princeton, NJ, 1975), esp. ch. 3. See also Sommerville, *Politics and Ideology*, pp. 58–9.
10. Deane, *Political and Social Ideas of St Augustine*, pp. 116–53; Tierney, *Constitutional Thought*, p. 39.
11. Quoting Blythe, *Ideal Government*, p. 5.
12. John Procope, 'Greek and Roman political theory', in J. H. Burns (ed.), *The Cambridge History of Medieval Political Theory* (Cambridge, 1988), p. 23; Robert Eccleshall, *Order and Reason in Politics: Theories of Absolute and Limited Monarchy in early modern England* (Oxford, 1978), p. 53.
13. Aristotle, *The Politics*, trans. Carnes Lord (Chicago, 1984), p. 35 (book 1, ch. 1).
14. Ibid., p. 37 (book 1, ch. 2).
15. Ibid., p. 101 (bk 3, ch.11).
16. Paul E. Sigmond, 'Law and Politics', in Norman Kretzmann and Eleanor Stump (eds), *The Cambridge Companion to Aquinas* (Cambridge, 1993), p. 220; Eccleshall, *Order and Reason*, p. 62.
17. Downing, *Military Revolution*, p. 30; Joseph R. Strayer, *On the Medieval Origins of the Modern State* (Princeton, NJ, 1970), pp. 65–6; Neithard Bulst, 'Rulers, Representative Institutions, and their Members', in Reinhard (ed.), *Power Elites and State Building*, p. 47.
18. Marsilius of Padua, *Defensor Pacis*, trans. Alan Gewirth (Toronto, 1986), p. 32. George H. Sabine, *A History of Political Theory*, 4th edition revised by T. L. Thorson (Hillsdale, IL, 1973), pp. 271–85, contains a useful discussion of Marsilius.
19. Walter Ullmann, *The Individual and Society in the Middle Ages* (Baltimore, MD, 1966), pp. 56–8; Antony Black, *Guilds and Civil Society in European Political Thought from the Twelfth Century to the Present* (Ithaca, NY, 1984), pp. 76–85; Tierney, *Constitutional Thought*, pp. 10–11; Downing, *Military Revolution*, pp. 19–22.
20. Tierney, *Constitutional Thought*, p. 17. On the significance of the conciliar movement, see Antony Black, *Monarchy and Community: Political Ideas in the Later Conciliar Controversy, 1430–1450* (Cambridge, 1970). See also Black's contribution in J. H. Burns (ed.), *The Cambridge History of Medieval Political Thought* (Cambridge, 1986), pp. 573–87. F. Oakley, 'On the Road from Constance to 1688', *Journal Of British Studies*, 1 (1962), 1–32, treats some of the connections between medieval theory and seventeenth-century practice.
21. Blythe, *Ideal Government*, pp. 248–9; J. N. Figgis, *Studies in Political Thought from Gerson to Grotius, 1414–1625* (New York, 1960), pp. 55–70; Tierney, *Constitutional Thought*, p. 93.

22. Blythe, *Ideal Government*, p. 248; Joseph Canning, *A History of Medieval Political Thought* (London, 1996), pp. 177–8; Antony Black, 'Conciliarism', in Burns (ed.), *Cambridge History of Medieval Political Thought*, p. 549; Tierney, *Constitutional Thought*, p. 95.
23. Skinner, *Foundations*, 2:117.
24. Quoted in Tierney, *Constitutional Thought*, p. 66. See also A. Black, 'Conciliarism', in Burns (ed.), *Cambridge History of Medieval Political Thought*, pp. 582–7; Canning, *Medieval Political Thought*, pp. 183–4, and Sabine, *Political Theory*, pp. 298–9.
25. Black, *Monarchy and Community*, pp. 3–6.
26. Figgis, *Studies in Political Thought*, p. 63.
27. Skinner, *Foundations*, 2:114.
28. Ibid., 2: 121–3.
29. Prynne quoted in Tierney, *Constitutionalism*, p. 82.
30. Howell Lloyd, 'Constitutionalism', in Burns (ed.), *Cambridge History*, pp. 287–8. Biographical information from Frederick S. Carney (trans.), *The Politics of Johannes Althusius* (London, 1960), pp. xiv–xvi.
31. Althusius, *The Politics*, p. 34.
32. W. A. Dunning, *A History of Political Theories from Luther to Montesquieu* (London, 1927), pp. 62–5.
33. Lloyd, 'Constitutionalism', in Burns (ed.), *Cambridge History*, p. 289. See also Otto Gierke, *Natural Law and the Theory of Society, 1500–1800*, trans. Ernest Barker (Cambridge, 1950), pp. 70–9.
34. Althusius, *The Politics*, p. 181.
35. Bonney, *European Dynastic States*, p. 308; Thompson, *Political Thought of Luther*, pp. 91–3; John Calvin, *On God and Political Duty*, ed. J. T. McNeill (New York, 1956), pp. xii–xiv.
36. Thompson, *Luther*, p. 92; Skinner, *Foundations*, 2:218.
37. Kingdon, 'Calvinism and Resistance Theory', in Burns (ed.), *Cambridge History*, pp. 200–3.
38. Skinner, *Foundations*, 2:223; Mousnier, *Assassination of Henry IV*, p. 90. More generally, see M. M. Knappen, *Tudor Puritanism: a Chapter in the History of Idealism* (Chicago, 1966), and Edmund Morgan (ed.), *Puritan Political Ideas, 1558–1794* (Indianapolis, IN, 1965).
39. Ponet quoted in Peter Holmes, *Resistance and Compromise: the Political Thought of the Elizabethan Catholics* (Cambridge, 1982), p. 4.
40. Kingdon, 'Calvinism and Resistance Theory', in Burns (ed.), *Cambridge History*, p. 216; J. H. Burns, *The True Law of Kingship: Concepts of Monarchy in Early Modern Scotland* (Oxford, 1996), pp. 185–221, provides the best coverage on Buchanan.
41. George Buchanan, *De jure regni apud Scotus, or A Dialogue, concerning the due Privilege of Government, in the Kingdom of Scotland* (Philadelphia, PA, 1766), p. 86.
42. Donald Kelley, *Francis Hotman: A Revolutionary's Ordeal* (Princeton, NJ, 1973), pp. 238–49, provides a useful analysis.
43. Francis Hotman, *Francogallia*, in Julian H. Franklin (ed.), *Constitutionalism and Resistance in the Sixteenth Century: Three Treatises by Hotman, Beza and Mornay* (New York, 1960), p. 55.

44. Ibid., 66.
45. Kingdon, 'Calvinism and Resistance Theory', in Burns (ed.), *Cambridge History*, p. 209.
46. Franklin (ed.), *Constitutionalism and Resistance*, pp. 30, 32.
47. Beza, *Right of Magistrates*, in Franklin (ed.), p. 108.
48. Ibid., pp. 110, 112.
49. Kingdon, 'Constitutionalism and Resistance', in *Cambridge History*, p. 211.
50. Quoting Herbert Rowen, *The King's State: Proprietary Dynasticism in Early Modern France* (New Brunswick, NJ, 1980), p. 37.
51. Franklin (ed.), *Constitutionalism and Resistance*, p. 40.
52. *Vindiciae contra tyrannos*, in Franklin (ed.), *Constitutionalism and Resistance*, p. 155. Ellen Meiksins Wood, 'The State and Popular Sovereignty in French Political Thought: A Genealogy of Rousseau's "General Will"', *History of Political Thought*, 4, no. 2 (1983), 292–3, emphasizes the corporate nature of Huguenot resistance theory.
53. *Vindiciae*, in Franklin (ed.), p. 156.
54. Ibid., p. 190.
55. On the Catholic League see Mousnier, *Assassination of Henry IV*, pp. 213–30; Frederic Baumgartner, *Radical Reactionaries: The Political Thought of the Seventeenth-Century French Catholic League* (Geneva, 1976); J. W. Allen, *English Political Thought, 1603–1644* (London, 1938), p. 344.
56. J. H. M. Salmon, 'Catholic Resistance Theory', in Burns (ed.), *Cambridge History*, p. 228.
57. Allen, *English Political Thought*, pp. 349, 354.
58. Holmes, *Resistance and Compromise*, pp. 131–5.
59. Mariana, *The King and the Education of the King* (1599), quoted in Bonney, *European Dynastic States*, p. 311.
60. Suarez quoted in Skinner, *Foundations*, 2:139.
61. Skinner, *Foundations*, 2:154–5, 160.
62. Suarez, *On Laws and God the Lawgiver* in *Selections from Three Works*, trans. G. L. Williams (Oxford, 1944), pp. 374–5, 383.
63. Quoting Skinner, *Foundations*, 2:174.
64. Guy Howard Dodge, *The Political Theory of the Huguenots of the Dispersion* (New York, 1947), pp. 6–7; Paul Hazard, *The European Mind, 1680–1715*, trans. J. Lewis May (New York, 1952), p. 83.
65. W. J. Stankiewicz, *Politics and Religion in Seventeenth-Century France* (Berkeley, CA, 1960), pp. 206–7.
66. Henry IV quoted in Rowen, *The King's State*, p. 51.
67. Quoted in Keohane, *Philosophy and the State*, p. 316.
68. Burgess, *Politics of the Ancient Constitution*, pp. 15–18. J. G. Pocock, *The Ancient Constitution and the Feudal Law* (Cambridge, 1959, reissued 1987) is the classic study of the phenomenon in England.
69. Weston, 'Ancient Constitution' in *Cambridge History*, p. 374.
70. Burgess, *Politics of the Ancient Constitution*, p. 3.
71. John Fortescue, *A Learned Compendium of the Politique Lawes of England* (Amsterdam, 1969), p. 26.

72. Weston, 'Ancient Constitution' in *Cambridge History*, p. 375. On Coke see James Reist Stoner, *Common Law and Liberal Theory* (Lawrence, KS, 1992), pp. 13–68.
73. Sommerville, *Politics and Ideology*, p. 92.
74. Burgess, *Politics of the Ancient Constitution*, p. 120.
75. Sommerville, *Politics and Ideology*, p. 88.
76. Hooker, *Of the Laws of Ecclesiastical Polity*, 8.2.11; 8.2.7. Robert K. Faulkner, *Richard Hooker and the Politics of a Christian England* (Berkeley, CA, 1981), pp. 99–117.
77. Sommerville, *Politics and Ideology*, pp. 11–12.
78. Arthur P. Monohan, *From Personal Duties Towards Personal Rights* (London, 1994), p. 281.
79. George Lawson, *Politica Sacra*, ed. Conal Condren (Cambridge, 1992), pp. ix–xviii.
80. Tierney, *Constitutional Thought*, p. 97.
81. Lawson, *Politica Sacra*, p. x.
82. Ibid., p. 226.
83. Ibid., pp. 25, 29.
84. Tierney, *Constitutional Thought*, pp. 99–100.
85. Lawson, *Politica*, quoted in Julian H. Franklin, *John Locke and the Theory of Sovereignty*, p. 78.
86. Peter Laslett (ed.), *Two Treatises of Government* (Cambridge, 1963), p. 72, fn #33.
87. Locke, *Two Treatises*, 2:220.
88. W. M. Spellman, *John Locke* (London, 1997), pp. 98–121.
89. Locke's early political views are expressed in his *Two Tracts on Government*, never published in his lifetime. Philip Abrams (ed.), *Two Tracts on Government* (Cambridge, 1969).
90. Richard Ashcraft, *Locke's Two treatises of Government* (London, 1987), p. 21. On Shaftesbury's career see K. H. D. Haley, *The First Earl of Shaftesbury* (Oxford, 1968).
91. John Marshall, *Locke: Resistance, Religion and Responsibility* (Cambridge, 1994), and Ian Harris, *The Mind of John Locke* (Cambridge, 1994), are now essential studies on Locke's political ideas during this crucial period.
92. John Locke, *Works* (London, 1823), 2:360.
93. Locke, *Essays on the Law of Nature*, ed. W. von Leyden (Oxford, 1954), p. 109.
94. *Two Treatises*, 2:76.
95. Ibid., 2:74, 105.
96. Ibid., 2:76.
97. Schochet, *Patriarchalism in Political Thought*, pp. 259–60.
98. *Two Treatises*, 1:52; 2:56.
99. Ibid., 2:52, 116.
100. Suarez quoted in Skinner, *Foundations*, 2:155–6.
101. *Two Treatises*, 2:6,8.
102. Ibid., 2:123.
103. Ibid., 2:124,125,126.
104. Ibid., 2:10,123.

105. Ibid., 2:2.
106. Ibid, 2:4, 6, 23.
107. Walter Ullmann, *The Individual and Society in the Middle Ages* (Baltimore, MD, 1966).
108. Ullmann, *Principles of Government and Politics in the Middle Ages* (London, 1961), pp. 19–26.

4   Republicanism Rekindled

1.   R. N. Berki, 'Republic/Republicanism' in *The Blackwell Encyclopedia of Political Institutions* (Oxford, 1987), p. 534; Herbert H. Rowen, 'Kingship and Republicanism in the Seventeenth Century' in C. H. Carter (ed.), *From the Renaissance to the Counter-Reformation* (New York, 1965), pp. 428–9.
2.   Quentin Skinner, 'The Italian City-Republics' in John Dunn (ed.), *Democracy: The Unfinished Journey* (Oxford, 1993), pp. 57–69; Margaret Canovan, 'Republicanism', in *The Encyclopedia of Democracy* (Berkeley, CA, 1968), pp. 3–5.
3.   Machiavelli, *Discourses*, ed. Bernard Crick (Harmondsworth, 1984), book 2, ch. 2.
4.   Arthur Herman, 'The Huguenot Republic and Antirepublicanism in Seventeenth-Century France', *Journal of the History of Ideas*, 53 (1992), 249–69.
5.   Quoting John Dunn, 'The Identity of the Bourgeois Liberal Republic', in Biancamaria Fontana (ed.), *The Invention of the Modern Republic* (Cambridge, 1994), p. 206.
6.   Blair Worden, 'English Republicanism', in *Cambridge History*, p. 443.
7.   Dunn, 'Bourgeois Liberal Republic', p. 208.
8.   Linda Kirk, 'Genevan Republicanism', in David Wootton (ed.), *Republicanism, Liberty, and Commercial Society, 1649–1776* (Stanford, CA, 1994), p. 270.
9.   For a discussion see William J. Bouwsma, *Venice and the Defense of Republican Liberty* (Berkeley, CA, 1968), pp. 3–5.
10. E. H. Kossmann, 'Freedom in Dutch Thought and Practice', in Jonathan I. Israel (ed.), *The Anglo-Dutch Moment* (Cambridge, 1991), p. 287. See also Jonathan Israel, *The Dutch Republic: Its Rise, Greatness, and Fall, 1477–1806* (Oxford, 1995), p. 215.
11. Eco Haitsma Mulier, 'The Language of Seventeenth-century Republicanism in the United Provinces: Dutch or European?', in Anthony Pagden (ed.), *The Languages of Political Theory in Early Modern Europe* (Cambridge, 1987), p. 179. See also Kossmann, 'The Development of Dutch Political Theory in the Seventeenth Century', in J. S. Bromley and E. H. Kossmann (eds), *Britain and the Netherlands* (London, 1959), p. 91.
12. Herbert W. Rowen, 'The Dutch Republic and the Idea of Freedom', in *Republicanism, Liberty, and Commercial Society*, pp. 310–12.

13. See J. L. Price, *Culture and Society in the Dutch Republic during the Seventeenth Century* (London, 1974).

14. Mulier, 'Language of Seventeenth-Century Republicanism', p. 187; Kossmann, 'Freedom in Dutch Thought and Practice', p. 288.

15. Kossmann, 'Dutch Thought and Practice', p. 290.

16. Martin van Gelderen, *The Political Thought of the Dutch Revolt: 1555–1590* (Cambridge, 1992), p. 271.

17. Ibid., pp. 262–3.

18. Ibid., pp. 263, 264, 273.

19. Blair Worden, 'Marchamont Nedham and the Beginnings of English Republicanism, 1649–1656', in *Republicanism, Liberty and Commercial Society*, p. 46. For the later development of these ideas in England, see Caroline Robbins, *The Eighteenth-Century Commonwealthman* (London, 1959); and in America, see Bernard Bailyn, *The Ideological Origins of the American Revolution* (Cambridge, MA, 1967).

20. Worden, 'Marchamont Nedham', p. 45.

21. Ibid., 51.

22. David Wootton, 'The Republican Tradition: From Commonwealth to Common Sense', in *Republicanism, Liberty and Commercial Society*, p. 5.

23. Glenn Burgess, 'Impact of the Civil War', in John Morrill (ed.), *Revolution and Restoration: England in the 1650s* (London, 1991), p. 73.

24. F. D. Dow, *Radicalism in the English Revolution, 1640–1660* (Oxford, 1985), p. 12.

25. Morrill (ed.), *Revolution and Restoration*, pp. 8–10, and Jonathan Scott, 'The English Republican Imagination', in *Revolution and Restoration*, p. 36.

26. Christopher Hill, *The World Turned Upside Down* (New York, 1972), p. 77.

27. David L. Smith, 'The Struggle for New Constitutional and Institutional Forms', in *Revolution and Restoration*, p. 16.

28. Ascham quoted in Wootton (ed.), *Divine Right*, pp. 340–1.

29. Hobbes quoted in Andrew Sharp (ed.), *Political Ideas of the English Civil Wars* (London, 1983), pp. 234–5.

30. John Sanderson, *'But the people's creatures':The Philosophical Basis of the English Civil War* (New York, 1989), pp. 128–9.

31. Martin Dzelzainis (ed.), *John Milton: Political Writings*, trans. Claire Gruzelier (Cambridge, 1991), p. xi.

32. Ibid., p. ix. See also Christopher Hill, *Milton and the English Revolution* (New York, 1978).

33. Dzelzainis (ed.), *Political Writings*, p. xii.

34. Ibid., p. xiii.

35. Milton, *Tenure of Kings and Magistrates*, in *Political Writings*, p. 18.

36. Dzelzainis (ed.), *Political Writings*, p. xv.

37. Milton, *Tenure*, p. 17.

38. Ibid., p. 8.

39. Milton, *A Defense of the People of England* (1651), in Sanderson, *Philosophical Basis*, p. 132.

40. Ibid.

41. Dzelzainis (ed.), *Political Writings*, p. xviii.
42. Milton, *A Defense*, in *Political Writings*, p. 108.
43. *Second Defense*, quoted in Sanderson, *Philosophical Basis*, p. 136.
44. Milton, *Ready and Easy Way*, quoted in Worden, 'English Republicanism' in *Cambridge History*, p. 456.
45. Wootton, *Divine Right and Democracy*, p. 39.
46. Quoting Andrew Sharp, *Political Ideas of the English Civil Wars*, p. 19.
47. Wootton, *Divine Right*, p. 17. For a representative selection of Leveller writings, see G. E. Aylmer (ed.), *The Levellers in the English Revolution* (New York, 1975), and Don M. Wolfe (ed.), *Leveller Manifestoes of the Puritan Revolution* (New York, 1967).
48. David Wootton, 'The Levellers' in John Dunn (ed.), *Democracy: The Unfinished Journey* (Oxford, 1992), p. 71.
49. Derik Hirst, *Authority and Conflict: England, 1603–1658* (Cambridge, MA, 1986), p. 272.
50. Wootton, 'The Levellers', in Dunn (ed.), *Democracy: The Unfinished Journey*, p. 82.
51. Perez Zagorin, *History of Political Thought in the English Revolution* (London, 1954), pp. 9–11.
52. Wootton, 'Leveller Democracy and the Puritan Revolution', in *Cambridge History*, p. 414. See also 'A Remonstrance of Many Thousand Citizens' (1646), in Jack R. McMichael and Brian Taft (eds), *The Writings of William Walwyn* (Athens, GA, 1989), pp. 225–6, for an early statement of the Leveller programme.
53. Pocock, *Ancient Constitution*, p. 126.
54. Ronald Hutton, *The British Republic 1649–1660* (London, 1987), pp. 13–14.
55. Zagorin, *History of Political Thought*, p. 9. See, for example, Walwyn, *Toleration Justified, and Persecution Condemned* (1645–6) in *Writings*, pp. 154–72.
56. John Lilburne, *The Free man's Freedom Vindicated* in Dow (ed.), *Radicalism*, p. 37.
57. Wootton, 'Leveller Democracy', in *Cambridge History*, p. 415.
58. Dow (ed.), *Radicalism*, p. 65.
59. Gerrard Winstanley, *The Saints Paradise* (abstract) in George H. Sabine (ed.), *The Works of Gerrard Winstanley* (New York, 1965), p. 94.
60. Hutton, *British Republic*, pp. 31–2.
61. Winstanley, *The New Law of Righteousness* (1649), in *Writings*, p. 159.
62. Hutton, *British Republic*, p. 32.
63. Zagorin, *History of Political Thought*, pp. 149–50.
64. James Harrington, *The Commonwealth of Oceana* and *A System of Politics*, ed. J. G. A. Pocock (Cambridge, 1992), p. viii.
65. Pocock, *Ancient Constitution*, p. 145.
66. Zagorin, *Political Thought*, p. 133.
67. Harrington, *Oceana*, quoted in Zagorin, pp. 134–5.
68. Jonathan Scott, 'The English Republican Imagination', in Morrill (ed.), *Revolution and Restoration*, p. 46.
69. James Harrington, *Oceana*, in Pocock (ed.), pp. 11–12; Pocock, *Ancient Constitution*, p. 129.

70. Harrington, *Oceana*, in Pocock (ed.), p. 13.
71. Ibid., p. 24.
72. Pocock (ed.), p. ix.
73. Ibid., p. xix; Zagorin, *History of Political Thought*, p. 137.
74. Blair Worden, 'James Harrington and the Commonwealth of Oceana', in *Republicanism, Liberty and Commercial Society*, p. 100; also Skinner, *Foundations*, 1:44–5.
75. *Oceana*, in *The Political Works of James Harrington*, ed. J. G. A. Pocock (Cambridge, 1977), p. 320.
76. Blair Worden, 'Oceana: Origins and Aftermath', in *Republicanism, Liberty and Commercial Society*, p. 318.
77. Worden, 'Republicanism and the Restoration', in *Republicanism, Liberty and Commercial Society*, p. 148.
78. Caroline Robbins (ed.), *Two English Republican Tracts* (London, 1969), p. 68.
79. Worden, 'English Republicanism', in *Cambridge History*, p. 461.
80. Ibid., p. 459.
81. Ibid., p. 156.
82. Ibid., p. 167.
83. Ibid., p. 460.

5   The Emergence of the Modern State

1. On the characteristics of the state see Antony Black, *Political Thought in Europe, 1250–1450* (Cambridge, 1992), pp. 186–7.
2. F. H. Hinsley, *Sovereignty* (Cambridge, 1986), p. 142.
3. Michael Zuckert, *Natural Rights and the New Republicanism* (Princeton, NJ, 1994), p. 120.
4. Kelly, *History of Western Legal Theory*, pp. 14–15.
5. Biographical information on Grotius from Tuck, *Philosophy and Government*, pp. 154–6.
6. For details on this dispute, see Israel, *The Dutch Republic*, pp. 450–60.
7. C. Bangs, *Arminius: A Study in the Dutch Reformation* (Nashville, TN, 1973).
8. Tuck, *Philosophy and Government*, pp. 184–5.
9. Hugo Grotius quoted in Tuck, *Philosophy and Government*, p. 186.
10. Ibid., 183.
11. Tuck, 'Grotius and Selden', in Burns (ed.), *Cambridge History*, p. 501.
12. Ibid., p. 506; *Philosophy and Government*, p. 173.
13. Grotius quoted in Tuck, *Philosophy and Government*, p. 173.
14. Richard Cox, 'Grotius', in *History of Political Philosophy*, ed. Leo Strauss and Joseph Cropsey (Chicago, 1987), p. 387.
15. Locke, *Two Treatises*, 2.6.
16. Grotius, *The Law of War and Peace*, trans. Francis W. Kelsey (Indianapolis, IN, 1925), p. 38.
17. Grotius quoted in Tuck, 'Grotius and Selden', in *Cambridge History*, pp. 516, 517. See also Grotius, *The Law of War and Peace*, p. 27.

18. Grotius, *Law of War and Peace*, p. 13.
19. Thomas Hobbes, *Leviathan*, ed. Richard Tuck (Cambridge, 1991), p. 109.
20. Ibid., 91.
21. See James Tully's introduction to Samuel Pufendorf, *On the Duty of Man and Citizen According to Natural Law*, trans. Michael Silverthorne (Cambridge, 1991), p. xx.
22. See Craig L. Carr's introduction to *The Political Writings of Samuel Pufendorf*, trans. Michael J. Sadler (Oxford, 1994), pp. 4–5.
23. Tully's introduction to *On the Duty of Man and Citizen*, pp. xvi–xvii.
24. Carr (ed.), *Political Writings of Pufendorf*, pp. 3–5. See also Alfred Dufour, 'Pufendorf', in *Cambridge History*, pp. 561–3.
25. Pufendorf, *On the Law of Nature and Nations*, in *Political Writings*, pp. 144–8; Dufour, 'Pufendorf', p. 566.
26. *Of the Law of Nature and Nations*, in *Political Writings*, pp. 151–2. See also J. W. Gough, *The Social Contract* (Oxford, 1957), pp. 119–20.
27. Pufendorf, *On the Duty of Man and Citizen*, p. 132.
28. Ibid., 7.
29. Ibid., 10.
30. Tully, introduction to Pufendorf, *On the Duty of Man and Citizen*, p. xxiii.
31. Ibid., p. xxvi.
32. *On the Duty of Man and Citizen*, p. 62.
33. Grotius quoted in Zuckert, *Natural Rights and Republicanism*, p. 122.
34. Grotius, *Law of War and Peace*, p. 104.
35. Brad S. Gregory, introduction to *Tractatus theologico politicus*, trans. Samuel Shirley (New York, 1989), pp. 27, 31.
36. For the most recent biographical sketch, see W. N. A. Klever, 'Spinoza's Life and Work', in Don Garrett (ed.), *The Cambridge Companion to Spinoza* (Cambridge, 1996), pp. 13–53. Also Gregory, introduction to *Tractatus theologico politicus*, p. 4.
37. Robert Rowen, *John de Witt* (Princeton, NJ, 1978); Israel, *The Dutch Republic*, pp. 726–38.
38. Rowen, *John de Witt*, pp. 436, 439.
39. Roger Scruton, *Spinoza* (Oxford, 1986), pp. 10–11.
40. Noel Malcolm, 'Hobbes and Spinoza', in *Cambridge History*, p. 547.
41. Spinoza, *Tractatus theologico*, trans. Shirley, p. 53.
42. Ibid., 10.
43. Alan Donogan, *Spinoza* (Chicago, 1988), p. 8.
44. *Treatise on the Emendation of the Intellect*, in Edwin Curley (ed. and trans.), *The Collected Works of Spinoza*, 2 vols (Princeton, NJ, 1985), 1:11.
45. Errol E. Harris, *Spinoza's Philosophy: An Outline* (Atlantic Highlands, NJ, 1992), p. 24.
46. *Tractatus theologico*, p. 293.
47. Ibid., p. 292.
48. Ibid., p. 298.
49. Scruton, *Spinoza*, pp. 93–6.
50. *Tractatus theologico*, p. 284.
51. Zuckert, *Natural Rights and the New Republicanism*, p. 3.

52. Jeremy Bentham quoted in Maurice Cranston, 'Human Rights, Real and Supposed', in D. D. Raphael (ed.), *Political Theory and the Rights of Man* (Bloomington, IN, 1967), p. 44.
53. Brian Tierney, 'Origins of Natural Rights Language, 1150–1250', *History of Political Thought*, 10 (1989), 615–46.
54. Richard Dagger, 'Rights', in *Political Innovation and Conceptual Change* (Cambridge, 1989), p. 295.
55. Patrick Collinson, 'Religion and Human Rights: The Case of and for Protestantism', in Olwen Hufton (ed.), *Historical Change and Human Rights* (New York, 1995), p. 39.
56. D. D. Raphael, 'Human Rights, Old and New', in *Political Theory and the Rights of Man*, p. 55.
57. Collinson, 'Religion and Human Rights', p. 40.
58. Kelly, *History of Legal Thought*, p. 189.
59. Richard Tuck, *Natural Rights Theories: Their Origin and Development* (Cambridge, 1979), p. 66.
60. Tuck, *Philosophy and Government*, p. 197.
61. Laslett (ed.), *Two Treatises*, pp. 137–8.
62. Hobbes, *Leviathan*, ed. Tuck, p. 91.
63. Harris, *Spinoza*, p. 100.
64. Ibid., p. 101.
65. Peter Jones, *Rights* (New York, 1994), pp. 73–4.
66. Jones, *Rights*, p. 74; C. B. Macpherson, 'Natural Rights in Hobbes and Locke', in *Political Theory and the Rights of Man*, p. 2.
67. See the discussion in John Yolton, *A Locke Dictionary* (Oxford, 1990), pp. 242–3.
68. Locke, *Two Treatises*, 2:27.
69. Bill of Rights, printed in Brian Blakely and Jacquelin Collins (eds), *Documents in British History*, 2 vols (New York, 1993), 2: 2–4.
70. Quentin Skinner, 'The State' in *Political Innovation and Conceptual Change*, pp. 90–2, 108, 110–11.
71. See the discussion in Iain Hampshire-Monk, *A History of Modern Political Thought* (Oxford, 1992), esp. pp. 2–8.
72. *Leviathan*, ed. Tuck, p. 89.
73. Johann P. Sommerville, *Thomas Hobbes: Political Ideas in Historical Context* (London, 1992), p. 41.
74. Harris, *Spinoza*, p. 100.
75. Spinoza, *Tractatus politicus*, p. 277.
76. Ibid., pp. 101, 102.
77. *Leviathan*, p. 110.
78. Ibid., p. 150.
79. Ibid., p. 153.
80. Ibid., p. 124.
81. Ibid., p. 144.
82. Parker quoted in Sommerville, *Hobbes*, p. 35.
83. Ibid., p. 82.
84. Pufendorf, *On the Duty of Man and Citizen*, 2.6.7 (book 2, ch. 6, section 7).
85. Ibid., 2.6.9.

86. Ibid., 2.6.5
87. Gough, *Social Contract*, p. 122.
88. Pufendorf, *On the Law of Nature and Nations*, in *Political Writings*, p. 214.
89. Skinner, 'The State', in *Political Innovation*, p. 112.
90. Dufour, 'Pufendorf', in *Cambridge History*, p. 579.
91. *On the Law of Nature and Nations*, in *Political Writings*, p. 234.
92. *Law of Nature and Nations*, p. 215.
93. *On the Duty of Man and Citizen*, ed. Tully, 2.9.4.
94. *Law of Nature and Nations*, pp. 242–4.
95. G. MacDonald Ross, *Leibniz* (Oxford, 1984), p. 26.
96. Mark Goldie, 'The Reception of Hobbes', in *Cambridge History*, p. 589.
97. Leibniz, 'The Common Concept of Justice', in Patrick Riley (ed.), *Leibniz: Political Writings* (Cambridge, 1988), p. 47.
98. Ibid., p. 56.
99. Filmer, 'Observations Concerning the Original of Government', in Johann P. Sommerville (ed.), *Patriarcha and Other Writings* (Cambridge, 1991), p. 184.
100. Goldie, 'The Reception of Hobbes', in *Cambridge History*, p. 597.
101. Baxter quoted in ibid., p. 591.
102. Parker quoted in ibid., pp. 592–3.
103. Riley (ed.), *Leibniz: Political Writings*, pp. 25–6.

Conclusion: Exit Divinity

1. Shennan, *Origins of the Modern State*, p. 112.
2. Marc Raeff, *The Well Ordered Police State* (New Haven, CT, 1983), pp. 19, 20.
3. Munck, *Seventeenth Century*, p. 382.
4. Raeff, *The Well Ordered Police State*, p. 41.
5. Wootton (ed.), *Locke's Political Writings*, p. 43.
6. Wootton, *Divine Right*, p. 41.
7. Ernst Bloch, *Natural Law and Human Dignity*, trans. Dennis J. Schmidt (Cambridge, MA, 1986), p. 49.
8. *Tractatus*, in Wernham (ed.), *The Political Works*, pp. 127, 211, 213.
9. See Richard Tuck, 'The "modern" theory of natural law', in Anthony Pagden (ed.), *The Languages of Political Theory in Early-Modern Europe* (Cambridge, 1987), pp. 102–3.
10. Thomas A. Horne, *The Social Thought of Bernard Mandeville: Virtue and Commerce in Early Eighteenth-Century England* (New York, 1978), p. 19.
11. Pascal quoted in Keohane, *Philosophy and the State*, p. 276.
12. Pierre Nicole, 'The Grounds of Sovereignty and Greatness', in Wootton, *Divine Right and Democracy*, p. 74.
13. Nicole quoted in Keohane, *Philosophy and the State in France*, pp. 297, 298.

14. E. J. Hundert, *The Enlightenment's Fable: Bernard Mandeville and the Discovery of Society* (Cambridge, 1994), p. 23.
15. Ibid., pp. 39, 43.
16. Ibid., pp. 1, 8.

INDEX